TALKING VIOLENCE

I0810860

TALKING VIOLENCE

An Anthropological Interpretation of Conversation in the City

Nigel Rapport

Social and Economic Studies No. 34
Institute of Social and Economic Research
Memorial University of Newfoundland

© Institute of Social and Economic Research 1987
Memorial University of Newfoundland
St. John's, Newfoundland, Canada
ISBN 0-919666-56-6

CANADIAN CATALOGUING IN PUBLICATION DATA

Rapport, Nigel, 1956-
Talking violence

(Social and economic studies ; no. 34)
Bibliography: p.
Includes index.
ISBN 0-919666-56-6

1. Conversation. 2. Social interaction.
3. Violence. I. Title. II. Series; Social and economic studies (St. John's, Nfld.) ; no. 34.

P95.45.R37 1987 401'.9 C87-094945-4

Cover design and illustrations: *Michael Sraga*
Book design and figures: *Sheila Gillard Studio Limited*

This book is dedicated to the authors of *Pig Earth,* John Berger, and *In the Land of Israel,* Amos Oz, and to Anthony Cohen and Robert Paine for directing me to them.

Contents

Maps and Figures

All understanding is at the same time a misunderstanding, all agreement in thought and feeling is also a parting of the ways.

Wilhelm von Humboldt

On the Differentiation of the Structure of Human Language...

Preface

This is an anthropological study of conversations about violence. It is intended as a commentary on the way individuals construct meaning and come together to constitute society.

The study is based on a period of participant-observation fieldwork which I carried out in the Canadian city of St. John's between July 1984 and August 1985. It is a traveller's tale, and it is subjective.

When Louch referred to social anthropology as a collection of travellers' tales, he was not being pejorative; he was pointing to the subject's strengths.[1] For here, he claimed, were accounts which would contribute to human knowledge as much as could more scientific enterprises, without aping the latter's experiments, measurements, predictions, or generalisations; here were accounts of acuitous and detailed observation, grounded and moral explanation, and rhetorical and reflective description, which were "sufficient unto themselves."

In writing this account, I have greatly benefitted from the support of many people. George Park, Tom McFeat, George Story, Alan Hall, Robert Paine and Anthony Cohen all read versions of the text, and without their criticism there would have been no book. Jean Briggs, Lisa Gilad, Jim Overton, Bill O'Grady, Raoul Andersen, Evie Plaice, Ron Schwartz, Louis Chiaramonte, Joanne Prindiville, Barbara Neis, Mary Dalton, Marc Gould, Hannah Franks, Iris Jean, Angela Lonardo, Gail Collins, Helen Peters and Victor Zaslavsky all shared ideas with me, and without their help the book would have been less rich.

While conducting the study, I lived on Freshwater Road and Goodview Street in downtown St. John's. To gather data, I frequented the morning and afternoon sessions of Newfoundland Provincial, District and Supreme Courts, and attended an extra-mural course at Memorial University as a student of criminology. I also worked part time each week as a volunteer at the Sisters of the Beatitudes General Hospital, and at the Lightship Community Rehabilitation Centre for Ex-Offenders. Evenings I spent in more informal visiting, as well as at near-by pubs like Tee Cee's, Milligan's, Brad's, and the Park Tavern, or at some further field like the Salon Paris. I am indebted to the people I met on this round, and to the friendliness with which most engaged me, and I apologise if my interpretations of their behaviour are misconstructions.

My research was generously funded by the Institute of Social and Economic Research at the Memorial University of Newfoundland, as part of an enquiry into violence in Newfoundland, and was initially arranged by Elliot Leyton. I am especially grateful to the Director of Research, Douglas House, and best of thanks go to Jeanette Gleeson, Daphne Benson, Shirley Atkins, Janet Oliver and Shirley Fraize of the ISER office.

Part I

A Conversational Journey Through 'Violence'

Man is a creature who lives not upon bread alone, but principally by catchwords.

Robert Louis Stevenson
Virginibus Puerisque

Introduction

Our language can be seen as an ancient city: a maze of little streets and squares of old and new houses, and of houses with additions from various periods; and this surrounded by a multitude of new boroughs with straight regular streets and uniform houses.[2]

I find Wittgenstein's image very provocative. Language as City. A city has a topography—a collection of roads, parks and buildings enumerated in a gazetteer which all inhabitants and visitors can own. Of course, use made of the topography, lives lived through it, will vary greatly. While everyone may use the major thoroughfares, only those from a given neighbourhood may use particular short-cuts or favourite lovers' lanes. And while only those from the same neighbourhood or club or street or family may know which draught beers the old pipes in the local pub frequently turn out flat and which the landlord always serves up a treat, only drinking partners or married couples or solitary lodgers may know how an evening pint of speciality ale regularly goes down just like nectar, after a snack lunch of salt beef sandwiches at that quirky delicatessen which keeps irregular hours.

In this book, I explore the use of one linguistic avenue, that of 'violence.' I trace the course taken by 'violence' from old borough to new, as it were; a by-way meandering past houses, shops and factories at one part, and then a highway racing on raised latticework to the suburbs and beyond: always the same public avenue and yet always informed in a more private fashion by the areas traversed and linked. For in 1984 and 1985 I found this avenue well-trodden; in everyday discussion, 'violence' was a catchword and part of a number of commonly exchanged phrases, and this is a study of that conversational usage: the way 'violence' was talked about and defined, the way 'violence' was part of and informed interaction in a number of different settings. City as Language.

The book is in two parts. This first is purely ethnographic; I reconstruct conversations which deal with violence in an attempt to reproduce their sensation and idiosyncrasy. The second part is more analytical, and I examine the tension between commonality of verbal form and diversity of verbal meaning: between language as a cultural institution and an abstract universe of words, and those words when personalised in a myriad of different arrangements-in-use.

In this introduction, I describe my initial and enduring impressions of Newfoundland, and St. John's its capital city, and prepare the way for the conversational journey which follows.

"Oh, you'll enjoy Newfoundland," I was assured by my fellow-traveller on his way to Halifax, on the Canadian mainland, and on the same Air Canada flight as me from London, "They have nine months of winter on "Newfie," and three months of bad weather!" We laughed and I was struck by the familiarity of his jibe: precisely the same phrase had been used by outsiders to the village in the Yorkshire Dales I had made a study of previously. It sounded out of context coming from my companion. Then he continued: "But it doesn't really matter to them Newfs, they're too boozed-up all the time to notice!" We laughed again; his comment was akin to that of another tattler, J.G. Millais, about the rural Newfoundlanders earlier in the century: "The purity of the air of Newfoundland is without a doubt due to the fact that the people of the outports never open their windows."

From the air, the Newfoundland interior appeared a land of forest and scrub. My map called it "Wilderness Area," and I knew that many of the province's inhabitants still lived in the small coastal settlements, "outports," of 500 people or so, although paved roads made these less isolated than formerly. Then a break in the fir curtain brought Gander International Airport. At Gander there was a four-hour wait before *Eastern Provincial Airways* flew us the further 25 minutes to St. John's (flying being the way to deal with North American distances), so I settled down to read an article on Newfoundland in a glossy complimentary copy of *Maritime Canada* magazine which was thus being advertised.

▪ the Province of Newfoundland includes the island of Newfoundland, 43,359 square miles, and the mainland region of the Labrador, 112,186 square miles...

▪ the population density is below four people per square mile.

▪ The island of Newfoundland [hereinafter called 'Newfoundland'] boasts 10,900 miles of coastline and a population of approximately 580,000, 1.5% of the population is of French extraction, and 98% of British (The West Country) and Irish...

▪ Newfoundland was officially discovered by John Cabot on St. John the Baptist Day, June 24th, 1497; and the English proceeded to stake their claim to the island, despite the native (Beothuk and Micmac) populations and other European (Basque and French) settlers...

▪ In 1855 Newfoundland achieved Responsible Self-Government for the first time; but the Depression forced a return to Commission of Government from London in 1933. This lasted until the vote to join the Confederation of Canada on March 31st, 1949. It is now the tenth and newest part of Canada: "The Happy Province"...

▪ As part of the Confederation agreement, Newfoundland retains schooling by religious denomination. Thus almost all schools are run by the Roman Catholic School Board, or the Pentecostal Board, or the Consolidated Board (Anglican, Presbyterian, Moravian, United and Salvation Army). All are funded by government...

▪ 28% of Newfoundland adults have an educational level of less than Grade 5 [i.e. 1st Form]; and 34% have less than Grade 8 [i.e. 4th Form], and are defined as functionally illiterate.

▪ Newfoundland occupies a unique North American time zone; half an hour before Atlantic Canada, three-and-a-half hours later than G.M.T....

▪ Newfoundland has a temperate clime, modified by the proximity of the northern North Atlantic Ocean, and the meeting of the Labrador Current with the Gulf Stream; and is characterised by craggy, deeply indented coastlines, evergreen forest, bare rock and shallow soil...

▪ The major industries are three: the inshore and offshore fishery which employs most hands and accrues c. $300 million per year in fish products; the forestry which generates the highest wages, and accrues $200 million per year in pulp and paper exports; and the mining of minerals (50% of Canada's total iron ore, as well as copper, lead, zinc, asbestos, gypsum, limestone and pyrophyllite) which produces the greatest export values of one billion per year. Future employment hopes reside in a burgeoning service sector, from feeding to retailing, and in offshore oil...

▪ In March 1978, the People's Commission on Unemployment, funded by the Newfoundland and Labrador Federation of Labour, found a "real unemployment rate" among the 249,000 strong labour force of 34.9%. The official Statistics Canada rate was then 19.4%. Now, the official rate is 20.8%.

▪ The province is policed by a federal force of the Royal Canadian Mounted Police. But the provincial force, the Royal Newfoundland Constabulary is extending its range. It now polices the towns of Labrador City, Wabush, Churchill Falls and Mount Pearl; and also the city of St. John's.

▪ The city of St. John's claims to be the oldest permanent European site in North America since its founding by Sir Humphrey Gilbert in 1583. However, to prevent exploitation of the fishery, year-round residence was forbidden by the English crown until the mid-nineteenth century...

▪ In the nineteenth century this city of mostly wooden structures was plagued by fire five times; the worst being the last, in 1892 when two-thirds of the community was laid to waste and $20 million of damage suffered...

▪ Now St. John's boasts a population of 86,600; with 143,400 in the extended metropolitan area. Its new university, enlarged in 1949 from the original 1925 college, caters for 12,000 students...

▪ Temperatures in St. John's range from minus 10°C to plus 24°C; the mean daily highs being minus 3°C in February and plus 20°C in August, 29 inches of snow can be expected in February, 14 days of fog in June, and 8 inches of rain in November...

Reaching St. John's at last, I hired a taxi to drive me on this July evening to the flat I had arranged to rent downtown. On the way I could already recognise some of the accoutrements of a city—suburbs, a Holiday Inn, large supermarket plazas and car parks. Next morning I awoke to another—record-players and radios whose stereo speakers seemed to be competing for attention from my neighbours' front window-ledges and cramped back gardens. It was a street of small, wooden, terraced houses, the road sloping steeply to give a good view of St. John's harbour and docks. This morning while listening to the commentators and pop-music on the local *VOCQ* radio station, the men of the street, bare-chested, but still in jeans and heavy boots, were sunning themselves on their front door steps, and smoking, and occasionally calling to their women and babies inside. While their parents thus broadcast membership and ownership, groups of boys or girls patrolled the area, intent upon their separate itineraries. The alley beside my flat seemed to be the rendezvous for a gang of six- and seven-year old boys. They were building a fort out of discarded wood and cardboard, with rusty nails, and stones as hammers. Then they ran around shouting "Enemy! Enemy!" and hooting like the pandemic police sirens until the 'attacked' fort was demolished and had to be rebuilt. While downtown St. John's was being 'gentrified,' and the old houses were being renovated, the process was slow, my landlord apologised to me before jetting off to his sabbatical year in The States; this was still part of a downtown core owned by local families, and largely 'untouched'...

Settling into my flat I explored the local books and papers which my landlord had left. It seemed a way of at least approaching the gross lineaments of a cultural landscape.

I found a number of images of Newfoundland and its inhabitants:

***In Search of the Newfoundland Soul* by C.F. Poole**

Newfoundlanders are a peculiar people, a fact noted by many native and foreign observers. Indeed a large number of writers (...) have gone so far as to refer to us as a race. None of these writers, of course, used the terms 'race' in its scientific sense. But it is revealing that they thought it natural to use the strongest term expressive of distinctness. It is stronger than 'tribe' or 'people' (...). I take it for a fact, then, that we are a singular people, or as our saying goes 'queer sticks.'

And we are all queer sticks, all bent the same way; for despite differences of origin, dialect and religion we are all children of the sea.[3]

***The Book of Newfoundland,* Volume I, by J.R. Smallwood**

Perhaps the very nature of our struggle, of our methods of wresting a living from nature, has helped to unfit us for creative and constructive effort. It is a fact that for centuries we have lived by *killing* cod and other fish; by *killing* seals in the water or on ice, and animals on land; by *killing* birds, and *cutting* down trees. Has this developed in us a trait of destructiveness, or narcotized what ought naturally to be an instinct of creativeness?[4]

Introduction to *The Greatest Hunt in the World,* by Ebbit Cutler

The Newfoundlander, if one judges from his history, would seem to be less violent than any other North American. Not that he did not have cause. For centuries, Newfoundland was one of the most outrageously exploited countries in the world, by both speculators from across the Atlantic (...) and by its own ruling classes, who (...) finally drove the country into bankruptcy in 1933 (...).

And all through these years of incredible hardship, no violent political protest ever seems to have occurred. While other Western peoples were having revolutions, revolts, riots and strikes, Newfoundlanders endured with unbelievable patience, keeping their kindliness and good-humour and dignity. Violence does enter the Newfoundland story in three ways, none of them political: in the religious strife that only very occasionally burst out between the varying Christian denominations of the island; in the fantastic enthusiasm and bravery with which Newfoundlanders fought Britain's wars; and the strangest way of all, in the seal hunt (...) blood, cruelty, filth, waste and hardship (...) a bloodbath unequalled elsewhere in the world.[5]

***House of Hate* by Percy Janes**

...that profound modesty which is such a distinguishing mark of our people as a whole that it amounts to an island-wide inferiority complex. (...) isolation, and its attendant horrors, was our island's chief curse, and men in obscure bays, and coves had to exist on a dole of six cents a day if no fish came to their grounds in a particular year.

We as Newfoundlanders were no longer the step-children of a distant and once-rapacious Empire. We were now brothers to one-half of a mighty nearby continent and that one great fact alone insured us for the foreseeable future against privation and the lonely death-in-life, both humanly and economically, that so many of our forefathers had known.[6]

***Our New Flag*, from St. John's Tourist Commission and Convention Bureau**

In this flag (...) White is representative of snow and ice; Blue represents the sea; Red represents human effort and Gold our confidence in ourselves. The Blue section, most reminiscent of the Union Jack, represents our Commonwealth heritage which has so decisively shaped our present. The Red and Gold section, larger than the other, represents our future.

The two triangles outlined in Red portray the mainland and island parts of our province reaching forward together. A Golden arrow points the way to what we believe will be a bright future.

But the design of the flag encompasses much more symbolism than this. For example, the Christian Cross, the Beothuck and Naskapi ornamentation, the outline of the Maple Leaf in the centre of the flag, a triumphant figure and our place in the space age. The image of a trident stands out. This is to emphasize our continued dependence on the fishery and the resources of the sea. Hung as a banner, the arrow assumes the aspect of a sword which is to remind us of the sacrifice of our War Veterans. (...)

and I found more images of St. John's:

***City of St.John's*, by St. John's Tourist Commission and Convention Bureau**

There is no other city like it in North America.

There are old cities, but none as old as St. John's; there are new cities, but none with as bright a future; every city has its people, but no other city has St. John's people.

The people are special. They are the unique element which captures the hearts of visitors whether they come for work or play. It is true that there is nobody quite like a Newfoundlander, and equally true that there is no Newfoundlander like a St. John's man. (...) What makes a St. John's man? Five hundred years of stubborn survival in the face of tyrannical oppression, inhuman laws, a harsh environment, invasion and pillage, holocausts, economic depressions, and violent politics. From this granite crucible has developed the unique St. John's culture, with the strong taste of pioneering optimism but the gentle bouquet of old world charm. (...) The coming of the oil age may well be the greatest single event in half-a-millenium of story-book history for the city. As it was in 1497, once again St. John's represents the new frontier of opportunity. It is the place to be.[7]

***Eastmall*, by Percy Janes**

The old St. John's, the world I grew up in and took for granted as permanent, is falling to pieces and being torn down in front of my eyes, and I guess there's a new city forming where I feel like a stranger. It's not so much that I'm against it as that I don't understand it.[8]

***Persistence and Change*, by the Department of Rural, Agricultural and Northern Development, Government of Newfoundland and Labrador**

A comparison of rural and urban crime patterns reflects distinctive forms of criminal orientation and patterns of change. Our cities (St. John's, Corner Brook and Labrador City/Wabush) have become more dangerous places to live. In fact they were 50% more dangerous to personal safety in 1980 than they were in 1974 (...). As the resulting rate for violent crime (except for sexual assault) is very high it is likely that this pattern of change reflects a real change in behaviour.[9]

Unarmed Police Push for Guns*, in Toronto *Globe and Mail

After 113 years, members of the largest unarmed police force in North America want to carry guns. In the wake of recent police murders in Ontario, the union representing officers of the Royal Newfoundland Constabulary says the day is gone when police can operate safely unarmed. (...) And in Newfoundland, armed robberies, mostly of service stations and convenience stores, have become common.[10]

Ray Guy's Column in *Atlantic Insight*

Time was when a movement, cause or a fad stayed with us for at least six months or a year. (...)

Now, the scope of a "cause" is narrower, its timespan shorter and its intensity more furious.

Pornography in March, Prostitution in April, Incest in May, Wife battering in June...child abuse, rape, mass-murder, sexual murder, drunk driving.

What the hell is this, the Abomination of the Month Club? (...)

The glaring spotlight lingers only long enough to jerk the knees of our legislators and moves on. Laws are bunged through in a state of semi-hysteria. There's barely time to pinpoint the alarm bells when they suddenly cease and burst out again in the bushes yonder.[11]

and then I switched on my landlord's wireless:

Keith's *Answer Line* on VOCQ Radio

...But what sort of perverted society are we living in? With violence increasing in Newfoundland and Canada and such an increase of violent and armed crimes in St. John's...Now there seems to be a general consensus—I don't know where it came from but there is one—that the hoodlum element is running rampant in our city and we're upset by that. A lot of crime and petty crime. Last night the police answered 220 calls for break-ins, and made 30 arrests! We seem to be losing our values and it kind'a lets you down. And this is so upsetting in a city known for its human warmth and the milk of human kindness. Is it drying up here? Because any of us could be victims at any time. Just one bullet separates you and the grave. You're living in the middle of it. So whatever did happen to the warmth and hospitality and the Newfoundland hospitality we always prided ourselves on? And are you dismayed and outraged to pick up the *Evening Telegram* every night and read about vandalism, hooliganism and violations all the time? And everything falling apart. All this crime gone out of all proportions. Doesn't that frighten you to death?

- we are all queer sticks...
- a trait of destructiveness...
- less violent than any other North American...
- no longer the step-children of a once-rapacious Empire ...
- St. John's represents the new frontier of opportunity...
- our cities have become more dangerous places to live...
- the day is gone when police can operate safely unarmed...
- a new city forming...
- such an increase of violent and armed crimes in St. John's....
- a general consensus that the hoodlum element is running rampant...
- a state of semi-hysteria...

Leaving my flat, I entered upon my year of largely covert participant-observation, and began the process of adding detail to these gross verbal images. For understanding them, fully bringing them to life, would entail a knowledge of their expression and use in people's everyday interactions, and would mean contextualising them in conversation with 'talking-partners' of my own.

My flat was situated in the old 'East End' section of downtown St. John's, characterised by terraced houses perched on steep hills; erected in a hurry, after the fire of 1892 destroyed the previous wooden structures. Also downtown were the busy Duckworth and Water Streets—bars and restaurants, small galleries, legal offices, mercantile headquarters, and new, high-rise bank buildings obscuring much of the view of the narrow entrance to the harbour. On the other side of the harbour there were the fishplant and the petroleum installations, large oil tanks advertising their multinational owners. On the hills overlooking the harbour were the one-time squatter settlements of the Battery and Shea Heights. Both were now officially part of the city and provided with amenities, but the unkempt aspect of the latter still preserved something of the stigma of pauperism. In this Shea Heights also resembled some of the newer apartment block complexes spread around the city such as at Buckmaster Circle, Virginia Park and Mundy Pond, and the subsidised 'town-houses' or 'row-houses' owned by the city council, such as behind the new modernistic City Hall, or near the picturesque, old fishing village and lake of Quidi Vidi. At the other pole were the posh condominiums of Tiffany Lane and Portugal Cove Road, and the elegant homes of Waterford Bridge and Circular Roads. Then, lining the city's outer approaches were the new, enclosed shopping malls, giant parking lots, service-stations, and 'fast-food' franchises; surrounded by the burgeoning metropolitan suburbs of Wedgewood Park, Mount Pearl, and beyond, the Goulds. Most houses were still made of wood: gaily painted box-like structures with clapboard siding, and its synthetic imitations, downtown, and newer and whiter bungalows on small plots of land in the suburbs; only the university, hotels, hospitals and office tower-blocks seemed predominantly brick and concrete constructions. Then the Supreme Court, Museum, Masonic Temple, Government House and old churches and cathedrals provided the imposing stone edifices.

Familiarising myself with a new physical environment entailed at the same time immersion in a new linguistic one. Local rules of verbal usage, criteria of belonging and exclusion I found strange at first, because in other superficial ways the language seemed the same. There was a familiar lilting Irish intonation, and yet the woman in the electrical shop looked at me with incomprehension as I repeated a request that she mend my tape-recorder; until I chanced upon 'repair.' People wore 'sweaters' but not 'jumpers,' and 'pants' but not 'trousers.' Men were 'smart,' but clothes were not. Women were 'fancy,' but dress was not. Customers waited politely, but in a 'line-up' and not a 'queue.' There were also new rejoinders to learn: 'is that right?' rather than 'really?'; and new abbreviations: here, a 'local' seemed to refer to a union branch rather than a nearby public house. And there was a host of exotic Christian inferences; from oaths: 'By the Lord Thundering Jesus,' to adjectives: 'Jeezly,' to their inversion as swear words: 'Holy Mother of Fuck.'

Indeed, verbal usage appeared rather eclectic. Ambivalence over the differences between British and American English seemed to issue as a wider tolerance, flexibility and laxity than I had been used to. So, sometimes the sign on the passing truck would read 'inflammable,' and sometimes 'flammable,' and sometimes 'flamable.' In one newspaper headline would be the word 'centre' and in the next 'center.' Radio commentators would talk about rates on graphs not just petering-out, but 'petering-up' and 'petering-down.' And plenteous, printed posters expensively advertising an 'upcoming' gala promised 'Exiting Times.'

As a stranger, still associating the English language, its form and grammar, with emblems of my home and friends, I was depressed. Everyone seemed to have been invited to re-write the traditions of the language; 'pioneering optimism,' I thought, or New World contrariness. I realised how unconsciously I had accepted verbal usage in the past, spelling for example, but now nothing looked quite right. I had been abroad before, of course, and lived in various parts of Britain, but never experienced so clearly the sensation of being a cultural outsider while using the same linguistic forms.

The process of un-learning linguistic habits was a difficult one, then. For example, I was surprised how insecure it made me to hear people talking about 'football' and know they were referring to American not Association Football. It seemed a challenge to the rectitude, the status, even in a way the reality of years of my own experience and enjoyment. For people not to 'know' the world that the shibboleth 'football' was part of for me, indeed to know of an opposite world and relegate mine to the slang 'soccer,' threatened part of the social identity I had been accustomed to believing I could communicate.

However, different feelings about the language would stem from a belonging to talking-relationships within it, and I set about negotiating these. In the Hive bar, for example, I found the regular meeting spot of a university-cum-artsy crowd. It was just over the road from the Longshoremen's Protective Union Hall, or the LSPU as it was more affectionately called (now a theatre), which seemed the centre of a renaissance of local drama and fine art. On Sunday evenings the Hive would become especially lively as local professional and amateur folk musicians performed, from 9:30 p.m. until 12:30 or so. One particular Sunday, ordering a lager at the bar, I was engaged by a slightly drunk man occupying the high stool to my left:

"Are you English?"

"Well, from Wales, yes."

"Welsh! I spent two days in Cardiff. Saw Cardiff Castle and the open market by the station. And I asked a woman in the bar where everyone was, and she said how weekends all the people from the north come in to drink so everyone from the south leaves to escape the crazies. (We laugh). Yeah, we hired a car and headed for Treorchy to see the Male Voice Choir. They were practicing but we arrived too late. You been there?"

"Uh. Yeah."

"No you haven't. You don't need to be polite. Then we went to the Rhondda Valley. We wanted to see what the English had really done to you. So we saw the slagheaps and the little valleys and we had a half-pint in every town, so we had twenty-seven before we got to Treorchy, eh! Look, boy, I'm drunk, so when you get too bored, just go, right."

"No. I'm fine."

"Hey! D'you know any Gaelic?"

"No. 'Fraid not."

"So you can't give us any Welsh oratory? Or rhetoric?"

"Nope."

"So d'you like Newfoundland?"

"I like St. John's, yeah. I'm not sure whether I could live in one of the outports."

"Well? That doesn't matter. That's Okay. Just leave "em to it. One man's meat is another man's poison. They like it and they're used to it so that's Okay...Hey!...You aren't a sociologist?!"

"Nuh!"

Phew! For a minute...Hey! You aren't an anthropologist?"

"Uh. Yes I am."

"Yes! Hey, John! Come over here! Loretta! (He calls over some friends chatting nearby.) Come and meet a Welsh anthropologist come to study us. Well, Mr. Anthropologist, this is Fred Penny, our Newfoundland poet. Give him a ditty, Fred. Loretta, give him a kiss. Isn't she a Newfoundland beauty! (I get kissed but then, realising my embarrassment, and their friend's tipsiness, they wander back to their conversation.) You know if Theresa had told me I'd meet a Welsh anthropologist tonight, I'd never have believed her. Not in my wildest dreams. But now this is a different...fish...a different ball-game altogether. I'm from Topsail, but my girl Theresa lives in town. So I'd like you to visit 'cause she'd really get off on seeing you. With you here now, I'll have to go to Wales to study you, you know...Jeeze! I'll have to watch my words or you'll be taking notes on me!...Okay, Mr. Anthropologist. Tell me what you know about the Australian Aborigines. (I laugh.) Go on!...So where's your notebook?"

"I haven't got one."

"Are you a Ph.D.?"

"Yes."

"Then why haven't you got a ring on?...Hey! D'you wanna have a fight? Later. Over there. 11:30? 11:45? D'you wanna fight?"

"No thanks. And I better be off now. See you again."

I retreated to another part of the bar to consider the exchange and its close; one moment he was inviting me home, the next to a fight. But all the way through I had been unsure whether my interlocutor was veiling friendliness in bluntness or dislike in politeness. My mind jumped to my contemporaneous difficulties negotiating the traffic around town. One moment it seemed impossible to jaywalk because whether downtown or on a four-lane highway cars insisted on the courtesy of stopping for you, while the next moment a screech of complaint from car tyres or brakes would be accompanied by a string of obscenities directed at women or joggers on the sidewalks.

I also recalled how anthropological monographs in the past had described the use of alcohol (and more especially among the men, beer) in the Newfoundland outports. Szwed, for example, had called beer-drinking a necessity for rendering public gatherings comfortable, and providing a framework for the initiation and maintenance of community relationships: "a constantly ready symbol of friendship and the occasion for its expression in an encounter."[12] At the same time, Firestone had explained that where there was most drinking there was also most fighting, often covertly pre-arranged beforehand and serving the function of legitimately displacing community tension and individual aggression.[13] And Szwed had agreed with this functional interpretation: fighting when drinking was rationalised as excusable, as alcohol talking, and a ritual of social reaffirmation was being effected, cathartically removing interpersonal hostility for the betterment of communality.[14] The rest of the time I knew, Newfoundland had been described as a society where sobriety was lauded, and everyone strove for harmony through a maintenance of reserve and impassivity. Dominant was an ethic of 'friendliness,' 'cooperation,' 'camaraderie,' 'intimacy,' 'tolerance,' 'familiarity,' 'equality,' and 'general goodwill.' Warmth and cordiality were a 'hallmark,' and calm and friendly expression a cultural dictate.[15]

Drinking and then fighting. Intimacy, friendliness and hostility. I was reminded of the list of contrarieties which Lison used to describe the paradoxical pulse of *village* life: antinomy, aggression and conviviality; conflicted solidarity; opposition in cooperation.[16] And the conversation in the Hive returned me to some of my own experiences in a small Yorkshire Dales village. Like interlocutors there, mine tonight, relaxed in his regular pub, deferent in conversation, had still expected at least overt reciprocity. The reminders were blunt, then, when his inquisitiveness for local information was not respected.[17] I might lie about my knowledge of Treorchy, but as his guest in Newfoundland, and possible recipient of his hospitality, ambiguity over my knowledge of anthropology and the information I may be extorting from him called for a more definite and honourable settlement.

The feeling of 'village-ness' stayed with me as I came to understand St. John's better: a city with the manners of a village or a small town, a dense network of closely-knit overlapping ties and disjunctions. No one ever seemed to have to travel far along lists of names before friends, even family, were discovered in common. And family names conjured up religious, historical, and economic connotations. Then, in gossip, local bigmen wintering in Florida still seemed bound by hostage indiscretions—local millionaires often claimed as drinking buddies or bed-wetters;[18] or, more usually, local sons and daughters always known as UIC (*U*nemployment *I*nsurance *C*ontribution) recipients. Market success, job opportunities or rather the lack of them, the declining fisheries, were known, if not felt by all.

Then again in their village-ness, people seemed extremely conscious of insiders and outsiders. Ethnically, maybe, St. John's was still very homogeneous—a smattering of Jews, Chinese, Greeks, Vietnamese, Philippinos, Pakistanis, Indians and American Indians, but overwhelmingly of British and Irish descent (St. John's and the Avalon Peninsula being areas of especially Irish settlement). But beneath this, play was often made of Newfoundlanders versus Brits and Yanks, Newfoundlanders versus mainland Canadians, Newfoundlanders versus other Maritime Canadians, and Newfoundlanders versus Labradorians. Furthermore, there was the important distinction *on* the island between townies and baymen, or 'baywops.' Only two languages were spoken on Newfoundland, a medical student from Montreal explained to me one night at The Hive: English and Baymanese; and he had been busy learning not to detain psychiatric patients who claimed that after leaving St. John's they were going 'direct to Paradise': it was a small settlement just outside town! Indeed, since St. John's was the only agglomeration boasting more than 30,000 inhabitants, 'bayman' often signified everyone else on the 'Rock'—all the inhabitants of Newfoundland's many hundred smaller communities. They, by way of reciprocation, derided the townies' sophistication and anonymity. They were nothing but the taint of an alien and monolithic Canadian mainland; and that was 'Sin John's'.

Of course, there were still more stereotyped oppositions and identities within St. John's. Many of the downtown bars, for example, possessed their own sets of members, and detractors. There was the Hive, of course, and not far distant I found Milligan's hosting a clique of young regulars. As a jukebox nightly serenaded them with their Top-Ten requests, all would raise a fist above their heads and, in unison, punch the air in time with the chorus:

> Born *in the U.S.A.*
> *I was* born *in the U.S.A.*
> *I was* born *in the U.S.A.*
> *I was born in the* U.S.A.
> Born *in the* U.S.A.

The gang seemed to be borrowing the belongings of popular heroes, and together escaping adults and adolescence, and unemployment in St. John's. In boarding school I remembered escaping and sneering at teachers' manners by aping the chants of distant football teams whilst waving imaginary scarves in time with the television set:

> *Well we hate Man. United and we hate The Kop,*
> *We'll fight Leeds United until we drop,*
> *'Cause we don't give a frig,*
> *And we don't give a wank,*
> *We are the Arsenal, North Bank.*

I would find a plethora of such local community distinctions, and a maze of cross-cutting individual identities in St. John's. However, it was also explained to me by a fellow-anthropologist that I, for one, would never really belong, never be a Newfoundlander or a local St. John's-man of any description. He had moved here from Ottawa fifteen years ago, even raised a family here, and, slightly embittered, he was still just a CFA, a 'Come-From-Away,' an outsider.[19]

Come-From-Aways. In the West Country, I knew they were called 'Up-Country Johnnies' and on Whalsay, Shetland, 'Soothmoothers.'[20] In my

Yorkshire Dales village, Wanet, outsiders were 'Offcomers,' or 'Offcomedens.'[21] They were the ones who were threatening to invade the dale: townies, government officials, bureaucrats and tourists, and no doubt in cahoots with more traditional 'neighbouring' outsiders and aliens. I had found the term 'Offcomers' to be a sign of self-consciousness in Wanet, of cultural vulnerability and peripherality. Sensitive to encroaching tides of change, the locals were beleaguered, frequently vocal in defence of their boundaries, and overt in their parading of emblems of belonging. But this introspection had been a matter of sport to outsiders: just something else akin to Wanetdale's homogeneity and inbreeding, and another part of the comic incestuousness of its longstanding internal network of relations. "Kick one native of Wanet," outsiders would joke, "and next morning you will see seven people limping!" Against the villagers of Newfoundland and St. John's, I found the sneering 'Newfie joke': "Did you hear about the Newf who locked his car-keys inside his car? Well, it took him three hours to get his family out!"

Newfoundlanders have been described by one local commentator as "touchy as boils" over the curse of these mainland jokes, and yet I was to find the genre in quite frequent and varied local usage, with a number of different shades of meaning attached.[22] Thus, when St. John's locals explained how the old train from the west end of the island to the east took so long to make the journey that American servicemen stationed here in the Second World War dubbed it 'The Newfie Bullet,' it was as part of local lore. An idiosyncratic emblem of common heritage was being recalled, as was, perhaps, a shared history of the war—its deprivations and, through work on the American bases, its compensations. Similarly, when townies' jokes mimicked outporters' habits and accents, there was also respect involved for the gruelling lives which forebears of so many St. John's-men had also led. Then, there were the times when partly assimilated newcomer professionals, on hearing of some further inefficiency on the part of the local government, or the hospitals, or the police force would be compelled to comment: "You know, I hate to say this, but it really is just like a Newfie joke." There was after all a more modern world outside to which they really belonged. But then again everyone in St. John's could enjoy the joke which reversed the original mainlanders' slur and instead played upon their ignorance about Newfoundland, their lack of subtlety. After all, only they would buy Newfie joke books and be so gullible as to take the tales at face value only. Through an inversion of the mainland joke, then, Newfoundlanders' pride in themselves could be bolstered. Thus, for example, in one of the many meetings between the outsider professional and the economically marginal and parochial Newfie, it is the latter identity which is championed below, and the superficial and credulous mainlander made into a clown:

Two Newfie pals, Jud and Gord, plan a vacation on the Mainland. Jud prefers Montreal, but Gord insists on Toronto: "Look b'y. I tell you, Dean Martin is singing in Toronto, right, and I knows Dean well, right, and if we goes to Toronto I promises to introduce you to him, eh?" "Is that right, b'y!" Jud is finally convinced and off they fly to Ontario.

No sooner are they ensconced and unpacked in their hotel room than Jud calls on Gord to uphold his side of the bargain. "No sweat, Jud, b'y! I tell you he's me buddy, and we'll see him tonight at 'is show downtown."

That evening they find a table at the front of the nightclub and start to really enjoy the show. After his first set, Dean calls a short break while he goes for a pee. Gord gets up too and excuses himself. Then, in the toilet, he explains the situation to Dean Martin: he's promised his friend, and pretended this friendship. Could Dean do him a big favour and walk up to the table after his second set and say 'Hello' to him? Just this once? Then of course Gord will take it from there.

Feeling sorry for Gord, Dean agrees, and sure enough after the second set he walks up to where Gord and Jud are sitting, drinking, and puts his hand on Gord's shoulder: "Hi there Gord! I thought it was you! How you doing?"

Gord slams his glass down: "Oh fuck off Dean! I told you I wasn't gonna speak to you tonight!"

Shortly after beginning to familiarise myself with my new environment in St. John's, I bought an old second-hand car—a very large, 1975, dark blue Chevrolet BelAir. Cars being widely considered indispensable, and mine being too blatant to miss, I soon garnered comment from my acquaintances. One said it was an immigrant's car, another that it was a real local's car, not like all these Come-From-Aways with their Datsuns and Ladas. Still others called it an American mobster's car, or tacky, or a tireless piece of North American workmanship (80,000 miles done but the engineering good for 120,000 more and replacement parts easy to come by), or a real bay-mobile for driving around the outports in, with two more people cosying up together on the front seat, or a car of someone with longstanding membership in North America's upper classes (above all the antics of *nouveau riche* Mercedes owners), or a mobile love-seat, with room for six people and twelve crates of beer, or a 'steal' at 1000 bucks, and artificially underpriced just because it was a bit of a 'gas-guzzler,' or the last of the real, big American cars... My Chevy became a node of communication: a catchword which I could easily and repeatedly exchange with people for the initiating and maintaining of conversation. Perhaps I alone knew all of the above associations connected with my car—I alone cognitively journeyed through this collection, using different parts of my family of remembrances with different acquaintances—but still the car was a cliché, something all my talking-partners used.

Another node of communication, a catchword common in my experiences of interaction in St. John's was to be 'violence.' Living in the city, I came to practise a weekly routine of visiting people and places, and my participant-observation involved recording as much as possible of any conversation which I took part in or heard. I did not use unsightly gadgets such as tape-recorders, nor did I resort to importing devices such as formal interviews, but as soon after a conversation as possible I would scribble down from memory key words, topics and phrases, and then use these as cues to reconstruct the direct speech in full when I reached home. I conducted this fieldwork for a year and composed a substantial diary of interaction.

On 'leaving the field,' and re-reading my diary I realised the extent to which the word 'violence' repeatedly appeared. Moreover, there was sameness in this repetition: a sameness of setting of speaker, and of type of violence each referred to, whether that of armed robbery, or bar-fighting, or drug-taking, or sexual discrimination, or religious prejudices or life downtown. There was a regularity in the conversations in the way the word 'violence' was used. That is to say, on reading my diary I became privy to habits of interaction which the actual living in discourse—the tangle of passing from interaction to interaction, of conducting conversation with oneself and others and at the same time experiencing the associations, the half-memories, the future projects which spring from words of the moment—tends to obscure. There were routine things that individuals would say and do when they met in specific settings, part of which entailed discussions of violence. It is these which I present as the ethnographical section of this book in the eleven scenes to follow: the habitual ways in which I heard my acquaintances associating the word 'violence' with other words in their regular and often detailed conversations with each other and with me.

It occurs to me that a useful analogy may be drawn between what my diary identifies as interactional routines and the singing of 'pop' songs. For in pop songs, words appear with particular repetition, linkage, rhythm, order and inflection, and in a context of lines, verses and refrains. The words may belong to one voice alone, or their emotion may be partaken of by an interweaving of singers in harmony; and the words are wed to melody, usually through musical accompaniment—they can seem rather odd if the lyrics are approached out of context. Then again, for a while a particular song may be played over and over, until, after a spell on the radio and in the charts, its popularity fades and it is superseded by new songs, new arrangements of the words and music.

The regularities of conversation which I shall reproduce may be seen to share many of the same features. These scenes are like locally penned pop songs which my friends had written and which I kept hearing performed during my fieldwork whenever they would meet each other. For here were words in particular aggregation, wed to habitual behavioural accompaniment, and the whole in frequent use. Of course no one person partook of only a single exchange, nor saw this to its conclusion on every occasion. Rather people moved from exchange to exchange, like a group of players who come together to perform and maybe repeat a pop song, or just a few bars of one, at one venue, before separating and performing other songs with other collaborators elsewhere. Also, here were solo efforts, songs performed as soliloquy with very little necessary accompaniment from other group members in attendance. Lastly, I would not claim any permanency for these interactional routines, for different playing partnerships and different melodies of words and behaviours will always be bidding for attention and the currency of fashion.

Part I of this book is composed of eleven scenes, then, narrated by a conversant observer. Without any conscious invention, I have reconstructed these scenes from the many conversations and snippets of conversation which my diary records for my set of acquaintances and myself around St. John's; like from the songs and snatches of songs heard from a number of radios in the city, here are some of the current 'hits' I came to know most fully.

I do not set out to stereotype a city or a society through this ethnography. Indeed, I shall argue in Part II that such a singular or essential representation would be a fallacy: that in terms of the meaning of individual interaction in which I am interested, society need lend itself to little common denomination; and an attempt at such a mapping could only proceed by corrupting the object of study and producing an inherently lifeless reduction. Instead, I set out below to describe some of my experiences of the city and convey some of my feelings as I lived them. As scene overlays scene, the diversity and complexity of attitude are the notes which I think are being struck.

By presenting my ethnography in this fashion, I wish to place emphasis upon certain features of interaction. Firstly, I want to portray the tenor, the flow and the colour of conversation which impressed itself upon me. As individuals construct their various versions of meaning in St. John's and embed 'violence'—sometimes deeply, sometimes less so—in the intimacies and intricacies of their debate, I hope one may hear in the laughing, shouting and singing voices something of the passion which one word has for the next; and as individuals meet in interaction, see the artistry of their games of metaphor and metonymy.[23] For it is as celebration of these that Part I is mainly intended. So, while I have changed the names of certain locations around the city where I felt sensitivities could be offended, and similarly disguised speakers' identities including my own ('Basil'/ 'Bas'), I have been at pains not to modify my understanding of the sense of this habitual exchange. Secondly, through this ethnography I want to present the data which I shall treat more sociolinguistically in Part II. These scenes of routine interaction, of habitual exchange, are the verbal residue of what I shall call individuals' *talking-relationships.* Individuals, I shall argue, are the sources of intention in society. They use cultural institutions to create personal meanings; for example, language: individuals possess their own preferences of verbal association, and they construct their words into particular egocentric worlds of meaning. Yet, it is through these diverse linguistic preferences that individuals come together in conversational exchange, albeit in meetings which may be momentary, situational and of variable closeness, and predicated upon opposition to those who would speak differently. Moreover, through an examination of individuals' verbal idiosyncracies and similarities, a picture of society as constituted by a sliding-scale of verbal sameness and difference is to be induced, from simple agreements of the many to more complex ones of the few: societal belonging as a spectrum of routine agreements over proper ways of speaking.

To arrive at this prospect for analysis, we shall review the regularities of my diary of interaction and trace out an ascending, if meandering, way from conversation to conversation around the city via the contingencies of overlapping topics of discussion or of individuals who are partners in them. As we proceed I shall introduce the different speakers and locations, but our general itinerary may be plotted from the numbers on the map on the following page.

We shall start at a party in a private apartment (#1) and move to a lecture at Memorial University (#2). This will be followed by an afternoon in St. John's Provincial Court (#3) and then a trip by car across downtown to the fishplant (#4). Next we shall return to the kitchen of the Lightship Community Rehabilitation Centre for Ex-offenders (#5) and then pay visits to Milligan's Irish pub (#6), the Salon Paris nightclub (#7), and Tee Cee's lounge (#8). These will be followed by a morning in Brady House Detoxification Centre (#9), and then an afternoon in the Sisters of the Beatitudes General Hospital (#10), firstly in a medical ward and finally in the Occupational Therapy Department, where our journey is complete.

Bon voyage.

City of St. John's

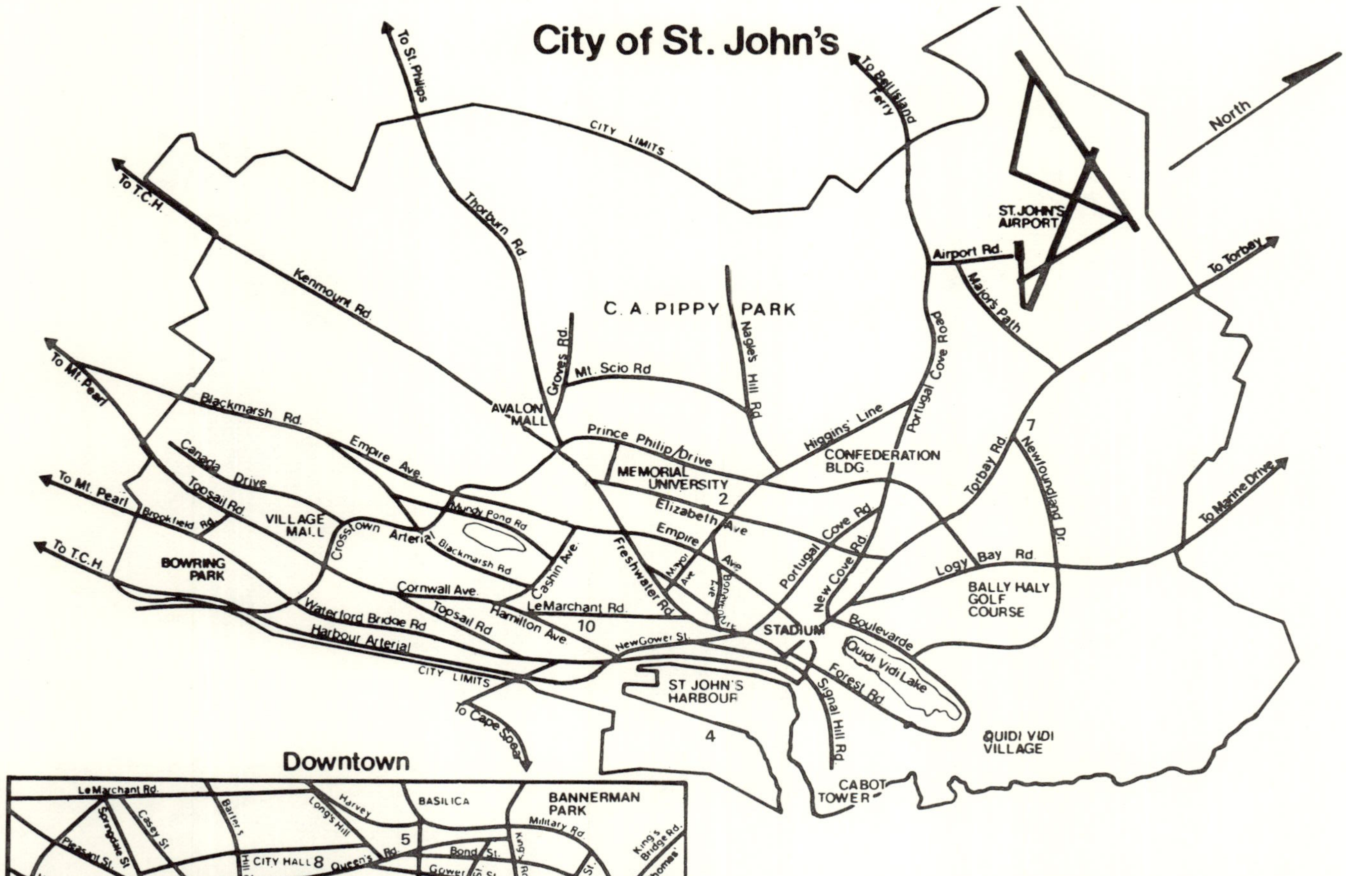

1: Private party; 2: Memorial University; 3: Provincial Court; 4: Fishplant; 5: The Lightship; 6: Milligan's Pub; 7: Salon Paris; 8: Tee Cee's Lounge; 9: Brady House; 10: Sisters Hospital

First Scene

Saturday night, at a party of academics.

After a weekend night at the Hive bar the university crowd appreciate a good party to move on to, and this Saturday it is Philippa Howells acting as hostess in her apartment on King's Road. Prefabricated and functional the apartment is newly renovated, with a fine view of the harbour narrows. All Philippa had to do was move in her books, cats, music, futon mattress and quilted eiderdown, and her collection of woodworking tools.

The St. John's academic community, a more or less transient group, still maintains a highly visible and eccentric aspect, and Philippa's party represents a motley meeting of cultivated a-culturated manners and styles. There are denim jackets, crew cuts, Donald Duck brooches, gypsy ear-rings, cowboy boots, plaid culottes, red sneakers, serious tortoise-shell spectacles, and explorers' beards. There are the men swigging out of beer bottles, and the refined and laidback sipping their wine or punch from plastic cups.

Philippa, in her late-twenties, is a post-graduate history student studying for her Ph.D. She was born in Vancouver, but has lived eight years in St. John's and is still single. Her party guests—invited, semi-invited, and forgotten-on-purpose-to-invite—are a regular bunch who turn up and find each other whenever one of them plans a get-together. Moreover, there is a casual mixing of university rank: from professor to first year; in the small college fraternity everyone knows everyone, by name or face or reputation or defamation, or at least knows of them. For example, there is *Professor Dwight Dewit,* of the Folklore Department: mid-fifties, divorced, born in Detroit but lived in St. John's ten years; and *Stella Spearns:* mid-twenties, single, just completing her folklore B.A., born on the Southern Shore but lived in St. John's five years; and *Lance Haines:* mid-twenties, single, reading for his anthropology M.A., born in Toronto and lived in St. John's three years; and *Sam Dyke:* mid-twenties, single, reading for a sociology M.A., born in Moncton and lived in St. John's four years; and *Chuck Lewis:* late-twenties, single, just completing his sociology M.A., born in Amherst and lived in St. John's six years; and *Professor Doyle Robbins* of History: late-fifties, married, born in Conception Bay but lived in St. John's since childhood; as well as Dave and Sherry and Tom, and many others. For as night turns to morning more make the short walk from the Hive and through Philippa's open door.

"I have my invitation, boy! I have my invitation!" The tall man pretending to be a stooped old man, shrouded in old clothes, gesticulates and points to the paper mask taped over his face. "See boys. I got me invitation!" There is generous laughter for Professor Dwight DeWit's Newfoundland-Mummer-entrance-to-the-party act. The other guests appreciate this avowal of loyalty to Christmas custom, even if that is months away and Professor DeWit is an American.

Still stooping and lurching around the room, Professor DeWit stumbles in the direction of Philippa Howells, the hostess, and squeezes and fondles her in shortsighted and senile embarrassment. But of course! This is the mummer's license for lewdness and the reversal of manners. The professor has read his stuff.

"I have my bags, see? I have my bags with!" Next, Professor DeWit reveals that inside the plastic Colonials supermarket bag dangling from his wrist are half-a-dozen more, carefully crumpled bags that need disseminating, graffiti-like, before a bottle of plonk can be disinterred and presented to Philippa.

But at last running out of props and aplomb, the professor unmasks, and reveals himself to the expecting crowd...Ah! That bulge in his midriff was a bath towel after all...and that bulge in his behind was not, mimes Professor DeWit, now Chaplinesque.

There are hurrahs for the professor as Phillipa takes the wine next door into the busy kitchen. Her party is taking up three rooms. In the living room, which has just witnessed Professor DeWit's display, people are sitting cross-legged on the floor smoking dope. Before the professor's arrival, Dave was wondering who to have as a fourth smoker if he rolled another joint; he had wanted to steer clear of Sherry: she went a bit weird on dope. But now Professor DeWit can be invited in.

Next to the living room, the furniture has been cleared in the bedroom, and the deep pile rug rolled up off the polished wooden floor, for dancing. The lights are dimmed, the windows are open, and the Rolling Stones' "Through the Past Darkly" blares out of the quadrophonic system, the record bouncing a bit here and there to the juddering of bodies. But most of the party is in the kitchen. People are watching their caches of beer in the packed refrigerator; or are watching the chilli bubbling away on the stove, ready to be served with french sticks later in the night; or are just leaning back against the counters which encircle the room.

"This way my old dear." Hot on the hostess' heels, Professor DeWit, still in the rudiments of his tattered costume, is led into the kitchen by Stella Spearns, one of his students, to find something to quaff. His costume justifies her attempts at sounding like an old Newfoundland maid, and her newly found high-pitched sing-song resounds round the room. "This way my dear. Oh careful there! Excuse us. Make way. My dear! And you not looking a day over eighty. Why, you must be ninety if you're a day." She witters on until the professor has his red wine; then her whine recedes again into the dope room.

"Now that still captures Newfoundland for me. Wild animals and tame peasants! I mean I really feel this is the gem of Canada. And I appreciate it more each time I get back. It's quiet and peaceful, no crime, just y'mummers and y'good times...Even if it can get a bit restricted in some ways."

"Is that right." Chuck Lewis has heard all this from his anthropologist friend Lance Haines before. It's 'cause Lance is from Toronto—and an anthropologist! He and his sociologist buddy, Sam Dyke, know differently. And all three are now squashed together by the kitchen table.

"It's 'cause of all the conflict avoidance customs, I guess," Lance continues, "and non-violent culture, and rituals of catharsis like mumming. So your only murders round here are common-or-garden, eh?"

"What about the Chinese laundry murder?"

"Oh come on Chuck! Read your *Alor:* a simple segmentation dispute. Three Chinamen in a laundry have an argument and one threatens to leave, and set up shop next door. They say they'll kill him if he does, so he kills them first. And gets hanged. No sweat."

"Still sounds exotic to me boy!" Sam laughs. "But you know that's never Newfoundland today, Lance. Seriously. The war brought in major changes. And there's been far more real crime since then. I guess crime must have risen 600 percent, right Chuck? And that's crimes of violence especially."

"But I still thought there was such a way of life of camaraderie and reciprocity and deference so it was only in situations of enormous emotional stress, like in the family, that you sometimes got norms like against murder overridden by people's emotions."

"Before the war Lance, maybe, yeah. Then it was just homicides 'cause of jealous lovers and bungled burglaries, eh. But since the war there's been more and more gruesome cases of nutters and psychos killing strangers. And rapists and sex-killers. And with the welfare state what was your own business suddenly becomes a public affair, see?" Sam explains the sociology of it.

"That's right, Lance," Chuck agrees. "There's been like a new dynamic here, a new process happening: more juveniles in crime, and more women, and obscene phone calls and arson and drunk-and-disorderly, and public mischief and insanity, and creating a disturbance and indecent exposure and all the rest, as well as your more high-profile crimes in the criminal code, like assaults with violence."

"Is that right?"

"Sure! And it should be scaring the shit out of people!" Sam adds. "This cop in my criminology class said they perceive an escalation in the general level of violence, and potentially violent people right through the system...and longitudinally, it's come since the war, see? I mean take murder. That's y'hardest data, that's y'clearest kind of violent crime, eh? But armed robbery has gone way up too, and the cop said it's only a matter of time before some soft touch gets shot up at a break-in. And then they get even more violent incidents that don't get charged on record, 'cause they pass as "insane" or something, eh!"

"Is that right?"

"Yes boy. It's getting really meaty here! And it's since the late-forties: these Newfs all start in on each other...And they still say only about one-third of crimes get to be reported."

Lance chances his arm at a statistic: "But I thought these crime waves sort of petered up and then petered down again?"

"But not since the war, see?" Chuck insists.

And Sam wades in: "Believe us, Lance, all y'exotic crimes of violence, like rape and murder and homicide, and infanticide, and assaults level one, two and three, they all suddenly escalated. This isn't mayhem city yet—not like the Northwest Territories—but it's not the most peaceful place neither! Whatever your commonsense perception says!"

"That's right. It's not all y'violence behind closed doors any more. I mean, Okay, a lot of violence is still in the home, but there's a kind of professional thief about now and all. And you can track them in the records: the 'stats' go down when Igor and Screw-Loose and Boris get sent away for a year or two!" They laugh.

And Lance is impressed: "Is that right! A regular career structure!"

"Yep. And most based round Buckmaster Circle: the nearest thing the city has to a working-class ghetto," Chuck continues. "But you find all of the inner city is becoming a kind of working-class core, and the middle classes moving out. So that's where all these armed robbers come from."

"Well this is fascinating!" Lance admits. "I mean I just been reading Matthews and Firestone and them about the expression of interpersonal violence being forbidden in the outports, right? But this sounds more like St. John's is disintegrating, and the centre is falling out of the society or something!"

"And this cop was saying, too, how it's people polluted with alcohol committing more crimes now. Or else they're the only ones they can catch 'cause the rest run off!" Sam laughs.

"Nah," Lance is back on firmer ground, "alcohol has always been used as a rationalisation the next day to explain what you did but can't remember the night before."

"Yeah. Right, Lance," Chuck agrees. "No it'll be economic hardship now causing an escalation of violence. It'll be crimes directed against the owners of property and against the means of production. And then that means violent reprisals and harsh treatment 'cause the bosses feel threatened economically and get scared of the social fabric weakening. And then of course the spread of urbanisation and oil, eh."

Lance ventures a medical insight: "Hey! You know I'd forgotten this, but all this fits what a psychologist I met at a party was telling me about the Medical Centre not too long ago. She couldn't believe how violent Newfoundland society altogether seemed to her. She said Casualty is always getting people stabbed and shot, or clobbered with monkey-wrenches, and they come in and say they just had a set-to with the father-in-law, or buddy in the street...Or it's this 65-year-old getting plastered and just going home and beating up the whole family. Hospitalising them! So they get all these head wounds and comas."

"This is what we find, Lance. And imagine how depressing it is never to find work. And just looking for ages. I tell you, it's more of a wonder they don't go round hacking themselves to bits, eh? They must be internalising so much of it still, I guess."

"It's called being civilised, Sam!...And having a cultural norm against it." Lance can anthropologise again. "See, it's not in the Newfoundland worldview."

"But it's sure starting to get to people, you know boys!" Chuck warns. "People are noticing there's a lot more violence about. It's a topic of great concern."

"Right. Look at Mayor Malone, scared of them putting them *Globe and Mail* vending machines round town 'cause it would give thieves more chance for more crime."

Chuck grins. "Yeah but Sam, his real gripe is that stores like his have to keep on selling them for fifty-six cents when people can get 'em now for fifty cents out of the machines!"

"Okay," Sam laughs, "he's a farce. But what I'm saying, Chuck, is even the Establishment is getting scared now. It's getting official, like in the courts, and the mayor, that crime and violence is escalating."

"Oh, no doubt, boy...And I guess it's not worth throwing the baby out with the bathwater. I mean the Establishment and what they think is still part of the society. But I'd be more interested in what the people really affected by this rise in violent crime are saying about it."

"Do you think as the city expands people's thresholds of tolerance kind'a contract?" Lance ventures. "So then they perceive an upturn of violence, domestic and the rest, and conceptualise it as illegitimate?"

"Yeah, Okay, Lance," Chuck is wary, "but it's not just perception, eh. I mean the real picture from the 'stats' is also a jump in the level of violence. Like a critical point has been passed."

"That's right. See Lance, this isn't just a small town any more. This is urban sociology now. Like before, for a small town, you'd expect an arithmetic progression in the 'stats,' eh? So a town of 50,000 won't have twice the violent crime of somewhere 25,000 'cause it's still a small town, right. And maybe the same right up to 100,000. But then you get take-off, and there's a quantum leap."

"And people are shocked," Chuck adds. "But they shouldn't be. These kids go to the mainland, make big bucks, and then blow the lot on women and booze and fast cars. So then they come home 'cause of oil, but it's hard times here still, so they get frustrated and start smashing the place up... It's easy to work out. And I bet they're responsible for 80 percent of the crimes of violence."

"So what would a causal explanation look like to you lot? Anything clear? General patterns?"

Sam has a go: "Well. Don't forget violence is a universal question of industrial society, eh. I mean to write a good theoretical analysis of violence, and its severity, and nature and that, you'd have to take formal sampling and look at class conflict. For y'social and economic causatives. Like the dialectics of capitalist society..."

Chuck's turn: "Right. And then relate ideology to a socio-economic infrastructure. 'Cause it'll be that which shapes society. And y'social trends, like. So you say there's violence 'cause of class hegemony. And then misperception of class membership means you get violence between members of the working class. 'Cause of false consciousness."

"Right. Instead of just competing with members of different classes and structural positions. And then, for your domestic violence you'd have to decide if you're gonna go along with the feminists and say it's patriarchy right across the board, and or if it's different for the upper classes."

"Yeah Okay," Lance halts the rush, "but how about an explanation in simple language? Have you got a feel for that?... I mean, forget y'behaviourism and y'existentialism. Just on the empirical level of a blow on the nose or a dead body, like your typical Newf could understand, Chuck?"

"Fine Lance. But you still can't get a real picture without y' 'stats' and some number-crunching. See? Otherwise it's just shooting in the dark... It's like one of those studies in the States Roy Black was telling us about. Remember Sam? They were using this cultural explanation to look at homicide and violence and they said it all came from the southern States that had slaves in the Antebellum. So when people moved from there they took this culture of violence with them and spread it and didn't assimilate or something," Chuck and Sam smile at the naiveté. "Okay, but then Roy and some other professors brought in some economic and social factors, and drew up a table of variables—like income and unemployment and social group and race—and showed there's something far more complex going on... Get what I'm saying Lance? You can't just make a simple argument about commonsense and culture, eh? It's more complex. 'Cause you got to relate violence to all these inequalities in Newfoundland society. The same as with all social problems."

"That's right. And see how patterns of violence relate to changes in an inegalitarian distribution of wealth and prestige in Newfoundland."

"Okay Sam. But I still don't see why that couldn't be made understandable to y'locals."

"Well, remember they aren't very intelligent here!" Sam grins.

"No, seriously, Lance. I see what you're saying," Chuck reassures him. "But take stranger-violence. Like that stabbing on the TCH. Some guy buddy had never seen before, and after he doesn't know why he's done it. I mean that's what people are shit-scared of, eh. Getting murdered walking the streets. And this is what they mean when they talk about a more violent society bursting out. 'Cause that's real violence against everyone. But to explain that, and why it gets folks so outraged you'd have to bring in Durkheim, eh, and say it's against all of society, while y'wife-battery or domestic violence isn't y'real Durkheimian violence 'cause it's more definable, right?"

Philippa squeezes over from stirring the chilli. "Chuck," she licks her fingertips, "be a love and pop out for some paper plates for me would you? For the chilli later. I thought I'd have enough but I miscalculated." She is matter-of-fact in her request. She and Chuck used to live together, and Chuck always respected the kind of European style in which she accepted his moving out: she didn't have to pretend the town wasn't big enough for the both of them any more. And she still invites him round. So, sensible likewise, Chuck nips off to the corner convenience store that's always open, and Sam and Lance decide to go along for a breather. Get another 6-pack of Heineken for the night too.

Seated by himself and his beer bottle at the other end of the kitchen table, Philippa can see, now that Chuck and the rest have gone, a rather tired and morose history thesis-adviser of hers: Professor Doyle Robbins. So she sways over to him: "I'm pleased you made it, Doyle!"

"Don't be so sure Phil. You know how your sociology lover-boys get up my nose!"

"What? Chuck? Oh come on. He's harmless enough. What's he been saying?"

"Oh, just the usual balderdash sociology has to serve up: 'Newfoundland isn't like it once was; it's got far more violent now; moan, moan,' you know!"

Philippa laughs. She has a soft spot for tweeditone, alkie academics, like misery-guts Professor Robbins. "But isn't it, Doyle? All this oil in town soon. And the police always calling for fire-arms?"

"Oh there's always been violence here, Phil. In the community round the bay next to my folks, I remember hearing about an eighty-year-old woman getting raped. And straw stuffed up her vagina. I forget the circumstances, but I mean it's always happened. It's just that traditionally people weren't interested, you know, so it never reached the papers and people didn't read anyhow. But it's our media now. They're getting as bad as in the States! Someone gets killed, and the very same day some woman is displaying her grief on TV, surrounded by all the blood and guts! People want news because they want security and satisfaction and they can't find any. I'll give you a for instance: a friend of mine had his car vandalised downtown, and the only thing everyone wants to know when they hear is 'was it locked?' You see? All they want is to distance themselves and know how to stop it happening to them."

"But I thought that was what the sociologists were saying, Doyle?"

"Oh all they want is to preach the moral breakdown of society and modes of social control, whatever that means! Get us all mouthing pop-theory... They already got the police pushing their angle: 'Anomie's coming to town,' I heard on one copper's lips," Doyle grins and shakes his head.

"Well it sure sounds good! With everyone saying it!"

"Precisely Philippa. Which means more jobs in the profession for the boys in future. And more juicy research grants. It's the same as bureaucracy: think of all the jobs lost if there was no unemployment!"

"But seriously, Doyle. Haven't crimes of violence increased since, say, the 1950s?"

"Well, hazarding a guess Phil, I'd say only by a tiny amount, just in line with the growing city. But it's all cyclical. And proportionally, St. John's isn't more violent, I'd say. Just the same pattern as any Canadian city since the war. But that's what these anthropologists should be doing: say comparing internecine violence in Quebec with here. Do Frenchmen, or rather people of French descent beat each other similarly to us? But so little of value is done. So there's just this widespread notion of peaceful, traditional Newfoundland, free of crime, till suddenly, Gosh! Beware the crime wave!... Bunkum!"

"Sounds like you don't put a lot of store by the old ethnographic monographs, Doyle!"

"Oh come on Phil! They're laughable. I told you before: the anthropologists would come round and my people would tell them all manner of white lies, and it would all be studiously written down and then published!... And they always provided a contradictory picture, besides. I mean on the one hand there's this tradition of painting the outport as 'peace to all men and goodwill to nature,' and on the other, we're all cold and barbaric seal-killers, and have to be 'cruel to survive in the environment'! See, it's all claptrap... And now they've hit upon "Violence" as the new in-word. It's what Foucault says about certain concepts suddenly becoming reflexive items of discussion, you know. Like 'Man.' Well it's 'Violence' now: books on books on books on it, from the States, or Canada. It's the new in-thing that professional sociologists and anthropologists can oppose Newfoundland culture to, you know. So all this garbage about urban violence, it's just the next import in line from the great U.S. of A. And then they start looking for economic factors here to 'base' this new cultural superstructure upon and 'explain' it! Huh!"

"So you don't believe all these new statistics they're always coming up with?"

"Load of rubbish! Crap, in a word. And that's all I have to say about the statistics business." Doyle surreptitiously looks about him. "I suppose I should keep mum rather than say that 'round here!" They laugh. "No, but seriously Phil, statistics by themselves are meaningless because there's no historical perspective. I don't just mean this to sound reactionary, you know, but you really do need historical perspective to make any sense of life on the 'Rock'. "

Philippa agrees. "I know. I've never really found these 'stats' wizards believable. They need critiquing."

"Ah, it's just all ideologues, Phil. Positivistic sociology is full of them. The States is choking with them. Find a narrow definition of crime, or violence, get lots of research money, go out and collect more statistics, and then you can bring your leopard home in a net for display, with you as the wild animal tamer. Awful! No, historically you can see how things here now are very much the same as they were in the nineteenth century. Even the eighteenth century. Maybe not the seventeenth century 'cause things do change, gradually. I'll give you a for instance. You ask any townie, and he's bound to tell you St. John's is the centre of administration and power, and everything else on the island, and has been since the 1850s. But really it's a seat of northern power! It's people moving in from Conception Bay and Bonavista and Trinity, moving in to work here. And it's always happening. Like all the Catholics coming in from Harbour Grace. They may be found everywhere now, but you check their parents and grandparents and they're all from Harbour Grace."

"So it's just us now believing in violence, or change change change all the time, so we see it. Not like the stability they saw before?"

"There's always been violence here, Phil. First it was all that foolishness between the English and the French. And then the nineteenth century ushered in more violent times: far more than your sociology friends give credit for. I mean per thousand of population there was an enormous police force here, trying to keep crime down, and still bricks were thrown through merchants' windows, and between 1838 and 1840, eight people were hanged by the authorities. See, this popular image of stability and order in the 1800s compared to now, that's just half the picture. That may have been true for the middle classes, but it certainly wasn't for the workers and the unemployed."

"Sure. But you don't read about them!"

"Right, and that's why a thesis like yours on labour history is so vital, Phil. I mean it was an oral culture here till the 1950s for fuck's sake, you know! Like I reckon the nineteenth century was full of Irish radicalism here. Influenced by the French Revolution. And all the priests were in on it, and then the church'd move them on when they got too active... But if you look I reckon you'll see the priests and the unions and the fishermen fighting mercantile capitalism to a standstill. And eventually bankrupting them and sending them out the province! I mean this is just a hunch, and I hope your thesis will elucidate it all, but I think it was the merchants' pressure that forced Newfoundland culture back into a pre-capitalistic subsistence mode, in a response to the commoditisation of their labour and social relations that the merchants wanted to capitalise on. Proletarianise them so they were even dependent on the merchants for their food and clothing, for fuck's sake! So you got an ideology of mercantile capital, and a legal system totally alien to outport life, and the merchants couldn't get the fishermen to use it—like come to court when there were thefts, as a witness, because the thefts were in fact a socially legitimate mode of borrowing they'd worked out, 'bucking', to distribute necessary subsistence goods between households, and withstand the enormous economic pressures... It was a covert rebellion, you know. Like you see with language too: they come with standard English, and change it to a distinct dialect... So, especially in the urban belt, if you can call it that, I mean St. John's to Carbonear and Harbour Grace, you get early on a politicised and radical Roman Catholic church, with priests garnering votes, and organising the locals to take over the local government that the merchants had set up in 1831, so by 1840 the merchants had had enough and insisted the Brits take the government away again! Or something like that anyway." Doyle's voice trails off as he realises his pet reconstruction has been getting the better of him again.

"That sounds great, Doyle. Really." Philippa is enthusiastic. "And that's just what we need, something general, 'cause it seems we're all trapped here, saying how unique every little part of the isle is, so these sociologists can come in and lay some gross abstraction on us."

"Well these sociologists just describe Newfoundland as baffling. And self-destructive. But you can see a covert battle going on right through Newfoundland history. And occasionally it just erupts, and you get the 1830s period of plebian collective violence. The 1832 sealing strike. And fishermen trying to gain more rights, and then getting violent at election rallies and the polling stations."

"Actually Doyle, this reminds me of some good stuff written about factional fighting in Ireland."

"Yes but that stuff tends to deteriorate into the drivel of descriptions of garden-parties, and functional fighting at special occasions. And that's just bourgeois window dressing for the most part. But you're right, Phil.... I mean it's a moot point whether religion or class is the more pertinent instrument for dissecting those 1830s disputes, but one thing they were not were ritual displays of an otherwise peaceful outport existence!" He grins. "You read some of the ballads from the time and you can just imagine the black Protestant faces and the Catholic tempers rubbing together and sparking. So the Harbour Grace Catholics go and shear off the ears of some Protestant speechifier one dark night in 1835 and then mail them back to him later, salted! Only to have the same fate overtake his publisher at the same spot, five years later! Marvellous stuff!... And you know Phil, I wouldn't like to recite some of those ballads in a beer-house in an Irish part of Conception Bay to this very day. I'd watch my ears carefully!" They laugh. "So even when it's hidden, it's there all the same... Take jannying, for instance. Now that gets far more interesting when you see mummers not as some 'rustic perversion of St. George and the Blue Knight,' " Doyle attempts an Oxbridge affectation and Philippa smiles," "but more local rebellion in disguise. I mean a sort of ritual of reversal of the relations of production imposed by the merchants, and in fact getting quite subversive, making boys into bishops and pissing in the holy water and the rest!"[24]

"Hey, now that's a really neat theory, Doyle!"

"And see, maybe that's why the authorities banned mummering in 1869 in Harbour Grace. 'Cause they felt threatened by some shenanigans the previous year... And by the looks of your Professor DeWit, by 1985 the repression and bourgoisification have finally won out. I mean what local working-class theatre do you see here now? None! It's all imposed from on top... There's not even street theatre like the old prizefighting. When we moved to town and I walked to Bishop Aloysius high school and back, in the thirties, you'd see bloodied men lying in the gutters along the streets all the time. And I'd be too scared to venture out after dark, because some streets were so rough. Full of boogey men waiting to pounce, we were afraid." Philippa smiles maternally. "But really, Phil. You could stand in a doorway on George Street, and watch prize fights every night if you wanted... And there were regular street fights too, only stopped when a measured tread heralded the policemen on their beats; towering fellows in those days, specially brought from Bonavista. They used to look seven feet high in their sealskin tophats. And they'd arrive just as the last round was completed, as it were, because word had magically got around that it wasn't Tom or Bill on the beat, ready to help you home, 'cause he knew you, but those wild baymen who really liked getting busy with their sticks, cracking heads. And sure, they'd lay men out left, right and centre, if they could... so it amazes me when people say Newfoundland is more violent now than before. Even Newfoundlanders my age. Dunno where they were in the thirties and forties!... And what about the food riots for fuck's sake! Looting and pitched battles in 1932 in St. John's, and storming the Colonial Building and police having to use tear gas. And then riots at Conception Harbour, and Carbonear and Spaniards' Bay, and Little Catalina. And Salvage and Twillingate... And then more at St. John's, and then Bonne Bay."

"Is that right? I never knew it was so extensive!"

"No one does, Phil. It's a neglected decade. So if you listen to these sociologists, it's like Confederation is year one in Newfoundland history! And no riots till Joey sent the Mounties in agin the loggers and suddenly proletarianised all the strikers!"[25]

"Well, historians should remind them."

"Right. Particularly since it was so much worse here than elsewhere. I mean before World War II saved everyone's bacon, as it were, including the Water Street Neanderthals, the merchants, St. John's was just a smelly dirty slum. They were calling all of Newfoundland in fact 'the slum of the Empire'... They even had to hand out vitamin-enriched flour here to help stave off beri-beri!... No. The whole social history of the period has yet to be written. And like how astute and socialist the workers were. Conscious of their political and historical positions, and realising they had to use violence as a bargaining chip, like hospitalise police and batter down merchants' doors, as propaganda, or they would get nothing from the government but retrenchments and more attempts to foist them off onto Poor Relief."

"The famous six cents a day!"

"Right. Or ten cents here in town."

"You know I wouldn't have guessed they were so politicised."

"Right. And it was all the police could do to try and find the ringleaders and arrest them when the trouble died down. And just pray St. John's and Grand Falls and Carbonear didn't riot at the same time or else the police force would never have coped. Even with all their special constables and gunboats!...But see, violence here is old hat, whatever the folk memory says."

"I guess it's a bad memory so folks wanna erase it."

"Well that includes today's unions, I'm afraid...Understandable, I suppose with less working-class consciousness. But I dunno...In the thirties, the unions instilled a sense of sort of entitlement, so action agin the government or the merchants was righteous if they didn't deliver what was owed. Like they even raided the liquor stores because they were refused their tots of rum!" They laugh. "Which is a nice thought!"

"Is that right! You'd never get that now. It's not collective rebuttals any more, just isolated individual incidents like cutting cables in the telephone dispute. Unless you say the armed robberies are against the shop owners. Or murder is an expression of workers' oppression or something."

"Watch it Phil! You're getting to sound dangerously like buddy, mastermind sociologist! No, the sorts of comparison that need making are like how the merchants calling for the return of the birch in the thirties, or else their shops would be ransacked and all hell be let loose, is just the same as the police today calling for the return of capital punishment. Or the same blackmarketing and thieving, and desperation then as now. You know, it's all the same—historical cycles: depression, violence, war; prosperity, affluence, recession, violence. I'm afraid Phil, plus a change, plus la méme chose! Nothing new." Doyle resigns into the staring-into-one's-beer pose.

But Philippa does not see. For Tom, her new boyfriend, tickles her from behind and steers her out the kitchen. The folklore clique has made a successful take-over bid on the music and found some of Emilé Benoit's jigs and reels cassettes. "My dear!" Stella's old maid's falsetto rises in exhortation of Professor DeWit from the dope-room, "This'll shake y'cockles and hoist y'mainbrace! And you not looking a day past 80!"

So Philippa and Tom join the ascendant folklorists. High time for ye olde step-dancing...

Second Scene

Monday evening, at a MUN criminology course.

After the weekend and its parties, Sam Dyke attends his usual criminology class at the university. The setting is a large, modern and steeply banked lecture theatre in the science building. Although a full-time student, Sam saw a copy of the flier below, advertising this extra-mural course taught by members of the local legal profession, and he thought auditing it would add valuable insight to his thesis, even if he didn't register for the certificate.

Memorial University of Newfoundland Extension Service
Fall Semester Offering

Principles of Criminal Procedure and the Administration of Criminal Justice:

Planning to work within the criminal justice system? Interested in law enforcement or just wanting to learn about criminology?... This course is for you!
Part of the certificate programme in criminology, this course will give you an overview of the Canadian criminal justice system, and take a detailed look at trial and court procedures, arrest, legal aid, evidence, sentencing, prison and parole.

Instructors: Hector Hussey and Lloyd Drodge
Fee: $125.00
Course: Classes will be on Mondays, 7:00—10:00 p.m.

It is 7:20 p.m. now and His Honour, *Judge Hector Hussey*, is about to start lecturing. The judge, a graduate of Dalhousie Law School, is now in his late-forties, but still unmarried, born in Twillingate, he has lived ten years in St. John's. His audience is a mixture: besides Sam, there are the housewives and hotel receptionists wanting to do something different; and the telephone workers escaping the boredom of being on strike, and the Sisters of Mercy preparing for a pastoral vocation at Her Majesty's Penitentiaries, and the women from the Military Police, and the nurses from the Oakleys Hospital Forensic Unit. There is also *Mary Kenney:* early-forties and married, a social worker in Ferryland, but born and living in St. John's and now intent upon working with Adult Corrections in the Department of Justice; and *Jane Purchase:* mid-thirties and married, born in Deer Lake and lived twelve years in St. John's, a secretary at a law firm but now aiming for a future in the RCMP; and *Sergeant Ted Nugent* of the Royal Newfoundland Constabulary: late-thirties, divorced, born and living in St. John's.

Now that His Honour and his leather briefcase have entered, the class is hushed; Cokes and chips have been hurriedly consumed. Seated in groups or couples or by discarded coats, and towards the front of the large hall and the lectern, the class is eager to imbibe more of its instructor's experience and wit. Note pads are at the ready, and pens raised.

"Well, good evening ladies and gentlemen. Let us begin with tonight's thrilling installment: punishment. Ah! What a word to roll around the tongue. Punish*ment*... The Law, remember, is a commanding mistress, as I was told at the bar, and it must be the reason I have yet to find time to marry!"

"What a catch he'd be!" Mary leans over and whispers to her neighbour, Jane. "And I could just do with a little marital fling about now. Remove the monotony it would!" Jane smiles.

The judge continues. "The Law is also an ass, and in more ways than one. In India they traditionally made an accused man hold a donkey's tail and if it brayed that proved he was guilty! Canadian law attempts not to be an ass too often, but delivered by judges, it can't boast perfection always. Even *we* do not always possess precognition." Hussey smiles. "Okay. Down to brass tacks. The system of law is there to protect the public, punish the offender and deter others. Sentencing must punish. Courts must respond to outbursts of violence like everyone else. So while not too long ago armed robbery in St. John's was not common, now we all know the difference: a spate of them and of course a public outcry against violence. Am I right? Of course. Did you see that programme on TV last night? Some wise guy whose personal history included his first armed robbery at age 11. I was imagining him standing on tip-toe to lean his gun on the counter, eh!" The class laughs. "But seriously, I am always alarmed by resorts to weapons; it strikes fear into everyone's heart. So the position of the court must be clear. I feel my bench must reflect society's concern and be strict if there is a propensity for violence being shown in a crime and the involvement of weapons. So. What can we do?" People look up from note-taking. "Well, the laws of sentencing, the rules, derive from the statutes of the Criminal Code as you know; statutes divided into Civil Law repairing differences between individuals, and Criminal Law between law-breakers and the state. Now you might think a bad driver is a danger to society, which needs protecting but most fender-bender cases are Civil... I bit my tongue. I was about to mention women drivers but we all know fender benders come in all shapes and sizes." The boys in the audience grin, and nudge girlfriends. "Okay. Where are we? Statutes provide the range of sentences. So break-and-enter, for example, could get you from a suspended sentence to life imprisonment. Pretty different hey! But maximal penalties according to the criminal code are almost never given, and the rhetoric of sentencing and the patterns of practical application are to be found in past cases. New sentences are usually kept in line with past ones."

"So criminals just get a slap on the wrist in other words, Sir!" a disgruntled Sergeant Nugent calls from his seat, and others nod.

"Well it depends what you mean by 'a slap on the wrist.' We choose this correctional procedure for a civilised country. Also, the western world is swinging to the conservative and the law is changing. Just look at Provincial Court. That's where 95 percent of cases are tried and where new directions really come from, even if it's higher Courts of Appeal which then crystallise provincial patterns. My younger cohorts more recently out of law school, so more learned, more educated than I...," the judge smirks to himself, "are better informed concerning all mooted changes, but, for example, kidnapping now also includes childnapping, the deprivation by one parent of the visiting rights of the other; and rape is now aggravated or sexual assault, with stiffer penalties."

But Sergeant Nugent is not satisfied. "We had a youngster who had a record of thirty-six 'B & Es,' right. Finally we got him on a fingerprint and the judge goes and gives him a month for each robbery—three years total, instead of life for any of them. Crazy! And four or five months after he's out, you'll see, he'll be in the paper doing it again."

"I sympathise Sergeant, but not if the culprit is properly dealt with and punished by his sentence. Now page 409 of your manuals, please." The judge looks up as some books are opened. "I see not everyone has yet invested in a manual, $20 I know, but I'm not to blame. I don't get any commission whatever, believe me. But nothing is cheap in this course, remember. Maybe in future we'll provide pocket manuals so you can remove them from your jeans on Water Street on Saturday nights and say, 'Hey! There goes a Section 85!' People laugh or look sheepish. "And not to worry if at first the manual is confusing. Even Appeal Court judges get confused over the law on occasion so you're in good company."

"I can see why girl!" Jane whispers to Mary.

"So. Punishment aims to deter, to repudiate, to compensate and to rehabilitate and reform the criminal and the wider public. These principles are centuries old. Like Deuteronomy in the Bible: 'Stone the rebellious son, purge the community of evil, and all Israel will hear.' A fit and proper punishment serves to protect society, prevent further breaches and support the police force which attempts to uphold the law. Then restitution is our attempt to restore victims to their positions before the crime. Reforming the criminal may be a more secondary principle of punishment, but retribution and the denunciation of the behaviour of the accused has certainly been around since the Bible. In fact retribution is gaining momentum and making something of a come-back. See, punishment goes in cycles and in ten or fifteen years, retribution should be a major aspect, from being near-to-nothing a while back. Now that's my personal view, and for the purposes of this class the correct view, right?"

"Proper t'ing!" Sergeant Nugent calls and others laugh.

"Okay. What can we do about the criminal? What do we have in our arsenal at Provincial Court? Well, one realistic and effective form of punishment is, of course, the fine. And, contrary to popular belief fines do not furnish the judge's retirement fund! No. And we never have to sue convicts, because we have the best way of collecting fines too. It's called 'The money or else the body', written on police warrants, and you'd be surprised how the money pours in!" The judge smiles. "Then, of course, there are prison sentences. Now, Newfoundland and P.E.I. are the only provinces with no federal penitentiaries so anyone sentenced to two years incarceration, or more, serves time off the island such as at Dorchester or Springhill Institution. You townies probably know about the debate over where to build Newfoundland's pen.; and more likely than not, St. John's will win the jobs and it'll be here. But the present 'pen' here from before Confederation—HMP—is really just a reformatory, a 'Newfie special' for short sentences. Or for compassionate grounds—like the ex-policemen who'd be killed if we shipped them up-along for their time-serving. But you know all these pens are fascinating places to visit, even if not to live in! It's rather scary to be locked in, but there's a whole different society inside. Like in women's prisons just about the only skirts you see are on the police officers! The inmates are wondering around in jeans and t-shirts, all their own clothes. And often finger-in-finger too 'cause lesbian sex is permitted in private, and they're allowed the unusual privacy of curtains across the bars of their cells. True!" The girls shudder as the boys grin at each other.

"Kinky!" someone shouts, amidst laughs.

"Those two women from the mainland who did the armed robbery on the Texaco service station in Chamberlains, and held up a taxi and stole it, remember—they were lovers from a federal pen. And you meet some pretty intelligent, classy ladies inside too. And there was even one sixty-five-year-old grandmother inside for armed robbery, I remember."

"I was involved in an armed robbery here this summer," Jane calls. "I mean as a victim," as the *double entendre* is realised. "And they all had supermarket bags over their heads and loose clothes. So I guess they could've been women too. I hadn't thought of it before."

"Well, most of them still are boys," the judge explains, "but it's possible. I know how difficult it is to tell genders now when women no longer wear rings of commitment, or semi-precious stones, and all these men dye their hair or wear it long. But it's certainly time for women to come out of the shadows and face convictions. Like the old saying said—'Behind every man of the moment there's a good woman!' So, as Judge Dindale of Provincial Court also says, if women want equal rights they also have to accept equal responsibility. Women often leave his court in tears. And I remember convicting one woman, not a gram under 350 pounds, a 'miss,' and rather rotund, who dangled her baby in front of me at the bar, attempting to use it in her plea. She got six years, if I recall." The class hums agreement. "There are no real security facilities for women in the province and they go to Stephenville lock-up. But they could be there for a while before trial, and there's less freedom there than in our HMP in town for the boys so I guess they could claim 'a cruel and unusual punishment'; and if they're innocent after all I'm afraid it's 'dead time' and their hard luck. Though not many complain at getting off, as you can imagine! Now, men's prisons are of course more security institutions and discipline can't be so lax. So all wear standard garb and like in Milhaven Institution if you look up you see all these fences topped with razor-ribbon (that's sharper than barbed-wire) and really intimidating machine-gun turrets, and a host of guards. And you enter through a string of automatic doors so you don't know where on earth you'll end up. If on earth at all! In Kingston they used to have a dungeon, for lunatics traditionally, and Lake Ontario used to seep in, so the authorities would drag bodies out of it each fall!"

"Eurgh!" Jane and Mary shudder.

"Then there is also Salmonier Prison Camp, or Work Farm," the judge continues.

" 'Salmonier Holiday Camp' more like!" Sergeant Nugent suggests. "That's just the easy life!"

"Well. It isn't hard labour anymore, and they can earn a wage for cutting wood. But they aren't a drain on society."

"But isn't it like these prisoners eating steak and watching colour TV?" Jane wonders. "And some of those cells are nicer than my home." Others agree.

"Well, I find nothing wrong in humane treatment so long as prisoners are working and earning it and even starting an industry. I know your view is often elegantly represented but rehabilitation must also be part of punishment, and is often the main logic behind our court decisions, for example, suspended sentencing. So you register conviction but don't pass sentence and give him a period of probation. Then if he goofs up and breaks any conditions anywhere in Canada—what he does outside Canada, in Greece or somewhere, on holiday, is the least of my worries—but anything *in* Canada and he's really in hot water. See? So probation is a flexible vehicle we can use if criminals seem upfront and cooperative and want to play ball with us. So we write a court order with deemed terms requiring certain behaviour of them, and then see if their probation officers speak well and highly of them. Like I always get lots of Mickey Mouse 'B and Es'; a snatch and grab who comes from a good home but just broke with his girlfriend, then I might award a suspended sentence and one hundred hours of community service on specific projects. You get lots of those. Sometimes I think I must've forgotten how it was to be a teenager!" The judge laughs, "Or if it's some dear old lady convicted of some minor breach of the Traffic Act, conviction may be registered, but no fine imposed. But don't go taking that as *carte blanche* over your senseless offences like drinking-and-driving. If any of you lot get picked up for that after taking this course you should be flogged!" The class laughs. "Or better, thrown down the Molson chimney so you drown in the hops!" More laughs. "I remember our 1984 Gold Medal Winner: thirty-three convictions for impaired driving, and sometimes on three consecutive nights! Someone deaf to plain English: 'Just don't drink!' Now, Judge Croft is Newfoundland's foremost expert on traffic law, and I'm a close second. And we only bend the technical rules sometimes. It's the same as with shoplifting. There's a real need to deter that because it's a problem in all North American communities, but if there are severe medical problems, say, or some student whose career would be ruined by a criminal record, then discharges can also occasionally be won here."

"But what about concurrent sentencing, Sir, like this lad with thirty-six 'B and Es'?" Sergeant Nugent still wants to know. "That's no punishment, either."

"Ah yes," the judge recalls. "Well, judges take a totality principle into account. So if I send someone away for two years for a break and enter, and a few days later the same man is before me on a 236, that's driving-while-impaired, and I sentence him to three months jail, then I feel it's fair to have them run concurrently."

"But why? He's getting away scotfree on the second offence," the Sergeant suggests, and his neighbours agree.

"Not really," the judge laughs at their 'logic'. "He's being punished for both simultaneously. So, as the saying goes, 'Cheat by the dozen,' I guess," he grins. "Now as you should know by now, it's us in Provincial Court who deal with most criminal cases while District Court judges settle more civil ones. So I feel quite free to knock them. You find some of them reading the Criminal Code during a trial for the first time. So one of them gave fourteen years in jail for a minor 'B and E,' and then when defence counsel reminded him the range was fourteen years down to a suspended sentence, the judge altered his decision to a suspended sentence!" Judge Hussey smiles as his class tut-tut in disgust. "Guilt of course is a matter of both a guilty mind—*mens rea*, in Latin—and a guilty act—*actus reus*—and the judge has to be convinced of both. Of course in Provincial Court the judges just toss a coin, and in Supreme Court you hear the jurymen throwing darts in their jury room—'a "ton" says he's innocent!' " The class laughs again. "Seriously, I often have a coin on the bench with me. I tap it around and get attention and respect, and criminals are attracted by the shine. And it holds Her Majesty's likeness—whom I represent. And *then* I toss it to decide! No, but after years of practice, watching people give evidence everyday, it becomes almost a gut reaction more than an intelligent one. You can hear the ring of truth in the strains of falsehood, or else they're excellent liars. But it's like you girls dating. Say on the seventh date buddy says 'I love you,' right, then you rely on your commonsense and your emotions and experience, and you say, 'what do I know about men?' and, 'what's in his eyes?' right!" The girls titter their agreement. "Well that's what hearing evidence is like. Most cases are so similar anyway that the relevant laws and sentences are all typed up in your head after a few years and it gets to be routine, rote. Of course you do still get some classic cases. On page 463 of your manual there's a classic case from the good old days. Take a look sometime: names changed to protect the guilty of course!" Some of the audience turn pages to follow up the joke. "Not your average 'St. John's Newfoundland,' this guy was from 'Casablanca, Morocco.' Been somewhere with the French Foreign Legion and then a French mental hospital in Marseilles, and then ends up here when the Queen's here, with a car full of guns! Then some cop dressed as a crook taping stuff in jail as hearsay evidence tapes him confessing in a conversation with God! But the judges rule that since God is not a person in their terms, no real conversation had taken place. Great stuff!" The judge laughs. "Of course you know that since 1976 there has been no capital punishment in Canada. Even if the Queen, or the Pope, was killed here, or if all the judges were blown up, or if someone poisoned St. John's water and thousands died, or some such macabre crime, then the state would still not take a life. At least not at the moment. That might all change in a more conservative age. Like the States changed back. But for the moment it's only dogs I can order executed in Newfoundland." People laugh. "And that's only if they bite twice too!...Of course I am still empowered to impose indefinite sentences. Violent or dangerous or sexual offenders who cannot control their impulses may be sentenced indefinitely, although the provision is rarely used in Newfoundland, even though it by no means infringes the tenor of the Charter of Human Rights. Just that you find some inferior Superior Court judges never having heard of the provision. On the other hand, if someone is that bad, at least most of them here would see that and award him 'life' anyway."

"That's still only twenty years, sir—fourteen sometimes," Sergeant Nugent throws in. "But I know a boy sent away recently as a dangerous offender, Sir. Eighteen he was, and repeatedly raped his sister and mother and aunt. And violent too. So he won't be coming out for a while!" He grins as the girls shudder and turn away.

"Yes, Sergeant. Well, like I said at the start, the courts, well my court at least, is strict where propensities for violence are found. We reflect society's concerns about any crime wave afoot. Okay? Talking of crime waves, and just before we break for ten minutes, if you like thrillers, full of deaths, rapes and thefts, I mean why not start in the gutter and go down from there, right? then a real good read with a bottle of scotch on the bear rug before the fire is the bestseller *Adam and Naive* by Norman Boem. A remarkable study of police investigation of violent criminal activity in California... Right. Ten minutes, before plea-bargaining. Grab a Coke if you want. Or anything else you can legally grab." He chuckles and begins to tidy notes as the class breaks into chatter, and people go out for a breather.

As they exit together, Sergeant Nugent explains to Mary that he's already read Boem's book. "Very entertaining. I read it over a weekend. All about gaining confessions. And not just the old good-guy-and-bad-guy routine! No siree. Down there it's six-foot policewomen in bunny suits beating on suspects, and policemen climbing through windows, in wet-suits. The works, I tell you girl." He grins. "And they change the routine so fast judges never get wind of it or suspicious, and the suspects just sound nuts if they complain about it to anyone! Good, eh?" Laughing, they leave the room...

Third Scene

Tuesday afternoon, at a session of Provincial Court.

The next afternoon finds Judge Hussey back in his chambers at St. John's Provincial Court, located behind the shopping precinct on the fourth floor of Atlantic Place, a modern tower block on Water Street. At his bench and away from the university the judge finds himself faced by rather different duties. It is 2 p.m. now and afternoon session is about to convene.

Atlantic Place: 'Bright, new shopping in the heart of downtown, old St. John's. Right on the waterfront, over twenty stores and services under one roof, close to ships and fishing boats, hotels, restaurants and night-clubs.' And close to the Criminal Division, Small-Claims and Juvenile Division, and Traffic Division of Provincial Court. The court has only recently removed here and all its fixtures are still bright and new: tile, plaster and polished wood.

In the well-lit foyer, business is brisk. Standing by the receptionist's desk in the middle is Judge Dindale, still in his waistcoat before he goes to befrock himself, complaining about having to attend mass this evening. Balancing on one stiletto heel and flicking her necklace, *Crown Prosecutor Fort* looks up at him, smirking, and wonders what engagement he will be missing. She is in her late-thirties and divorced; born in Ottawa, and a graduate of Ottawa Law School, she has lived in St. John's ten years.

Nearby, there are huddles of lawyers, each with his long worsted overcoat, deliberating together before parting for different court-rooms. There is *Crown Prosecutor Sharpe:* late-forties, married, a graduate of the University of Western Ontario Law School, but born and living in St. John's; and defence lawyer *Dermot Earle:* early-thirties, single and recently graduated from University of New Brunswick Law School, born in Harbour Grace but lived in St. John's two years; and also *Walter Hoolihan,* a defence lawyer with the Legal Aid Office: early-forties, married, born in Halifax and trained at Dalhousie Law School but lived fifteen years in St. John's.

At the sides of the room there are three female receptionists leaning on hatches which open onto different offices, and each has her parade of uniformed police officers admiring her gay attire. Files in hand, the policemen are all set to enjoy an afternoon off the beat.

Meanwhile, just outside the foyer, by the elevators and water fountain, nervous summonees are milling round and reading the noticeboard of charges and court-room schedules. They can see the names of *Tanya Martin:* late-teens, separated and unemployed, born and living in St. John's; and *Moira Godden:* mid-twenties, single, a federal government courier, born and living in Torbay; and *Gerald Purdy:* early thirties, single and unemployed, born and living in St. John's neighbourhood of Shea Heights. The summonees are waiting and smoking, and encouraging denimed accomplices with jokes, and shoves. Every now and then one of them answers to a name called out by a court clerk, and follows the busy, be-suited official through the crowded foyer to an ante-room outside the court-room where his case will be heard. The clerk, *Ford Lethbridge,* is in his late-fifties and married; born in Whitbourne he has lived in St. John's twenty-five years.

There are five court-rooms, each furnished alike with flags, portraits of the Queen, red carpets and fluorescent lighting. In the ante-room outside Court No:2 are three impatient and rather uneasy men: *Leo Normore:* early-twenties, separated, unemployed, ex-convict and ex-resident of the Lightship Rehabilitation Centre, born in Corner Brook and lived in St. John's intermittently for seven years; and *Walter Oates:* mid-twenties, single, unemployed, born in Springdale and lived in St. John's, at the Lightship for six months, and *Ken Holloway*: late-twenties, married, ex-resident of the Lightship, now working on the oil rig supply boats, born and living in St. John's. The three are back in Provincial Court, this time to support their friend *Rick Hudson* as he acts as unwilling witness for the Crown in the prosecution of another friend, Gerald Purdy, for armed robbery. They feel sorry for Rick. Rick, early-thirties and separated, ex-taxi driver and resident of the Lightship, born in Shea Heights, has already been up before this court, and then Supreme Court, on similar charges to Gerald's. He was found guilty and sent away. Now he's being told to do the same thing to Gerald!

Leo looks at his watch and curses: "Late already. Bet it's the judge finishing his dinner. Taking his time!"

"Yeah!" Ken sneers, "and getting the vodka off his breath. Who'll it be?"

"Not Dindale," Leo reckons, "'cause he does more first appearances. Least I hope not!"

The *Evening Telegram* reporter, Betty Ryder, walks past them to sit and wait in court. Leo and Walt make kissing noises at her and flick tongues in and out. Then they all laugh at her withering glare.

"She writes everything down. Cunt!" Walter complains when she has gone. "Wrote paragraphs on me last time."

Ken and Leo grunt agreement.

There is a sudden hush throughout the foyer, as two armed constables lead a chained Gerald Purdy from the holding cells through the crowd to Court No. 3. Ankles shackled to each other and to his waist, Gerald smiles, accepting the respect of his audience and clinks his way into court, followed by his girlfriend and buddies.

Walter, Leo and Ken follow suit and the court-room is soon full. Two long wooden benches are filled by Gerald and his entourage; a third one at the back by police constables, the reporter, some other women waiting to appear and a Salvation Army officer taking notes, "Blood and Fire" written on his cap. A female stenographer prepares on a desk in the corner, but the lawyers' tables and chairs and the raised, spot-lit judge's dais are still empty.

The accused, Gerald Purdy, seems in fine form. Girlfriend on one arm, her hair brushing his neck, he amuses his fans with his other. He remembers doing one of those life-skills classes as a parolee in the past, "You know, where they show you how to do a proper interview to get a job, and videotape you, then show you all y'mistakes and not talking or sitting proper and all. Well, we did a court once, and I was the judge, eh, and I gave buddy four years for 'B and E'! I reckoned 'why not? I got it! So him too.' Hope this judge isn't as strict as I was!" His friends laugh, and the constables and the reporter suppress grins.

A man pops his head in at the door, sees the full court and realises wrong room: "Whoops. Right church I guess, but wrong pew." He leaves.

Then Gerald Purdy's lawyer puts his head round the door and clicks his tongue at his client. Gerald obediently hops out for a short whisper and hops back a minute later: "Jeeze! I'm getting so used to these chains,

I won't be after walking properly when I get'em off!"

The clerk, Mr. Lethbridge, enters, hot and harrowed, followed by Crown Prosecutors Fort and Sharpe and Defence Counsel Earle and Hoolihan. The benches go silent as the chattering lawyers remove files from briefcases and arrange themselves towards the Crown or Defence end of their table.

"All set, Mr. Lethbridge?" a cheery Leonard Sharpe enquires. "Dunno about justice in this heat, Mr. Sharpe!" and the clerk leaves by another door behind the bench to find the judge in his inner sanctuary. A minute later he returns holding the door open for Judge Hector Hussey in black gown and red braids, with manicured beard and Pepsi cup. "All rise! I declare this court open in the name of the Queen." Hands clasped before him, the clerk bows as Hussey ascends his dais and sits. The court sits and the clerk crosses to his table to find the stenographer whispering at him. He conveys the message to Judge Hussey.

"Afternoon, ladies and gentlemen. Uh, excuse me. I hear a voice from this side of the house." Hussey listens to Lethbridge. "Thank you Mr. Clerk. A slight technical hitch. No functioning tape-recorder. Good start. So Mr. Lethbridge will find one before we properly convene." The clerk leaves, twiddling his fingers in anxiety. "No point starting without one in case anything from this bench goes to appeal and then you have no record, la la la, so we'll just wait and then you can take any complaints to whoever you please." Hussey drains his Pepsi and licks his moustache.

After a few minutes, Mr. Lethbridge plus tape-recorder returns and Judge Hussey opens his first file. "Umm. Terence Power." No response. Hussey checks the file again. "Mr. Terence Power?"

Miss Fort rises. "Crown has withdrawn that case, Your Honour."

"Ah! I thought you had that look on your face, Miss Fort, that counsel have sometimes when no one comes or—anyhow one less." Hussey lays the file aside, on a new pile.

"In fact Mr. Power passed on, Your Honour."

"Even better, Miss Fort! Death conquers all, eh!" Hussey and Fort exchange grins. "Moving right along, then. Tanya Martin?"

A woman leaves the benches and approaches the bar of the court, and promptly has her old seat taken by a noisy latecomer who enters brandishing a plastic Colonials bag.

"Tanya Martin," Hussey continues, "You are accused that on or about January 20, 1985, in the city of St. John's, Newfoundland, you did shoplift from Colonials store on Hamilton Avenue. How do you plead, Miss?"

"Guilty, I guess."

"What d'you mean 'you guess'? Are you guilty or not?...Look. Do you understand the charge?"

"Yes."

"So what's the story? Come on girl, where's the pleasure in this?...Have you seen a lawyer?"

"I can take care of myself."

"You can take care of yourself! Well that's all very nice, but this court isn't to be taken lightly you know. You get a criminal record if you are found guilty, Miss. Okay? So you shouldn't just say 'guilty' if you aren't sure how to plead. Right? Why not discuss it with Legal Aid?"

Tanya slides her hands deep into her jean pockets and slouches. "It's okay. Guilty."

"Guilty. A plea of 'guilty.' Right Miss. Conviction registered." Resigned to her lack of interest in the procedure Hussey writes it in her file. "Miss Fort. The facts if you please, and anything on sentencing."

"Yes, Your Honour." Miss Fort rises and scratches a stockinged calf. "On January 20, 1985, Mr. Dicks of Colonials security stopped Miss Martin outside their Hamilton Avenue store, St. John's, Newfoundland, and found two pounds of steak in her purse that she could produce no receipt for."

From the back of the court, the latecomer holds up his Colonials bag and swings it back and forth until Hussey notices and gives an exasperated nod of understanding. There is stifled laughter and a holding of noses from Gerald Purdy's entourage.

Miss Fort continues. "Thank you, Mr. Dicks. Mr. Dicks then identified Miss Martin by an unemployment cheque and some personal possessions, read her her rights and gave a police caution. The value of the meat stolen was $9.56. No previous record Your Honour."

"Thank you, Miss Fort. Anything to say in your defence, Miss Martin? Before I pass sentence?"

Tanya shakes her head, shifts her chewing gum from one cheek to the other and leans forward on the bar.

"Fined $150. Or, in default, fifteen days. Thirty days to pay the fine. Understand Miss?" Hussey concludes.

"Can't afford $150. I wanna change my plea."

"What! What!" Hussey chokes. "Don't be ridiculous, girl. Why? You can't change your plea after conviction is registered just because you can't pay! I suppose if I had fined you $25 you would still be 'guilty.' Ridiculous!"

Tanya smirks affirmation.

"Surprise, Surprise! Look Miss! My court is no joke. It's not a mess-about here. And you just better smarten up and act sensibly and maturely and fast! You're acting like some first-class prize jerk. You're nineteen you know now. Time to grow up. But I'm not y'mother. Go on. Get out! Out of my court. Go and find Mother Goose outside or something. Out!" Hussey dismisses her with a final wave.

Tanya turns, still smirking. "Pushover," she mouths to the crowd as she precedes the clerk to the offices outside.

"And probably next time you come to my court, you could remove that gum from y'mouth, Miss. That would be a great help!" Hussey calls angrily after her retreating back. "Now, where are we! Oh yes. Moira Godden. Miss Godden?"

"I represent Miss Godden, Your Honour," Mr. Earle answers, rising and indicating to Moira to stand at the bar of the court. On the bench, her mother fidgets without her, a crucifix held in blanched knuckles.

"Moira Godden." Hussey begins again. "You are charged with shoplifting from Z-Mart stores, contrary to Section 294 of the Criminal Code. How do you plead?"

"Not guilty, Your Honour." Dermot Earle again responds. Hussey enters the plea on the file as the clerk comes back, bows to the bench again (as all the court-officials and lawyers take time to do upon entering or leaving the room) and returns to his table. The judge motions Moira to a chair by the bar. "The facts, Miss Fort?"

"Yes, Your Honour. On December 17, 1984, Gwent Haines, private investigator with Z-Mart, apprehended Miss Godden in the parking lot, Torbay Road, St. John's, Newfoundland, at 2:30 p.m. and found $48.44 cents worth of unpaid-for-items in her possession. These included a comb, some make-up, a chair cover and a package of DuMaurier cigarettes. She was identified by a driver's license, read her rights and given a police caution. Mr. Haines is unfortunately outside the province at this particular moment in time but he claims to have observed Miss Godden in the store for over half an hour, never more than an aisle away, and she made no attempt to pay." She sits down.

"Thank you Miss Fort. Mr. Earle? The defence?"

Earle stands, "Thank you, Your Honour. You know Your Honour it's a great shame Mr. Haines *is* absent because on Monday, December 17, that man made a mistake. Now I'm not blaming him: he must have many many cases. But on that day Miss Godden's behaviour was not theft, but sheer forgetfulness. She was shopping with her mother—and you do not go out to shoplift with your mother! And when she is in the witness box you will see she does not *sound* like a shoplifter, either."

Earle indicates to Moira who smiles and mounts the box at the side of the clerk's table.

Mr. Lethbridge hands her a Bible. "Hold the book in your right hand and speak the words on this card."

"I swear by the Almighty God that the evidence I shall give to this court will be the truth"— "the whole truth," Hussey prompts her as she stumbles— "the whole truth and nothing but the truth, so help me God."

Moira smiles at Judge Hussey as the clerk retrieves his props and sits down.

"Now, Miss Godden. In your own words what happened?" her lawyer prompts.

"Well, I was shopping with my Mom. She was in Wrigley's Drugs and I went to Z-Mart and I remembered she had my shopping list and so I went to get her and forgot I'd already put the things in my bag. Then the man stopped me and took out the stuff and, honest to God, I nearly died. I forgot they were there, see! Honestly."

"Do you swear that on an oath before God?" Earle prompts again.

"Yes. And I thought I was gonna have a heart attack on the spot. I started screeching and I could hardly walk to his office. I'm allergic too, and on two pills a day, and I didn't control myself till next day when Mom phoned you. I could swear—well I am aren't I—as sure as I'm standing here today, I'd have paid for the stuff if I hadn't forgotten. I mean I'm not looking to rationalise it or anything, but it's been some awful this past few months, and I don't... " She begins to break down and sob. "Sorry. Excuse me."

"Your Honour! May I give Miss Godden some water?"

"Sure, Mr. Earle! It's here for your use. Mightn't do you any good, mind, but, please. Feel free." Hussey half-grins.

Her lawyer pours her some water, but Moira only cries more uncontrollably, so in the end Earle has to lead her back to her seat and her worrying mother.

"Your Honour, I'm afraid my client cannot continue at present." Mr. Earle excuses her, "So I shall have to stop there."

"Thank you, Mr. Earle, I believe you have put your message across," Hussey chuckles. "So, Miss Fort. Anything more from you in summation?"

"Thank you, Your Honour," Crown begins again. "Your Honour, unfortunately this court has seen many a case of middle-class people suddenly shoplifting without reason. But in this case the facts are clear. It was not mere forgetfulness. The items were all stashed in a shopping bag. An act of concealment had taken place which Mr. Haines witnessed. Therefore, theft Your Honour."

"Thank you. Final statement Mr. Earle?"

"Your Honour. I won't labour the defence because it must be obvious, quite obvious to Your Honour. This was forgetfulness, and anyone could have this happen to them. For example, I was at Canadian Tire last week and thirty seconds before I reached the cashier I found an item in my pocket I had forgotten all about. Thirty seconds more and if a security man had been watching that forgetfulness would have been theft." "Let's stay with the evidence of this case, Mr. Earle, and keep personal stories out, okay?"

"Your Honour. This boils down to a question of credibility. Crown has proven no evidence of intent. And we all know security guards are not infallible. They are as human as the rest of us. Plus, Miss Godden has no prior offences, and this is her first encounter with the law. It is totally out of character. You see she suffers from anxiety problems and has suffered a lot out of embarrassment and expenses since the arrest. She has grade eleven and spent two years at MUN. Since, she has worked for the federal government full time as a courier. This is a bonded post and if she gets a criminal record she may lose her job. Meanwhile, she pays her mother rent at home, and therefore contributes *vitally* to their mortgage payments because this income is their main support. Her father has only recently died, and her mother was working, but isn't at the moment. Your Honour, I ask for an absolute discharge in this case." Defence sits.

"Thank you very much, Mr. Earle." Hussey finishes writing his annotations and looks up. "I don't know. It seems cases like this one are becoming far more prominent in this court. Okay. In a case of theft, for conviction to be passed, intent to absolutely or temporarily deprive the owner of his possession *must* be satisfactorily proven. Moreover, unless the plea elected is insanity or total inebriation, then intent must be adjudged from *actions* not from rationalising words. In this case I have some difficulties understanding the young lady's mind. She seems perfectly normal, so what exactly does it amount to when she says she cannot recall placing the items in her bag. She can't be quite as dense as she pretends. I find that a very likely story, frankly! So, guilty as charged." Hussey writes as Earle looks down, a bit sheepishly, and Moira is soothed by her mother's hand. "However," the judge continues, "I shall not register a conviction. Under this system of law, there is a difference between the terms "to take" and "to steal"; they do not connote quite the same things even though those outside the law are apt to forget this. I think Miss Godden fully intended to *take* those items, but not to *steal* them. Therefore, without a pre-sentence report, I am going to complete this now and award Miss Godden an absolute discharge. This was a mistake made by a young person undergoing strain and therefore forgivable. I deem this court-case and today's proceedings punishment enough.

"Thank you, Your Honour," the two counsel mumble together.

"Oh, thank God!" Laura Godden exclaims. "I'm so happy it's over."

"But will my name still appear in the *Telegram*?" Moira looks up from her mother's tear-stained shoulder. "Oh *please* no!"

"Miss Godden," Hussey snorts, "I control this courtroom and its proceedings but I still do not control the press and what they may see fit to publish. Now you've had a bit of a bargain here today, anyway, and you're on thin ice. So don't make us call you again because next time I might not be so reasonably disposed. And may I also say at this point that I regard ladies shopping with open bags, and not the trolleys provided by the stores as a silly and dangerous practice. It causes accidents that are hard to explain. Now, this pronouncement is not going to change the shopping habits of all you women, but just be more wise in future... Now, I see I'm down to my last... not dollar, but information." Hussey jokes as Moira and her mother thank their lawyer and leave with the clerk.

Miss Fort and Mr. Earle also stand, pack up, bow and leave the court-room.

The reporter and the constable by her side stop their crossword-puzzle and look up, eager for the main case of the afternoon.

"Mr. Gerald Purdy, come forward again please," Hussey asks. "I represent the Crown again Your Honour," Leonard Sharpe half-rises to say.

"And I Mr. Purdy," Walter Hoolihan responds.

"Thank you, gentlemen. Just to recap," Hussey arranges his notes, "Mr. Purdy you stand charged with armed robbery of Discount Stores, contrary to Section 312.1.9 of the Criminal Code of Canada. How do you plead, Sir?"

"Not guilty, Your Honour," Hoolihan answers and waves Purdy and his chains to a seat where he continues stroking his girlfriend's hair.

"Mr. Sharpe? A summary of the facts, please."

"Yes, Your Honour." Crown rises, and sums up the case as it stands on this, the second day, and just before the last of nine witnesses. Leaning over his files on simian fists, he recaps the prominent events and explains the central role which witness Rick Hudson should play. It seems that on August 17, 1984, at 9:00 p.m., in Ivan Lawlor's car, Rick Hudson, Lawlor, and Ray and Thomas Farrel had picked up Gerald Purdy at his home on Shea Heights and driven to Freshwater Road. There they got out, donned ski masks and three entered the Discount Stores. Thomas Farrel waited outside as look-out while Purdy kept the car 'revved up.' Inside, Hudson held a baseball bat and Ray Farrel a pellet-gun while Lawlor robbed the tills and loaded the cash into garbage bags. Then all ran for the car, Ray Farrel, the last to leave, being spotted by witnesses removing his mask by the car door. All drove to Shea Heights, and left the cash in the car. Later that night, all met at a party at Lawlor's, although Hudson was late, having to complete his taxi shift first. At 8:00 a.m. the following morning, Hudson and Lawlor were arrested and at 11:35 a.m. Hudson pleaded guilty and gave a statement at Fort Townsend to Sergeant Kavanagh. For his cooperation, Hudson was sentenced in Supreme Court, January 30, 1985, to two years less a day, thus remaining in provincial jurisdiction; and served fourteen months in total. Since his release, Hudson has been on day parole at the Lightship Centre for Probationers and Parolees.

Having brought things up to date, Crown looks up from his notes and signals to the clerk to call in his witness, Hudson, from the ante-room.

Rick Hudson, nervous but managing a lop-sided grin to his mates, follows Mr. Lethbridge in and mounts the witness stand. The clerk swears him in and turns him over to the prosecutor.

"Please state your full name and address for the court records," Sharpe begins.

"Richard Hudson. The Lightship Centre, Killick Road."

"St. John's, Newfoundland," Sharpe completes for him. "That's a halfway-house, the Lightship, isn't it? And how long have you been there, Mr. Hudson?"

"Uh. About four months."

"Four months. And," Sharpe checks his notes, "you were sent back to the pen, twice for drinking infringements... full parole, if all goes well, at the end of September."

"It *will* all go well."

"Fine. So, tell us about the robbery, Mr. Hudson. In your own words. No hurry."

"Well, to be quite honest with you boy, uh Sir, I can't remember the details. I was drunk at the time. I remember doing it so I pleaded guilty but I forget the details and next morning when I gave the statement I was stoned so I don't remember any of that either."

There are titters from the gallery. Purdy's buddies.

"Hey! This is a court-room. Any more of that from you lot and you can go, the lot of you. What do you think this is!" Hussey shouts at the benches.

Crown continues. "Okay Mr. Hudson. Let's go back a bit. Do you recall driving taxis?"

"Yes."

"Good. And completing a shift after the robbery?"

"Yes."

"Rather pointless exercise anyway, wasn't it? You already had a job that paid."

"Yes, Sir."

"But you can remember nothing of the actual robbery?"

"No, Sir. That's behind me, in the past, and I prefer to leave it there, forgotten."

"Didn't you say you never saw the money? That Lawlor was meant to give it to you the next day?"

"I don't remember."

"Wasn't $3,000 stolen?"

"I thought it was $2,400. I read it in the paper. Everyone knew that."

"Do you recognize these six photos of Lawlor's car?" Crown hands over a file. "And didn't you say this car was used in the robbery and was licensed in his mother's name?"

"This is Ivan's car, I don't know if we used it. I've forgotten."

"Didn't you say you never got any of the money but the police took $150 from your house?"

"Definitely! The police took $150 from my house, from my taxi work, but I can't remember where the money from the robbery went. I'd never be 100 percent sure of that, boy."

"There seems to be an awful lot of forgetting here this afternoon!" Sharpe is becoming increasingly exasperated; unsure how to get his witness to perform properly. "Your Honour. Would you mind reminding Mr. Hudson that under The Charter of Human Rights nothing he says here today may be used to incriminate him, and that his own trial cannot be reconvened."

Hussey nods. "That's right, Mr. Hudson. As the prosecutor has just explained, you are free to say anything in this court, just so long as it isn't perjury."

"Thank you, Your Honour." Crown, hoping for a change, begins again. "Now, Mr. Hudson. Don't you remember giving evidence in Supreme Court against Mr. Lawlor last year? When he pleaded guilty? Surely you must."

"No. I was on medication and pills last year."

"Surely you remember. It must have been an awful experience. Being in the dock. Something it is understandable you would want to forget."

"I don't remember."

"Your Honour!" Sharpe's patience snaps. "I claim Section 91: Mr. Hudson is resisting examination and being a hostile witness."

"No he isn't Your Honour!" Hoolihan jumps up in defence. "Mr. Hudson has not once contradicted his earlier statements. He just can't remember them, and that's only natural. I do the same sometimes and forget things."

Leo, watching, is impressed. "Good man, he is!" he whispers to Walt.

"Your Honour!" Crown continues. "May I draw your attention to the case of Alberta vs Weber, Section 91?"

"Yes I am aware of the precedent, Mr. Sharpe, thank you. I allow your definition. Please proceed."

"Thank you, Your Honour." Crown smiles at Hudson. "Mr. Hudson. Do you know what 'perjury' means?... It means lying under oath. And it carries a sentence of fourteen years jail. So come now, Mr. Hudson. You *must* remember Supreme Court. Just up on Duckworth Street. Giving evidence. Mr. Drodge cross-examining you before a twelve-man jury? That must have been the most stressful day of your life!"

"Well, see, to be honest with you, you're still losing me there."

Two of Purdy's retinue stand up and begin squeezing their way along the benches to go out for a pee and relieve the tension.

"And you can stay out!" Hussey orders them. "I'm not having this court turned into a fairground."

The two grin with embarrassment. Gerald Purdy takes the opportunity to hobble over and whisper a question to his lawyer. Then he hobbles back and bows respectfully to the bench like he saw the clerk doing earlier, before conveying the answer to his girlfriend.

"Mr. Hudson. Is it likely you would plead guilty in Supreme Court for something you could not remember?" Crown starts in again.

"I can't remember."

"Ha! Mr. Hudson. That's a good answer sometimes, but I'm afraid it won't do here. I want an answer from you this time! So what's it to be?"

"I dunno if I would or not. I could've said it or not. I can't say."

"Does it make sense that if something is true in Supreme Court then, that it's not true now?"

"I don't understand y'question."

"Does it make sense that you would forget now but have remembered in Supreme Court? Or that, if it was true then, a year closer to the events, then it is less true now?"

"I don't know. I'm not up to this!"

"You seem to remember other details of the intervening time—Christmas Day at home in Mundy Pond with your family. Why would you plead guilty in Supreme Court to something you did not remember Mr. Hudson?"

"So I'd be out the slammer by Christmas."

"So you would be out of jail by Christmas...Mr. Hudson." Crown, baffled, tries a different tack. "Do you remember telling me half an hour before this court how you had a hard time in jail?"

"I don't remember. You can keep on cross-examining me but I'll say the same. I don't remember."

"Don't you recall them calling you a 'rat'?"

"No."

"Didn't they have to segregate you? Put you in protective custody?"

"No."

"Mr. Hudson. Do you know the people who have appeared before court today? And have you spoken to them about the case?"

"No."

"I thought you said Bob Purdy phoned you this morning?"

"Oh yes."

"Oh yes!" You remember now." Crown gives Judge Hussey a glance to check he is registering what is implied.

"And did you also see a lawyer today, Mr. Hudson? By any chance?"

"Yes."

" 'Yes' I see." Sharpe shoots the blackest of grimaces at a rather smug Hoolihan, before sitting down, beaten. "No further questions of this witness, Your Honour."

Defence has none either, so Hussey informs Hudson that he is now free to step down and then calls a twenty-minute recess for tea. Tempers need to cool and decorum to return. Hudson wastes no time, even rushing out before Walt, Leo or Ken can reach him with their pats of congratulation.

After recess, Hussey calls upon both counsels to sum up their cases. Crown is first. Sharpe realises his last witness did waffle a little, and was hesitant, but he did admit that he would not lie under oath. Therefore it is possible, nay even probable, that his earlier Supreme Court statements were true. That being the case, then it is commonsense that when Hudson's previous statements are put alongside those of Crown's other witnesses yesterday and today and seen to corroborate them, that a far higher plateau of probable incrimination concerning Gerald Purdy is reached. In conclusion, as Supreme Court Judge Blackey argued, Crown pleads use of Hudson's previous giving of evidence be used in this case, even if Hudson has since forgotten it.

Defence cannot agree at all. Crown has no evidence whatever linking his client, Gerald Purdy, to the crime. Not a scrap. And all Crown witnesses contradicted each other; like who held the baseball bat, and what colour the ski masks were, etc. etc. And as for Judge Blackey, whom learned counsel Sharpe mentioned, well the Supreme Court of Canada voted 5:1 *against* that interpretation; about the legality of using statements which witnesses have forgotten, and continue to deny even under perjury cross-examinations. "So," Hoolihan concludes, "Your Honour, to find Mr. Gerald Purdy guilty would be a draconian measure similar to the legal system of the Soviet Union where a mere suggestion leads to a conviction. Whereas here, under normal circumstances of Criminal Law, it must be proven beyond any reasonable doubt. Thank you."

Summations complete, a hushed courtroom waits for Judge Hussey's decision. "Thank you, gentlemen," he begins. "The facts of this case of robbery with violence seem pretty clear to me. Earlier witnesses such as the supermarket manager, Mark Moores, have described the scene in the store. However, only Richard Hudson it seems could incriminate Mr. Purdy, and he, we have all heard, swears under oath, and mindful of perjury, that being inebriated, he remembers nothing. Obviously the credibility of Mr. Hudson is highly suspect, but under our system of law, whatever the charge, innocence remains until guilt is proven, *beyond a reasonable doubt.* And in this case I tend to agree with Defence Counsel that some doubt remains. So, whereas in a preliminary hearing, doubt is weighted in favour of the Crown, and the accused placed in jeopardy of a trial, in full court, doubt must be weighted in favour of the accused. I close this case then and declare Mr. Gerald Purdy..."

A young lawyer rushes in, bowing, and whispering to Crown Prosecutor Sharpe.

"Your Honour!" Sharpe rises. "Uh, I'm not sure how to say this but the witness wants to change his testimony!"

There is a hum around court, and heads turn. Threatened with more jail for perjury, Hudson must have been held in an outside office and then buckled.

"Order!" Judge Hussey reconvenes, frowning at the irregularity. "Well, it's a bit late Mr. Sharpe. The case is really closed... Uh, I shall be advised by Defence Counsel."

Hoolihan rises, adamant: "The case is closed, Your Honour." "Yes, I agree Mr. Hoolihan. I'm afraid the case is closed Mr. Sharpe. You are a bit late. Of course, Crown can use this information at a later date in another trial as it sees fit."

Another young lawyer rushes into court but Sharpe turns and gloomily signs 'too late' and the lad stops running.

"I declare this case of armed robbery dismissed," Judge Hussey concludes. "Further charges of break-and-enter and assault-with-violence against Mr. Purdy will commence in tomorrow's session. I declare this court closed." The judge rises, and the rest of the court copies, watching as he leaves for his rooms.

Gerald Purdy checks with a buddy what 'case dismissed' means, and then turns to hug his girlfriend, delighted.

The clerk recites his closing phrases, as the lawyers pack their briefcases and follow the excited voices of Purdy and his now-confident, backslapping crew out into the foyer. At least Purdy has survived court for another day...

Fourth Scene

Wednesday lunchtime, driving downtown looking for work.

"Ha! Listen to this, boy: 'Richard Hudson of the Lightship half-way house, Killick Road is' ...uh, 'up for perjury, for contempt of court, for altering evidence he had previously sworn to, in the trial of Gerald Purdy on charges of armed robbery.'...uh, 'Purdy was acquitted, but Crown may appeal the decision.' Ha! How's that?" Seated in Basil Smith's Chevy the following day, a more relaxed Leo Normore slowly reads from the latest *Evening Telegram* and grins. Basil and Leo are driving across downtown to the National Sea Products fishplant on the south side of the harbour. Leo needs a job, the fishplant has advertised for fish-trimmers and packers, and Basil's big old car is doing the ferrying.

Basil is in his late-twenties; born in Wales he has lived two years in St. John's and just completed a social science degree. His girlfriend works as a counsellor at the Lightship Community Rehabilitation Centre for Probationers and Parolees, so, with some free time on his hands now, Basil volunteered to drive some of her clients — such as Leo — around town in their daily searches for work; she said how very appreciative the Lightship would be.

The Lightship provides a half-way house, and counselling, to aid the rehabilitation of deserving ex-offenders. Its brochures explain this in terms of the responsibility all citizens have towards working with the correctional authorities to reduce crime in the community: that part of the blame for a criminal act lies with the perpetrator's social environment so he must be taught a more socially responsible attitude towards the law. A central part of Lightship services are courses assisting ex-offenders to become 'job ready'; for meaningful and stable employment is seen as a major means of providing these unfortunates with a 'positive self-concept.' So they are shown how to write job résumés, analyse the skills called for by the labour market, and present themselves to prospective employers. The government Departments of Justice, and Employment and Immigration also assist by allowing ex-offenders to take part in the various government 'make-work projects' such as the 'Volunteer Initiative Programme' or 'Section 38.' Under these schemes, people still remain technically unemployed, but the government subsidises their unemployment cheque. In this way, ex-offenders may get job experience, and employers are encouraged to take advantage of 'bondable,' 'pre-screened' and 'motivated' cheap labour; and after the weeks of the government programme are completed, a worker just might be offered more full-time employment.

Leo recently moved out of the Lightship, his months of parole completed. However, he still pops back frequently to see his buddies and listen out for any jobs on the go; even with chronic unemployment the Lightship might just deliver, one of these years. Today, he found Basil and cadged a lift. Basil promptly complied: he is still getting to know his role but keen to ingratiate himself with 'the lads'; and a drive over the railway tracks, past the oil tanks, to the fishplant and back is a good chance for a chat.

So now on their way, when Leo starts reading about Rick Hudson in the newspaper, Basil is quick to show his own intimacy: "I thought Rick said they couldn't prove it?"

"Right boy. He's 70 to 80 percent sure of getting off, he says. Or just getting a bit of time added to his parole in the Lightship. Not a new sentence."

"He's served enough time as it is."

"Right. But at least the Lightship are good people...Now I'd have gone for those lights, boy." Leo explains as Basil slows at a junction. "Folks just dunno how to drive proper in St. John's. Or else they drive some fucking fast...Y'motor sounds good, boy. How old is she?"

"Yeah. Runs Okay. Touch wood!" Basil taps his head but keeps his eyes on the road. "Uh, 1975."

"Pretty good shape...What did you pay? Five? Not worth more than five, I'd say. When did you get her?"

"Last summer. Thousand bucks."

"I'd never pay more than that for any car. You'd never get that for this again, boy. Never. Book value must be two or three hundred, I reckon. Put y'foot down flat. Let's hear it." And on an open stretch of New Gower Street, Basil complies.

"I bought a V8 Grand Fury off Walt at the Centre for eleven hundred, but that's got more options than one of these. He'd done it up real nice but then he bumped it so I took it 'cause I'm a bit of a hand at that. It's in Torbay right now getting some body work on it. Bigger than this and all."

"Well this is big enough for me, mate!" Basil chuckles.

"See, I'm used to driving big cars as taxis, boy. And I love 'em. Never have one of these small ones you see all these women about driving now. And I can really drive a big car, boy! You better believe it!... I got the length perfectly coordinated for turning, as a cabbie."

"I hate how taxi-drivers drive!"

Leo laughs. "Yes boy. 'Course. Most folks do. But that's it. You gotta be fast to make a buck. Or you get nothing. Only trouble with big old cars is these bored cops always stopping you." Leo ventures as they pass an RNC squad car. "Hey! See those two cops sweating their arses in that car? Those were them what came after me one time for a bike I stole. Jeeze! I'd recognize 'em anywhere." Leo laughs at the memory. "Yeah. It were one of them mini-Hondas. Tiny thing. And they turned my place upside down looking for it, boy. Then round to my buddy's so he just said 'Get off my fucking land!' and they had to give it up... I guess they're still after me for it, but they won't find it now boy! No chance! It's at the bottom of the harbour now boy. Blow-torched." He chuckles. "Never get me on that now, they won't!"

"Was that when they sent you away?" Basil wonders.

"No. That was before I went out on the dredgers. Gave up the cabs; boss'd never smile, right, just sit at his desk and look glum, so gave up the cabs and went dredging. Now, captain on the boat, boy, he was a good boss. Like he used to understand you. And good boys to work with and all. Skip' bet me five bucks once, I couldn't lift the sinker of this net 'cause it weighed about 750 lbs—350 kilos, eh, and I dunno how I did it boy 'cause we couldn't drag it back between us, but I did, for the wager, right across the deck and they couldn't believe it. And after I got drunk down the Legion." Leo laughs. "I was 205 lbs then. I'm only about 185 now. That's no home cooking, boy!... Holy Jeeze! See the tits bouncing on that?" Leo turns round to stare as Basil drives past some girls standing outside the shelter for battered women. "Jeeze boy! Some fluff there, and not a black eye between 'em. What they got to complain about? I'd soon give 'em something eh boy! Soon give 'em what for. Get the old scrotum out and shake it about! What?"

"Still a boy at heart, I see, Leo," Basil responds jocularly.

"There was a real bit of nice fluff, and no mistake boy. Worth getting y'dipstick wet for was that. Holy Fuck!...Okay: Why is sex like snow? 'Cause you never know when you're gonna get it, nor how much, nor how cold she's gonna be after!" They laugh.

"Very good...So where do you belong to, Leo? West coast isn't it?"

"Right. Born in Corner Brook. And I was down there Christmas, and we had a great time 'cause I hadn't been there for a year and I spent the $600 I'd earned. That's why I got none now!...I like St. John's but sometimes I miss people there and wanna get back, eh?"

"Got folks there?"

"Right. My parents are in Corner Brook now, and they won't leave 'cause my brother died there recently. His heart. He was a teacher, then he decided to become a missionary priest. Then he died of his heart...And I got another brother, sixteen or seventeen now, but he's already 6 foot 2 and 190 lbs and he's gonna join the RCMP. There's eight of us altogether, I think. Also, I got a kid sister. And my older sister's in here now with me. She's a secretary, eh, at the Medical Centre. She and buddy are separated now, and she's saving to buy back her furniture and get her own apartment. She looks after my bank balance for me and stops me getting to the bank book to spend it all—even when I feel I just gotta get to it to get out of town for the weekend, eh, she don't let me. She's good."

"D'you like getting out and about then Leo?"

"Yes boy! I used to hitch it into here from Corner Brook all the time. And in winter. And before that I used to hitch twenty miles round the bay every night to see my girl. And if there was no rides, I'd walk it."

"Yeah! Sounds like you liked her!"

"She was okay. But that's no more than any guy'd do for a girl he's seeing, eh. Like hear of that boy killed on the Trans Canada last year?"

"Knifed over some argument?"

"Right. He and buddy hitching together, let off at the same place, and he's pissed and goes crazy. He was hitching to his girl...But you know I hitched all over Canada. Got 4000 miles of hitching behind me boy."

"Really?"

"Yes boy. Ontario, Calgary...everywhere. I mean it's like you gotta go out and meet people, eh? Go round and form y'own opinions of things and then compare it to the books and decide who's right. I even had me own business in Calgary—carpenter. But one day I decided to just come home so I packed it in and did. And then I got into trouble when I got back. That was my mistake. But that's how I do it. Like when I left here first, I just decided and got my cheque and I was away. I didn't tell anyone I was gonna leave the job, I just did. 'Cause you gotta take pride in y'work and I reckoned I'd been there long enough, 'cause I was getting lazy and slacking. So it was time to go... Then it's always I get back to here and I get into trouble. See, I got relatives in Ontario, and also in Atlanta, Georgia and I was building, in Ontario—London. We were doing lawns and gardens for new constructions. And after, you get to hose down the new sods and that's when the fun starts—with hoses, and a gang of guys! Y'know! And it's just for a bit of fun, eh?... But one thing I couldn't take was camping in tents. I just couldn't hack it, boy! For the love of Jesus. The smoke always got to me. And in them swirling winds, it gets everywhere, boy—y'hair, y'eyes, y'clothes. I had to wash my hair twice a night to get rid of that smell and I still couldn't. So I said, 'Sod this! I'm not doing this no more!' And I came home."

"How long were you there altogether then?"

"I had three years on the mainland, boy. And then I had enough... A year here, six months there... Then I got into trouble when I came back. The first time and all. I had a clean record before, so it was only an easy sentence."

"So do you miss not being on the mainland, Leo?"

"Holy Fuck, no boy! They're wild over there. Like Toronto, eh. I was living there and there was this bikers' bar opposite, right, and this guy from B.C. told the owner I was a cop, so buddy threatened to kill me. See, I was the only one with short hair 'cause they was all from out west, B.C. and Saskatchewan and the rest. So I was different... And I got a sort of multi-face, eh? Like some women think it's a criminal's face, and then criminals think I'm narcotics police. See, it depends what you want... So the cops had to put me away for a night for my own safety. And this big sergeant says how I'm gonna die all right, but not in Toronto. So they sent me home... But it's like they don't understand you in Toronto and Ontario. Like they speak too fast, and butt in, and won't let you finish what you're saying. It's like they all speak before they think there. English folk speak slow I noticed. So they probably mean what they say like Newfoundlanders do eh? I mean we got all different dialects in Newfoundland—like Corner Brook and up the coast, St. Anthony and Port-au-Fleur. And then it's all Irish and different sounding down here...I been all over, see boy. But in Newfoundland they all speak slow and have time to think. Not like up-along Toronto and the rest. Newfoundland's a good place. And they're not ignorant here like New Brunswick and Nova Scotia and them places. I've been there and they all think you gotta have money and that to be someone, eh? And if you got none you're a nobody. And that's plain ignorant. So they're all over you, won't leave you alone so long as you got the dough. And then they're gone. Jeez! Sometimes you think you should never've left home. Hey! See that Spencer's, boy?" Leo calls out as they drive past a supermarket. "That's who I robbed two-fifty bucks off." he laughs proudly. "Can't show my face there now boy!"

"Is that why they put you away?"

"Yes, boy. And fighting. I beat up on the owner and his store and his car. And his house...He had it coming...I made $3400 damage! So they sent me away. See, I was drinking and I didn't know what I was doing. But it was 'cause the owner said he'd kill me, for something I knew about him...They threw me out of school and all for fighting and not coming. And fighting the teachers. But don't worry boy! I never beat up on someone who didn't have it coming to him. I just got drunk that time and I got a bit excited. See, I had a bit of a problem before 'cause the beer was going straight to my brain and I couldn't take it. But not now 'cause I gave up. Generally...like before, I said no one was gonna stop me drinking, and I broke parole a few times like that and they sent me back to the Big House. But I stayed out of trouble a year now." Leo chuckles. "I had a few beers last night, mind, and they went down real well! But now I'm just trying to keep out of trouble."

"How long were you in jail for then?" Basil is inquisitive while not trying to sound nosey or officious.

"Uh..." Leo calculates. "Twenty-one months altogether. And a half. Fifteen months first, then three more, then two more. Last time they had me cooking for the boys in a camp in the woods. Seven days a week. No pay. That really pissed me off..."

"Lumber camp?"

"Yeah...But that time I beat up on buddy. I just snapped right? See he owed me twelve hundred bucks 'cause I built this log cabin for him. But he said how he wanted to sell it before he paid me. But I knew he had the money already. So I beat him up, and after, I gave myself up. But I just snapped 'cause I was under a lot of pressure...See, it's not that I'm dishonest or criminal or that, it's just there was a lot of pressure on me at the time...But I suppose those are the breaks."

"What was it about, then, mate?"

"See, buddy was my wife's brother: Grace's brother. And he raped her. And her mother's nuts too, and has a few marbles loose. And Grace was scared of her. True, boy. Even Monsignor O'Dwyer who married us said that. She was crazy, boy, and she wanted to take Grace away from me...Her father was okay, but he had a bad heart and had to take it easy and he was scared of his wife too. And when Grace got pregnant, her mother didn't want her to have it. So when she was in hospital she told the security guards not to let me in. So I went to administration and they told me all about these lies my mother-in-law had said. The old bitch! Like I was violent, eh. And beat on the wife. And the rest, which I never. Right?"

"Sure. Then what?"

"So then they saw too how the old woman was gone cracked...Then the week after the baby came, they had it whacked through for baptising without telling me. And I only got to see it when Grace and her mom came after the christening. And her mom said she'd stay outside but she didn't and we had another fight and I threw the old bag's coat outside in the rain and said how she better get, or she was going after it. So she did." Leo laughs and looks to see if Basil is also enjoying the repartee. "But I knew I'd never get custody. The old cunt never liked me...You know they own three houses. Waterford Bridge Road. And I used to clean them cars for 'em, and wax too and do carpentry, 'cause I got my professional carpenter's diploma, right, and she still wasn't friendly...And I used to do everything for Grace. I used to be up and cooking her breakfast in bed, and cook her a little lunch, and then leave the house at seven and work eight till eight, and then come home, cook dinner and wash up. And she'd be watching TV all day, boy!"

"The easy life!"

"That's it boy. Grace had it easy with me. Then I got home one day and all the furniture was gone. Not a bit left!"

"Really!" Basil sympathises.

"Sure. Her mother had been in...And you know what she said to my father when he came in here? He could only see the baby if she thought he were good enough. The frigging grandpa! Now is that nuts or wha'?"

"How old's your mother-in-law?"

" 'Bout sixty-five. And good for twenty years...Wish she wouldn't last twenty hours boy!" Basil laughs at Leo's fanciful wish. "But see, all this was on top of me when I done Grace's brother," Leo continues, serious again. "Like you can only push someone so far, eh...But Holy Jeez! I wouldn't even have Grace back now. No way would I! Sod her. I'm not the sort who goes crawling, crying after women. I never have any trouble finding women...And at least I'm not the sort what has to have women pay for them when they go out. No sir! I've not reached that level yet...Nah! Let Grace walk out if she wants to. She isn't coming back. Sod her! And her kids is her own problem. See, she had two from buddy before and all. So she's got them to handle now...Know what I want boy?"

"What's that?"

"I wanna find another woman, say with two or three kids. Her guy's left, so I move in, nice and easy, and then she helps me find work, underhand like, through her brothers or something. Easy. Like there's work around town, eh, but only if you got friends to give it to you. And then if she's working too, it's perfect."

"So get out and find her, boy!"

"Oh, I will! Look under every stone if I have to," Leo laughs, then pounds his fist in his palm. "I gotta get a summer job, then I can stay in town on UIC with a girl after. I got a girlfriend now but she's just a kid—nineteen or twenty or something. She's back in school right now, learning book-keeping 'cause she had to leave at grade ten before to have a baby. But I'm not gonna marry her."

"What sort of work you after then?"

"Any sort boy! Labouring. Shops. I'm gonna go begging to every fucking store owner I can find if I have to...But I'm not lazy you know boy...Take a look at these hands." Leo holds them up and turns them round. "Real workers' hands. See boy, I got no brain. I got the brain of a peanut!" They laugh. "Really. I just work with my hands. I can't work with my brain hardly. I mean they chucked me out of school before I got grade six so I can't hardly read. Only newspapers a bit. Reckon on learning some day, though...But 'til then I'll have to con my way into a job, right? But I'm gonna find one boy. Even if I gotta turn over every goddamn stone in this city."

"Ken Holloway's just landed himself a good one I heard," Basil boasts his knowledge.

"Too right! Supply boats for the rigs. And they're already sending him for his medical even before he's done his training course! And you better believe that'll be good money boy! I'd soon do that and all...I heard Corrections may get twelve jobs there, and it'd be great: twenty-eight days away, then fourteen at home. And you save money, though I guess you spend it all when you get home. But I bet I wouldn't get too drunk. Yep, I wish the Lightship could hook a 'Section 38' for me for the summer!"

"Well maybe there'll be something still at the fishplant."

"Right, boy. I wouldn't mind that neither. And I should get a job there 'cause I trimmed fish for years. And buddy on the phone said they need trimmers... So it should be easy to get a job. Anyone can trim fish! I can trim fish right down from their eyebrows... Or I wouldn't mind going out on a trawler again. But a fish plant's a good place: lots of women about... And that's easy, too!" Leo exclaims as they drive past a gang of road-workers laying tarmac. "I'd love one of them jobs. They must be on $11 or $12 an hour, and I bet they got a forty-ouncer of scotch in the truck cabin too!" He laughs. "Maybe I should go to trade school first and do a course on working the roads. I know they got a college on the west coast that does it; maybe here as well! And then I could get Manpower to pay, get it off UIC."

"So you reckon on staying in town a while now, is it Leo?"

"Looks that way boy. Dunno. I got an uncle in Atlanta, Georgia, says I should visit. He's an alkie and all. Crazy! He sends me these photos of him in battle fatigues, right. With a gun and bayonet. And he says if a guy hassles him then he goes and blows their car away with his gun! And he smuggled up a Nazi bayonet for me to fit to a rifle. He said I should visit. So I could try something different. 'Cause I ain't been to the States. But I dunno. Newfoundland is okay. And sometimes I think I should never've gone away. That's how I got into trouble. And I'm just getting used to it in town again... But sometimes I'd like to move back to Corner Brook and get into some sports again 'cause all my sporting buddies are over there."

"Sportsman, eh, Leo. What did you used to play?"

"Anything. Hockey. Baseball. Broomball. And I had so many buddies I could always get a game. Not like here. In the 'pen' we had some real good hockey workouts and all. One time we had a team against the guards and the police, and we practiced for weeks, like. But they were dirty cunts. I lasted six minutes."

"How come?"

"They played dirty, see. It was meant to be a gentleman's game right. No bodily contact. But this big fat copper came for me when I had the puck in a corner, and I could see him all the way give me this elbow in the neck, like. And I knew his number and said I was gonna get him so I give him a two-handed swipe on the arm and they disqualified me. Sent me off. But that was okay. I got him back, eh. And I had enough by then. Police behaving like that and all."

"How did the team do after?"

"Got into the play-off then lost. But I'll have to get a job and save up before I get into sports again proper like. And lay off the booze. Gets expensive. I mean I'm not like some of these boys, can't go home nights without a beer. I can't understand that. And I'm not a darts player. I don't mess with that stuff. I never have and I never will... In fact I'm not into beer so much. The gas fills me so after six that I've had enough. No, it's Screech I go for. But a twenty-six ouncer of that'll last me a few weeks. Unless the boys come round then it goes some fast!" Leo grins at the thought.

"What about Barcardi?" Basil licks his lips.

"No, boy. But I loves tequila. When I went home last time my buddies took me out for an evening of double tequilas and I tell you boy, that was some real time we had—till seven in the morning! I was as drunk as a cunt! So my friend had to put me in a cab, and I slept until three o'clock!"

They arrive at the fishplant to find the shifts changing. The area is busy with people. Basil parks at the side of the road and locks up as Leo jumps out.

"Not locking the car boy! What? Scared the seats'll be stolen!"

"People like you about..." Laughing, Basil follows Leo towards the door.

Fifth Scene

Wednesday afternoon, at an introduction to the halfway-house

Later that afternoon, back at the Lightship, the counsellors are called to their weekly staff meeting by Tony Murrin, the centre's director. "Last call for staff meeting, please! Last call."

"Last call? I didn't even know we had a bar here! Where's the bar?" Norm Ward laughs at his own joke as he emerges from the staff toilet to find Tony leaning over the microphone on the secretary's desk. *Norm* is the centre's cook; in his early-fifties and now divorced, he was born in Pouch Cove but has lived in St. John's thirty years.

"Ah, Norm. Meet Bas Kean, our new night supervisor," Tony introduces the man standing behind him and has another drag of his perpetual cigarette. *Tony* is in his late-thirties, born, married and living in St. John's. *Bas,* in his late-twenties, is a university anthropology graduate; still single, he was born in Britain but has lived in St. John's two years. "Bas," Tony continues, "maybe you could help Norm in the kitchen for a while, and I'll see you again later after our meeting. And here's the house keys, Norm." Tony hands Norm a big jangling bunch, and Norm leads Bas away.

Norm likes afternoons when the counsellors are in conference. The Lightship is a large, wooden, rambling Victorian house with enough room to accommodate up to twenty probationers, day- and full-parolees and temporarily eligible absentees over the last few weeks or months of their sentences, and during the staff meetings if any residents or callers need something from one of the house's locked cupboards or rooms then they have to come to Norm, not the secretaries, for the keys.

Norm is to be found in the inner kitchen, deep inside the house, past the counsellors in their offices and the residents vacuuming staircases or playing darts or mooching around on sofas. The kitchen is just Norm's size and he keeps it spic and span—at least the visible surfaces: he can't budge the fridges or deep freeze by himself, so sometimes a few scraps accumulate behind them, when his helpers sweep them there, but every few months he has a spring-clean anyway. And the resident assisting him is carefully chosen, for everything is in place and to be kept that way. Moreover, Norm keeps a keen eye on everyone entering his territory—past the long tables and benches of the outer kitchen and towards his provisions. For there are vegetables in the lower cupboards, and perishables locked away in fridges, and tins and dry goods stacked on shelves along the walls and up to the ceiling; and Norm's cigarettes and matches hidden behind the bottles of coffee whitener.

"Welcome aboard, Bas!" Norm chuckles and shows Bas to a chair by the sink, brushing some cigarette ash off it onto his palm first.

"Thanks, Norm. What's cooking?" He gestures to the two large tureens of meat boiling on the electric stove.

"Soup! I love making soup. Sometimes I'll come in in the morning, even on a day off, and twenty minutes later I'll have a big pot of soup boiling up... I eat a lot see. And I force myself to even when I'm ill. So I don't lose strength. 'Cause I'm on me feet here all day. Busy as hell. 'Cept for a short game of cribbage and that. See I'm up at 9:00 with the alarm and I'm shaved and got my shirt pressed and ready to go by 9:40. Then I'm here from 10:00 'til 6:00, 'bout... But I dunno, I'm putting on some weight now!" Norm blows out his flat stomach by arching his back and then taps it. "And I'll soon have you doing the same, Bas. You see!"

"Smells all right anyhow!"

"Sure. Boys shovel up all I give 'em." Norm is a nervous man, with a spare, wiry frame; his jaw just starting to jut, and his eyes to sink. He unpadlocks a fridge and pours himself an orange juice, then unpadlocks a freezer and shows Bas the array of frozen meats. "And the cost of food in this house is 3,300 bucks, Tony told me. 'Cause these fellers are worse 'n youngsters for food. I mean we baby 'em, but even after I'm done at night they're at the food again. So it costs."

"Wholesale is it, Norm?"

" 'Less there's an offer on, yeah... See all this toilet paper?" Norms points to stacks touching the ceiling, "Well that was on offer at Colonials. This big sign up, then this ignorant clerk tells me it's through, and

I says 'not while the sign's still up it's not buddy!' So he had to let me have it, and I said I'll have two big cartons, and he says 'Jeeze! You must be running a hotel or something, a boarding house,' and I says 'No boy! But I got eighteen boys to watch out for.' Right! And buddy goes 'What! Eighteen sons! Jeeze!' And all the time Tony is listening behind and killing himself laughing. And I never told buddy no different. So I got a good deal there, see? And then it's a real riot getting it all into Tony's Nova and all these people standing round saying how it'll never fit. But it does, though you can't push a finger between all those boxes I tell you!" Norm laughs at the thought. "And we spent 700 bucks last time out!"

"Is that right! What are they getting for supper tonight then?"

"Fish and brewis tonight boy. And the lads'll soon finish that when I put it down. Heads down! Then they get up and it's 'thanks for the grub, cook' and they're off. And I always wash the saltfish through a few times before, and I still like mine with a bit of sugar on top."

"Me too. Gets less of that salty taste."

"Right. And like they say, 'where there's a will there's a way.' So it's the same as some folks eating something sweet after, eh...But you can't give these boys a salad. They won't eat it. And they call it 'high-class food.' 'Give us some simple grub, cook!' " Norm mimics and laughs. "And you give 'em a touch of garlic and half of 'em end up smelling like wops!...Then they're all over you, complaining 'bout not liking tomatoes, or peaches and that and you just gotta say: 'You fucking eat what's given! Or you fuck off and get y'own some place else!' " Norm stabs the air with a finger and Bas laughs at his contortions. "No, but they won't get fed like this when they leave here! That's for sure. Lot of 'em end up at take-outs all the time. Like four guys I remember lived together after here, and one of 'em 'd buy groceries and then the rest of 'em 'd eat it, see. No organisation. And they told me they ended up in cafes 'cause that was only twice as expensive each, nor four times like a home, right!" Norm shakes his head and laughs. "Hey! What time d' you have, Bas?"

"Uh. Three-thirty."

"Frig! Should have the potatoes on!" Norm transfers a pan of peeled potatoes from draining board to stove.

"How long you worked here then, Norm?"

"Coming up for two-and-a-half years, boy, and I never wanna go! And that's some unusual for me 'cause I always wanna move on after a bit...No. I worked everywhere. Bell Island mines and then Colonials.

And then I was cook at the Musgrove and after that at Newfoundland Hotel. I always find work. And my brother says how I'm a charmed bastard 'cause he never can. And how you gotta take y'brother's burden as y'own!" Norm laughs. But I reckon this'll be my last job now to end my days, 'cause they been really good to me. Even if I got offered more money 'cause I got lots of contacts in the trade, see... Like, I want whatever I can get outta life without breaking the law, or hurting someone else. And I been okay so far."

"Knock on wood!"

"Right. But they been unbelievable to me here. Manpower put me onto 'em—first fucking thing they ever done for me. Ever. And I still didn't want 'em looking through my papers. And they said did I know about the Lightship? And how I should see this guy Tony Murrin. So there I was shit-scared, down on my savings a bit, and expecting some big businessman in a suit. Then, there's Tony with his arse hanging out of jeans!" They laugh. "And he's a fantastic boss. And he says right out, 'Don't worry 'bout the residents and what they say. Just fuck'em, the bastards!' That's what he said. 'It doesn't fucking matter what they say.' You'll see how Murrin speaks. And then I tells my mother and she says 'Oh I prayed for you to get another job, Norman. I prayed for you!'... So are you another student Bas?"

"Yeah. Least I was."

"Well you'll enjoy it here. And you'll find something different every day, almost. Some days it's like clockwork and then the next it's all 'bout to collapse!" He laughs. "I was a bit scared when I came. Like I knew it from outside, but I didn't wanna be alone with all these ex-cons, right. Like I thought there'd be this bunch of greasers, all hard and fighting all the time, spit in y'face as soon as hear a cross word, but no one's hardly said 'Boo' to me! 'Cause they don't take violent criminals here, see. Rapists and murderers. And arsonists, or them's caused bodily harm... And no drug-pushers nor child abusers and them with too deep problems. And the other boys'd attack any like that they did get in, see? And rats too. Informers. The boys beat up on anyone who squealed in the Big House 'cause they hate them."

"Is that right?"

"For sure. The Lightship don't take violent criminals. They're mostly just here for 'B and Es.' Well, there's Roy did an armed robbery, but that was on the mainland, not here. So now he's paroled here back home... And he only used a pipe, see, not a serious weapon. People here'd not use a violent weapon like a gun or a knife. And there's a big difference, you know. And even if they did use a gun it'd only be an imitation one, or broken or something... And anyhow, Tony says these violent offenders and those on firearms offences keep it all inside and don't let it all go and get violent and threaten you. And that's just as likely to be them on 'B and Es.' So you'll be okay here, boy. We'll make sure of that."

"Hello, Mr. Cook!" A long-haired lad in denims and baseball boots pokes his head round the door. "Just came to say hello. That's all."

"Now. I want a word with you, Des. Know why we ran out of cutlery for you yesterday?"

"No, Mr. Cook."

" 'Cause Tony and me found it wrapped in a cloth upstairs! Ready for ripping off! And there was more someone chucked in a bin instead of washing it. So you tell the rest of the boys they better watch it 'cause Tony and me's not going out for more knives all the time. It'll be everything locked up at night next. And bringing more rules and institutions down on you... And another thing. Georgie found a great glob of green spit in the corner of the outer kitchen. And that's gross. Must be someone new 'cause we not had that for a time. But that better change 'cause Georgie's only on seven bucks a day for helping me out and he isn't paid to clean up that mess. It isn't fair on him. And you know he's one of the best boys we ever had in the kitchen. So you tell 'em, Des. Or they'll be getting their arses kicked. It's not that I don't trust 'em 'cause I do. Most of 'em at any rate. And I'm not being suspicious, eh, but you gotta be careful."

"Right, Cook. Gotta go. Oops! Nearly squashed my ciggie."

"And no smoking here next time!" Norm calls after him and grins. "No. He's a good boy is Des. But we nearly lost him last night for drinking and infringing a parole. He skipped house and got drunk but he came back all right and admitted it, so he's grounded now. Two weeks. Tony gave his probation officer a call and he said we could keep him, so he's lucky. If the police'd caught him, it would've been straight to the lockup. But Des is a good boy. He goes and plays cards at AA to kick the habit. Doesn't moan... He used to help me out here before Georgie and he was never saucy. Just followed orders. Like he said, he never cooked before, just ate it! Not like some of 'em I had. Like Eugene. Jeeze boy I wanted to choke him sometimes! Squeeze him 'til he died!" Bas laughs as Norm strangles an imaginary neck. "I guess he was a cunning animal in his way but he drove me nuts, like. Always behind me, talking at me. Like when he was first hanging 'round I thought that's normal enough. Most of 'em do it for a day or two 'til they gets their own buddies here. But this guy never stopped. And going on 'bout his feelings all the time and getting convicted and how he felt this was just like still being in prison here; like that. And then he was calling me 'Dad,' and saying how this boy was sleeping with that boy upstairs, screwing. And the other boys saying to him 'Don't get on the wrong side of the cook or he'll soon have his cock in y'mouth!' " Norm laughs. "The bastards! He wanted a parent so I says in the end how I'm not being his fucking father! I had four sons of my own and that was enough. You married Bas?"

"No chance, Norm!"

"Good for you! I thought I'd try it, see. But Lord Jesus! Five-and-a-half years of crucifixion! Jeeze! I still see the cunt 'round town sometimes, but never again. Been separated nigh on fifteen years now too...Best guy I ever had helping me here was this old feller, Murray, in for killing his wife. Now she was a bad sort. She drove him to it, and he took an axe to her. But it could just as easily have been the other way about."

"Is that right."

"Yeah. It was like we were father and son. 'Cause he was seventy odd. Been away ten years when he got probation or he was about to die inside he told me. And I used to look forward to coming in Mondays and hear all these new goings-on from him. And he used to hear me coming over the parking lot and then hear my boots in the hall and he said how he knew they were 'fucking' my boots not 'fucking' Murrin's boots 'cause of the weight!" Norm swings his arms in the air and they laugh. "Murray always used to say 'fuck' and get excited with his hands all the time he was giving me the gossip...And once he said he was gonna tell me about what he done to the wife and I said, 'No. What's past is gone. Paid for.' 'Cause I wanted to remember him like this, and he said how that's the nicest thing anyone said to him. And he hugged me... 'cause Tony told me 'bout him anyhow. He was drunk, see. They both were, really putting it away, and he killed her in a fight. And then he tied her behind his truck, like meat, 'cause he was gonna dump the body in the woods!" Norm laughs. "I tell you I just cracked up when I heard that. Dragging her behind the truck when they saw him!"

"Is that right!"

"Yeah. I mean a life is a life, especially a human life, but it was the alcohol did it, not him. Or he'd never truly've killed her. So I bought him bed linen for here, and that, and made him a big cake for his birthday. And we used to work non-stop. Eighteen hours a day. Strong as a horse he was, my son...But he hated the other boys. Ooh yes!... 'cause they stole his last sixty bucks from his pants under his bed one night. And we know who it was and all. 'Cause he only slept from three 'til five like, nights, and this young feller went to the washroom at four, another feller said, but he never saw him come back 'cause of how he crawled back and ripped Murray off. Took his smokes and all!"

"Is that right!"

"Yeah. Lost everything 'cept thirty cents that fell out. Then the young feller left next day so you couldn't prove anything...But Murray said he'd have killed buddy if he caught him! Stuck a knife so deep in his fucking gut so you wouldn't see the handle. And I said he wouldn't and he said he would if he was gonna lose all his money he worked for, 'cause his life was over anyway...Jeeze but he used to work some hard, my son! Even one Good Friday I remember. And I said, 'Them Protestants and Salvationists got proper respect for the Lord Almighty! They aren't working today! And here's you! A good Catholic and all!' And he cracked up. And I was no better like, and on the beer. And then next day he broke his toe an' had it in plaster and I was on about it being his punishment, and he loved that!" Norm laughs fondly. "No. Great times, my son. And he'd go wild to see me again."

"Where's he to now?"

"Home. Twillingate...No we had some great fellers here. They got some old photos up and all, by the stairs. And business diploma and certificates and all. All these fellers who left here and made good. In their own business, or like working for Canadian Tire or something."

"Oh yeah? I'll have to see them later. It's upstairs you say."

"Yeah. By them new offices they built last year. You'll find y'way 'round, Bas. 'Cause this is some big old place. Used to belong to Paul Spencer. Him what owned all Spencer's stores. Then his daughter got it and she leased it to the Sisters of the Beatitudes Hostel, like, and then us...No. We'll take care of you here, Bas. Feed you up!"

"Not too much, Norm!"

"No. But I'm really happy here, my son. It's like a big family, eh. Like I know I'm sentimental but I have a job saying 'No,' if the boys want something. Even if I'm tired. Or I feel bad after a few hours. I'm built like my mom like that. And I do everything for 'em, soon as they ask. Repair their clothes, everything...And I never cheated the Lightship neither. Like took food for myself before the rest of them. Oh, one thing you gotta watch out for nights is bums. Derelicts. I guess Tony'll tell you 'bout them later. You'll get to know 'em. Ernie Guzzwell and Craig Fleming and the rest. They'll be after you for fifty cents so you just say 'there's none here' or they'll really bug you. They aren't allowed in anyway, and I'm surprised some of the boys let them."

"Just bums, are they Norm?"

"Yeah. And you'll know them 'cause they'll freak you out if you try talking to 'em. I remember Ernie just sitting in the lounge one day and there I was thinking him a regular resident, right!" Norm laughs. "But he's been banned from the mental hospital and Tony says he's well known to the criminal system too and got his photo in six police stations. He's a paranoid schizophrenic something, one psychiatrist said. So you have to ask 'em to leave... And another one's Billy Reid. 'Billy Gluehead' they call him 'cause he comes and asks for a glass of water and then he goes sniffing glue in the washroom. He's 'gone' as they say. And you can smell him a mile off." Norm laughs again at Bas' distaste. "I tell you, my son, you get a real insight into life working here. But don't worry! You'll do okay. We're a happy family here... And I never had any violence from the boys... And I remember only one boy ever assaulted his counsellor. Threatened to punch his face in, 'cause the boys had something going on in the house, so Murrin called in the police and that was the last we saw of him."

"What was it about?"

"Nah, he was all fired liquored up, something bugging him and ready to beat the world, and with the alcohol it came out, is all... But I had no problems here, Bas, since I came. Never happier. And that's how it's gonna stay. 'Cause I've worked hard for what I got, boy, and I reckon I deserve it." Norm clenches a serious fist and grits his teeth. "I got rights on the face of this earth, and no one's gonna say something against Norm Ward again, or if they do, they'll find themselves at my feet. And if I can't do it then someone in this house'll do it for me... I mean it, my son. We know how to look out for our friends 'round here. You'll see... Anyhow, staff meeting'll be out now and you better see Tony in the front office. And I'll cook you up something nice for supper here... You know where I'll be!"

"Thanks, Norm. Great!" Bas vacates his seat.

"Sure. You'll do okay."

"Catch you later."

Sixth Scene

Wednesday night, fun at Milligan's Irish pub

That evening, all the introductions over with, Bas repairs to George Street and Milligan's Irish pub for a beer or two. He is pleased to have the job but it will mean less time relaxing over a drink once he starts...May as well make the most of it now.

George Street is the backside of Water Street and New Gower Street, where one sees behind the facades of the busy downtown shops and traffic. This was once home to warehouses, but now O'Malley's wholesale grocery operates in a street dead to the day. Now, bars and their parking lots jostle for space, and it is at night that Plastic Bertram's, and Swiler Jake's Bar and Museum, and the Broadwalk, and Milligan's really come to bustling life.

Mayor Malone once met a Torontonian who said that even though he had never been to St. John's, he had still heard that George Street was the hottest spot for clubs and bars in the country! Now, to attract more tourists, there are council plans afoot to make George Street into a pedestrian precinct, with the Parisian ambience of open-air cafes, umbrellas and cobbles.

Bas likes George Street because the bars are mostly not pretentious and still do not have the cover charges of the more pucka-pucka clubs. And Bas likes Milligan's because it is safely in the hands of a young local set who can meet here after a day studying at college, or working as shop-assistants, or after another day tramping the streets and handing in job résumés like lottery ticket stubs. In the cramped and cosy darkness of Milligan's, with its beer-smelling wood and token piece of

Irish tartan framed on the wall, the etiquette of the workaday city may be forgotten. Between 4:00 p.m. and 7:00, you can douse yourself in the two-drinks-for-the-price-of-one happy hour, and then carry on at a normal pace into the early hours of the morning.

Gord Sutton likes Milligan's too. Gord, a hotel page in his mid-twenties, single, born and living in St. John's, likes coming here from his regular bar, Tee Cee's, in order to see the beautiful downtown women. In Milligan's, naked women decorate the bar area, and lewd signs the walls: 'Beer Drinkers Make Better Lovers,' 'Catholic Lover: 24-hour Service: Rhythm Method My Speciality,' 'We Do Not Serve Women: You Have To Bring Your own,' 'To All Employees: New Incentive Plan: Work Or Get Fired.' And the place is always full towards midnight, tables of girls drinking away and Gord's buddies always good for a laugh. There is *Paul Lawrence:* mid-twenties, single, unemployed, born and living in the neighbourhood of Shea Heights, and *Art Knight:* early-twenties, single, unemployed, born and living in the Buckmaster Circle area; and *Sue Welch:* mid-twenties, single, a student at the Fisheries College, born and living in Shea Heights; and *Bernie Hickman:* mid-twenties, single, a fisheries student, born and living in St. John's; and the bouncer, *Bruce Pearce:* late-twenties, single, born and living in Buckmaster Circle; and even a reasonable owner, *Frank Murphy:* early-forties, divorced, born in Belfast but lived in St. John's fifteen years; and then regular singers like *Jerome Tirk:* late-twenties, single, born and living in St. John's.

Milligan's hosts a fair crowd tonight, and Bas parks himself on a stool at the bar.

Nice legs, shame about the face,
Nice legs, kick her in the face!

Jerome sings from the opposite corner.

"Hey! " a lad rushes in, "does anyone here own a beige Nova? 'Cause it's parked right in the middle of the parking lot and it's blocking me. And I got to go!"

"I've got a Nova, but it's not beige. And it's at home," Sue answers from a packed table of her girlfriends.

"Well this one's in the middle of the parking lot, and if no one owns it I'll move it myself."

"Why not bounce it out of the way?" Gord shouts.

"I know well enough how to move it, boy. I done it to a Plymouth before: ram her from behind with my four-wheel drive and she soon moved all right!"

"Wrong club, buddy; it's all freaks here!" Jerome jokes as the lad leaves in disgust.

"Got any tokes?" Gord asks Paul. They and Art are seated at a table near the bar. But they can still watch the bevy of females coming and going at the big table in front of Jerome's stage. "Hey! I heard Lance was done. Monday night. For impaired driving and possession of twenty-five grams of hash with intent to traffic." Paul and Art didn't know. But then Lance is a bit of a freak. "Yeah! He said he convinced the cop who arrested him that he smokes that much himself, so it was just gonna be 'possession'; but then the Crown Prosecutor decided it was more like 'intent.' So he's gotta have a preliminary enquiry first, and they'll see if they got enough evidence on him to bring him to trial. But Lance said he's got a good case and there won't be a trial... Or if there is, he'll go for a judge and jury, and at the end just pay a little fine for possession and that'll be it."

"He must be making a buck on them rigs."

"Good job, yeah," Gord agrees, "but he may be out of it September... Remember when they caught him with hash at home, round the bay, and took him to Harbour Grace lock-up for the night! He told me how his old mother kept on at him 'you should be ashamed, ashamed, ashamed boy!' " Gord squeaks and laughs, "And he just said back, 'the only thing I'm ashamed of is being caught,' and that shut the old lady up for a spell!... Then next morning he drove to court smoking a reefer! And he hadn't finished it by the time he got there, so he drove round a bit and then went into this bar for a beer. And all through the case he was stoned out of his mind! And this cop saying to him, 'The lab reports confirm the substance is hash,' and Lance said, 'He suspected it might!' So the cop got furious and took him for a breatherliser but they couldn't find anything 'cause being stoned doesn't show up!"

They laugh. "That sounds like Vaughan," Art says. "He was late for court, so he grabbed his jacket and dashed out, and got fined $120 for hash — this is a few years back, mind — then he found he'd forgotten his wallet and he only had $13 on him. And he also found he had twenty dimes of hash in his jacket! And he knew they wouldn't let him out without paying $60 at least, and it meant time in the lock-up, so he had to hide the hash down his pants! With three cops watching!... Then he had to give his keys to his house and his locker where he also had some coke and seven bricks of dope! And they found none of it! Lucky for him... Vaughan's also got done for assaulting the police. Said they got violent and started beating on him. And he had four grams of hash in his pocket then, that he had to stuff down his pants."

"Crazy!" Gord agrees. "Only Vaughan'd assault the police with dope in his pocket!.... And you could spit in his face and he'd not get riled. Couldn't. And he'd smoke eight joints a night! Magic feller."

"Says he only does drugs every eight months now. And that's coke."

"I could stop like that," Paul boasts. "I can do anything like that."

"Want some hash, Paul?" Gord pushes. "Come on. Get down and party! I've been doing it a bit lately... Let's have a few beers first, smoke some dope, then play that new video in the arcade."

And here comes Art with his pecker in his hand,
'Cause there goes Sue with her titties in her hands,
And Gord ain't getting any!!

"Fuck off, Tirk!" Gord shouts as Jerome finishes his song and people laugh.

"Gord can't be getting any, because his car is always in the street when I get back at night," Jerome continues from the stage. "You can always tell the men who aren't getting any: they just drink beer all the time! Sorry I left y'party the other night, Gord, but all the beer was gone so I came down here. Then I got stoned and walked home... But I've never known twelve Canadian go so fast. Next time I'll sit on the frigging twelve-pack!"

"Fuck off then, Tirk! You're on cheap drugs. You're crazy!"

"Hey Gord! You wanna go to this bar I was at in the States: 'Liquor in the front and pok-er in the rear!'... Or maybe Sue over here is free?"

"Free, but not easy!" Sue's friends scream and giggle.

"That last song, for Gord, was also from the Monks' album. And there's another good track on it: 'Drugs in my Pocket.' That's good too. But I don't usually do that Gord-song. Makes me sick!"

"Then why do it here, boy?" Bruce the bouncer shouts from his high stool by the door.

"But I do it at Milligan's. Frank, the boss, says I'm not allowed 'cause of the rude words; so I could lose my job. And not be allowed two-for-one happy hour. And it's not the pink slip I'm scared of but losing the two-for-one!... Hey Frank! How about half an hour happy hour after this?" Frank shakes his head and smiles, from his stool at the bar. "That's Frank: the only Irish Jew in Canada!" Jerome laughs. "Frank'll have two-for-one tomorrow. Pay for two and get one! Great way to stop drinking!"

"Doing this for drinks, are you Tirk?"

"Well I'm not being paid!"

"Hey, Tirk. What does it take to get you warmed up?" Sue calls again.

"A good pair of lips!" and the girls squeal coyly at Jerome's repartee. "Hey, Bruce boy. Did you hear of the rabbi who signed on as a bouncer? He heard he'd get four-skins every night and as many tips as he could handle!"

"Jerome, have you heard of the leper who carried three fingers in his pocket? Photos of his wife and kids!" Jerome laughs with Sue and fits a harmonica around his neck, licking it wet. "How does it feel, Jerome?" Sue giggles.

"Bring it up and I'll tell you!"

Sue's girlfriends forcibly shut her mouth, and apologise: "She's so small she creeps up behind you!" "Yeah, up and down Shea Heights with her forty-ouncer!" "And every night she walks right into it!" "Yeah, and says 'Keep it up'!" They break off, laughing. "Hey Jerome! She's got two tests tomorrow, you know."

"Well this is a good way to prepare!... I took sexology. You could probably take your master's in that tomorrow, Sue."

"Play some Beatles!" a boy shouts as he staggers in, melodramatically, and dances before the clapping girls before collapsing in their midst.

"Right":

Picture yourself in a boat on the river,
With tangerine trees and marmalade skies,
Somebody calls you, you answer quite slowly,
A girl with kaleidoscope eyes.
Lucy in the skies with diamonds,
Lucy in the sky with diamonds,
Lucy in the sky with diamonds,
Ahhhh.

People applaud the song, and the girls' hero flails his arms.

"Hey. The relations must be here! Or else I owe someone money!...No. Thank you very much. You know, usually my singing clears a pub by 11:30. I've got a good record!" Jerome laughs. "Thank you. 'Lucy in the Sky,' LSD. Heavy trip...Now you know what's a really nice gesture? To buy the singer a beer. They really appreciate it. I went into the Prince of Scotland and I saw the singer beer-less and I went and bought him one. So you feel free to do the same to me! I'll accept."

Gord laughs and signs to the waitress, who carries Jerome a beer.

"Cheers, Gord! All these beers, I'll be fried by one o'clock. But it looks better if you sing with a full glass behind you and there's room for about four more bottles up here before they start falling all over the place, so keep 'em coming. Of course you know if you go to the bar tonight and buy any Carlsberg products you get a ticket for the draw on this cigarette." Jerome holds a roll-up to the room. "Now I didn't roll it, so I dunno what's in it. It doesn't smell like tobacco; and it could be horseshit. But it could be weed." He sniffs it. "It could be tea leaves or it could be the weed. Actually it smells more like horseshit!" The crowd laughs. "No. Joking aside, I know it's not a toke up here... or the police'd bust me. Right, Frank?"

"Proper t'ing!" Gord shouts as Art and Paul smile.

"You know, boys, as well as this beer strike, there's also a hash strike on. Hash is $50 a gram!... Has anyone here a gram or a half to sell. If so see me after this set. 'Cause it's gonna be a hectic day tomorrow, and best to buy some now. I been seeing nothing but nuts and bolts of starting motors all day and my nerves are shot to hell. If I carry on like this I'll have to smoke the black hash I was saving up for tomorrow. Okay. Anyone who guesses the name of this next song can buy me a beer. Hey, I'm really getting into the music tonight, and I'm not even stoned!"

"Play some Rush!" the drunken lad emerges from the girls to call.

"The Doors!" Art counters.

"Sorry, Art. Don't know any, though I've nothing against them. Great on video. The only difference to the Beatles is that McCartney didn't overdose!... But it's bad when people ask you and you don't know a song."

The waitress appears with a birthday cake, and carries it to the drunken lad being cushioned on the table of girls. The cake takes the form of two breasts with candles atop the nipples. It reads: 'Here's the big ones you always wanted!! Happy Birthday Bernie.' The girls laugh and applaud, and prop Bernie up to receive it, with his beret perched on his quiff, and his leather jacket over one shoulder. "Do a 'Happy Birthday,' " there is a request. Jerome obliges, and everyone joins in the chant:

Happy Birthday to Bernie,
Happy Birthday to Bernie,
Happy Birthday, you bastard,
We hope you get plastered,
Happy Birthday to you.
We hope you live to make it home,
We hope you live to make it home,
Now that you're here, get drunk as a skunk,
We hope you live to make it home.

"Buy him a Milligan's special!" Jerome suggests. "After that, boy, all the girls look good. And you keep celebrating so long as they buy the beers! Look how confident Sue's got, since she's been on the beer with the boys!"

"Bernie's going away tomorrow," Sue shouts.

"Going off to a job?" Jerome wonders. "Going Alberta or somewhere, Bernie?"

"Just Lab City," Sue explains.

"Hey! I was up there last June. Had a good time. Though I dunno how mean they'd be in a beer strike! No, they're good people... Hey, Frank! It's past midnight. Do I get double time?" Frank just smiles. "I knew I should've joined the union..."

" 'I'se the B'y,' " one of the girls requests.

" 'I'se the b'y who kissed the fish and brought it home to Liza'!" Jerome mimics. "That's what happens when you get a few shots of Screech. Jeeze! I'm not singing here again: I'm gonna go ossified!"

"That's what we're trying to do, boy!" Sue shouts.

"Okay. Here's one from Ron Hynes for all the old hands about":

Sonny lives on a farm; on a wide open space,
You could take off your sneakers and give up the race,
You could lay down y'head by a sweet river bed,
But Sonny always remembers what it was his mamma said,
And she said:"

All the girls are harmonising with each other, looped-armed and swinging side to side in their seats. They sing and whoop, and toast Bernie and raise their bottles to Jerome:

Oh Sonny don't go away,
I am here all alone,
And your daddy's a sailor who never comes home,
And the nights get so long, and the silence goes on,
And I'm feeling so tired, I'm not all that strong.

"Hey Gord. Let's go and have a joint in the washroom," Paul suggests. "Bruce'll keep an eye out for us on the door. And I'll pay you the end of next week."

"Friday! Seventy-five dollars... And no need to go to the men's. Just light up here. They don't mind. Frank's probably toking up right now in the manager's office!" Gord takes some dope from a matchbox and hands it to Paul. Paul sniffs it, then burns and crumbles a small chunk of it on the table. Then he adds some tobacco and rolls a thin cigarette. Lighting it, he, Gord and Art take drags until it is too small to hold, even with Paul's tweezers.

Frank Murphy walks from behind the bar, past Bas, and pretends to go sniffing around. Gord calls over to him: "Hey Frank. It's the narc police! 'Come out with y'hands up: you're under arrest!' " They laugh.

And the girls are still singing and swinging along with Jerome:

And it's a hundred miles to town; Sonny's never been there,
And he goes to the highway and stands there and stares,
And the mail comes at four, and the mailman is old,
And he still dreams his dreams, full of silver and gold.
Oh Sonny don't go away,
I am here all alone,
And your daddy's a sailor who never comes home,
And the nights get so long, and the silence goes on,
And I'm feeling so tired, I'm not all that strong...

Seventh Scene

Thursday night, a chin-wag at the Salon Paris nightclub

Jerome's act is not always such a 'hit.' At another bar, the Salon Paris, Shirley Blanchard, the barmaid, recalls him differently. "Sure we tried to liven things up a bit with some live music like everywhere's getting, so Cal got in Jerome Tirk and Billy Bennet, but soon as he left they started in messing around like they owned the place, you know? Acting up like they was better'n the rest of us. And I been here too long for that: my nerves won't take it."

"Sure all these bands round town now are lazy bums," Garland Jefferd agrees, seated on the other side of the bar. "Still, bit dead in here now. Sheesh! Cal got any more bands lined up?"

"Well those two won't be back! Cal caught 'em stealing steaks one time. It's like he's never been a judge of who to hire on as staff! Be different if this was my place, I can tell you."

Shirley and Garland are old friends. *Shirley,* early-forties, married, born on the northern peninsula but lived in St. John's periodically for twenty years, has worked at the Salon Paris since it opened almost a decade ago. But, *Garland,* mid-forties, an unemployed labourer and separated, born and living in St. John's has not been in for a while. For the Salon is a couple of miles from the city's centre, on one of the city's main arterial routes, Torbay Road.

Torbay Road presents a less neon-infested approach to the city proper than other arteries but it is modernising. Recently widened, partly in honour of a Papal entourage, it also boasts its hypermarkets, cheap apartment blocks, expensive suburban estates, doughnut-cum-video outlets, and large, concrete, new-looking bars such as the Salon Paris. Over its decade of life, the Salon has passed through a number of managements and facelifts. Now the building is divided in two: a pub and games-room to engage the youth, and a larger strip-joint to attract any adults bored with downtown and looking for a more stimulating night out. Stag parties come here — and hen parties — and randy students, and groups of Japanese sailors celebrating dry land.

However, the strip-joint still feels unfinished and makeshift; dark, cold and cavernous. Black low ceiling, stucco walls, small, frosted windows, and plentiful tables arranged around a large square dance floor, and a small stage boasting a mere jukebox.

Almost midnight now, it is a quiet evening: too near the weekend. But Shirley and Garland do not quite have the place to themselves, and at odd tables there are a few men waiting for the next half-hourly show to begin. With nothing happening, the men seem bored, muttering and looking about them uneasily. The embarrassing silence is drowned out in three-minute bursts by the crackling jukebox, light bulbs flashing in time. In between selections, three waitresses and a cashier by the door, skimpily dressed in bright negligees and dark g-strings call to one another in French, and exchange stage-screams and giggles over some running gag.

Then, a pair of high heels clatter over the wooden floor to the jukebox again, and at this sign, men and beer get up and jockey for the best tables at the dance floor railings.

Selecting three of her favourite tunes of the moment, one of the erstwhile waitresses does her regular three-part striptease; always timing her dance routines so that she is back safely at base, by the relatively distant stage, when the protective beat of the music and the lyrics she can mouth have stopped.

In the first song the girl teases and suggests, checking the faces on each table. Seven secretaries out for a night on the town with their male escorts, getting ribald at a table in one corner, she avoids.

Her second song is slower. The negligee is lowered by one table and removed by another; a g-string likewise. She offers her chest here, and her fanny there. She taps her bum at him, and winks at them.

The third song is sensual, and she shows off intimately, from various angles, writhing on a furry rug on the floor.

Meanwhile, for those who can pay the price, the other waitresses do more private stripteases on top of movable benches before particular tables. These men are then personally invited to inspect their waitresses' charms, as she daubs them with her lingerie.

At the secretaries' table, introductions are underway: "Gwent, meet Sally. And this is Rose. She works for Whelan Dindale you know!"

"You have my sympathies, Rose! No not really. But you can tell Judge Dindale you met Gwent Warford of Grand Falls. He'll know who you mean."

"Tell the judge we were all at the Salon Paris, shall I?"

"Oh he's okay. These judges may look like they're so stiff if you put a board down their backs, the board'd split first, eh! But get a few beers down 'em and they're same as the rest of us!"

But oblivious to all these antics, Shirley and Garland keep drinking and chatting at the bar. 'I used to be disgusted. Now I'm just amused,' a sign hanging from the bar announces above their heads.

"So that Portuguese has gone, you say, Shirl?"

"Right. He was only renting this place. But he drank away the profits."

"Typical Portuguese I remember. Five-foot-nothing and always after wining and dining the girls!" Garland scoffs. "And what about them old beer-bashes we had here then, Shirl? Four to seven at the Paris!"

"Gone too, me old son. Got too wild. Them fisheries students got drunk on cheap beer, then they'd destroy the place. Even the girls' washrooms, mirrors trodden on and I don't know what. So you needed someone down there all the time, keep an eye on things. And you'd call the police and get rid of the troublemakers, then there'd be more in a few weeks. So now Cal wants a different clientele, and I can't honestly say I'm sorry."

"Just say 'No Students.' The rest were all right."

"Can't do that... Mind you, we still get the odd confusion down here, Garland! Like last week, woman sitting over there in bright red whore-boots, screaming at buddy as how he's not taking this other woman home, and him saying he is, and then she slaps him and he gets his arms round her and says how he's not doing friggin' time on her account, or something, and then she's on about how if he was a real man he'd take his hands off her and apologise and buy her a beer—"

"Is that right!"

"—and next thing you know the two women are at each other, fists flying 'cause you could see they'd both had a skinful and just itching for a fight, and then missus is laid out on the floor saying how her neck's broke, and there's blood coming out of her nose and her eyes. So Cal called the cops and the ambulance and all the time this other woman's kicking her saying as how she'd get up and fight if she was a real woman, and how she's ugly as her arsehole, and hitting anybody else who got near. So in the end the police had to carry her out in an armlock 'cause she still won't give it up, screaming."

"Yeah! Just like the good old days. Sorry I missed that! Sounds like a bit of fun. Y'old fighting party."

"Yeah sure, but you gotta watch out when these big women get going, Garland. 'Cause they can be some fast! And unless there's a whole bunch of you, you can get hit yourself if you jump in. And for me, like, unless I just walk away and forget it, I have to get involved if I sees a fight, eh?"

"Sure, Shirl! Can't just stand around and watch. And there'd be lots of ways you'd get a recreation fight before, downtown; folks going out to a bar just to get in one!" He chuckles. "I must've been only a young feller, going on seventeen when I got first slung out of Brad's by this big bouncer for calling him 'gander-neck,' 'cause his neck was some long!" They laugh. "And he told me not to come back. But the boys were always at him. Seeing if they could take him, eh?"

"Right. Bernadette told me how they got this real character as bouncer there now. Only little guy but he's done it all—logging and mining in Canada—and he thinks he can reason with these guys, eh? Logically like."

"Is that right! Sounds a bit of a nut. Nah. You gotta beat guys out, 'Cause they're just out for a fight... Remember my buddy Mort. Always in a fight and that's the God's truth!" Garland laughs and shakes his head. "What a guy! 'Cause he had some mouth on him people didn't know his bark was worse than his bite, like. One time he got in a fight 'cause he accused buddy of drinking his beer when he'd finished it himself! And forgotten. And another time he hits buddy for dancing with his girl when she's already been round the whole floor!"

"Yeah well, that's how it was, boy. And then they'd set to it."

"Another time, Mort's watching these heavies scrapping. You know, tatoos and all, punching the shit out of each other, and he says, 'My watch goes on buddy,' right? So no one's gonna back down then! And Mort gets lined up against 'em too, and wakes up under some table and he says to me he thought he were dead he felt so bad!" Garland laughs. "No I tell you, Shirl, it's all pussies downtown now. You don't get fights like you used to, say ten years ago."

"No, that's for sure. Bars aren't what they were... Whatever happened to Mort? Short guy weren't he?"

"Right. Always being picked on. Dunno. Last I heard he was telling me how he woke up at the lock-up, 'cause he called the cops 'cock-suckers,' and wouldn't sign this release notice about appearing in court, when they arrested him for being drunk and disorderly."

"What?"

Garland laughs again. "That's Mort! Standing up for his right to be drunk, he said, but they wouldn't stop victimising him. So when they told him to count his money down the lock-up he tore it up and threw it at them, so these supercops laid into him or something. I dunno. He was drunk when he told me. But he was a real 'un was Mort. Don't make 'em like that no more, Shirl, and that's for sure!... You can drink more with y'eyes shut than these pussies downtown now! Same old boring faces. So thought I'd get out of it for a night, see how you was getting on."

"And I'm pleased you did, old son. And Cal's hoping folks'll get fed up 'cause it's like a strip, all them bars downtown now. Like me and Jeff come here on my nights off too. He used to go to Tee Cee's regular for a game of darts and I never used to go 'cause there'd be all this cursing and swearing on you if you didn't get a ton, or if you never got away, eh?"

"Sure. Not just a game down there."

"Right. And Jeff'd say with me around he got into far more fights if anyone so much as looked at me, so I used to keep away. Like last time we was down to the Park Tavern, boondocks, and this fat barmaid won't serve me 'cause it's men only and she says there's no ladies' washroom, 'cause that's the excuse they use, eh, so I say I'll use hers if I need to go, right? So then buddy walks up and sticks his neck at Jeff and says he doesn't like him, or something, and everyone staring, and then buddy hits Jeff as he goes to take off his coat and breaks two bones in poor Jeff's hand, right, so I just had to pull him out and say, 'don't be stupid, leave it,' or I was about to get hysterical myself."

"Nah. It's changed downtown now, my girl. Like the Musgrove. I dunno what you'll see walking out of there, but it won't be men, for sure."

"Oh, gays you mean. And they had that stabbing there mind, a while back. Buddy killed. And same at Pat's Place. Transvestites from Toronto and all this. And Jeeze boy, what a cesspool Toronto is now, eh! Like all the world's misfits and dirty scuzzes walking round with empty faces. Sweet Jesus.... You been into Pat's at all, Garland?"

"No chance, Shirl! Not 'til they ship the lot of 'em back to Canada!"

"I know what you mean. But me and the girls had a look not too long ago for old time's sake, like. 'Cause when I was to the university a gang of us'd go out for a night's boozing and we'd start the evening there. Ten, fifteen of us. But it's all different now. Loud music, and everyone rowdy and shouting and smoking. A rougher element like... And I heard they get lots of thefts there too, Garland. Girls put their purses down, and next thing someone's whipped it down to the bathroom and cleaned it out."

"Nah. Not like it was down there, Shirl. It's 'cause they're trying to clean it up too much now. Or else they torched all the old decent bars for the insurance money. I dunno."

"Know what you mean, Garland. But this girlfriend I got, works at Brad's still, Bernadette, she says how they keep it the same and not too fancy or people'd not come. And she's a big girl, mind. She's thrown her share of rowdies out down them steps when they get to swearing on her, and the bouncer's busy. And she said they had the paddywagon round there three nights in a row last week 'cause of fights when they were shutting up for the night."

"Is that right?"

"Yeah still a good place for fights. And they had this gang of Irishmen in, sailors, what was really scraping the barrel, she said! Broken beer bottles at each others' throats. The works!"

" 'Course! But best of mates next day for sure."

"And she said they also got this mongol boy down there, not normal, and he joins in the band on stage, screaming away, and that really gets 'em going... Don't think I'd work there. I've had enough of neighbourhood bars, personally. Just a personal opinion like, but you been there recently, Garland?"

"No girl! I've gone too soft now and all! Have to get fit again then give it a go."

"Well, like I say, everyone's entitled to their opinion... They also had a couple of Indians in there before, Bernadette said, getting drunk and mouthing off, and in the end these longhairs from that bikers' bar laid into 'em with their feet, blood everywhere, and they ended up in the Medical Centre and all!"

"Good job! They shouldn't give these Indians booze. It thins their blood and they can't take it. They got no control."

"I heard in Labrador, in their natural setting, like, every penny of their welfare cheques go on drink. And they can get through a twenty-six-ouncer a day, and then go unconscious, and keep that up for two weeks. That's ridiculous! Shouldn't be allowed. Kids got nothing to eat. And then they're fighting all the time and fornicating and I don't know what. It's just not rational. You can't enjoy drinking like that, can you?"

"Nah. They should've done up in Labrador like we did on the 'Rock': shoot the lot right off the bat, and, Hey Presto! No Indian problem."

Shirley laughs "Oh you're bad, Garland! But you got a point, I gotta admit. They just gotta smell the cap off a bottle..."

"And it's like they say, Shirl: the white man alters it all wherever he goes. And that's progress."

"Right... I used to go up them ways fishing with my brothers before. From Port-au-Fleur, eh? They had this twenty-eight footer in the sixties, early seventies."

" 'Course. You belong into there don't you girl. Now I bet they had their fighting families up there in them days, eh?"

"Oh yeah! I could've shown you round some of 'em then! Bit untamed up there they were! Lived by their own rules and they wouldn't have any other!"

Garland chuckles. "Oh I know girl. And fishermen and all, so they'll be fierce guys."

"For sure. They wouldn't listen to no Mountie preaching at 'em, and I saw it all 'cause I was working to this bar up there then, and Mounties 'd stick well clear 'cause they was so outnumbered. Just went round confiscating kids' drugs so they could smoke 'em themselves!"

"Right. So what was the bar like? See lots of good old fights like down here then? Chairs getting thrown through windows and that?"

"Oh, for sure! They'd have been fighting every night up there if you let 'em. Always spoiling for a fight... And with the alcohol you really saw folks in a true light. Like the booze brought out the real person, 'cause they lost their defences, and conventions and self-control, and you just see what's underneath . . . And it's funny who you end up respecting after you see 'em like that, eh? And how you change y'opinions. Like some of 'em 'd need the beer to get up courage to fight, and then they'd be sitting at the bar and foul-mouth everyone else, and too cowardly to get to scrapping themselves."

"Yeah. I met that sort and all."

"Yeah. And then we'd ban 'em for two months, and then they'd be back next night with this sob story about how they'd had more trouble with the wife. Some backwater, you know... My cousin Jim had a real violent temper, and all. Always in a fight. Then one day he turns up at the bar in these dark glasses and I just cracked up laughing when he said how the Saunders boys just give him a lesson, ganged up on him, and how now he was gonna change his ways. See Saunders were a big family and they'd always have brothers round to back them up."

" 'Course. Like you would."

"Right. But they could get nasty, too, mind. Fingers in eyes and scratching and the rest...Dunno what's gonna happen to Jim. Keeps saying he wants a woman, but he's too old now for a woman to straighten him , I reckon. And his sister's the opposite. Real sensitive. Like she always hated the other girls talking coarse and on about getting blasted every night. And I remember her considering getting hitched, serious, to this guy up there, and she comes to me and says how she's not sure 'cause he drinks and comes home late and bangs the door and wakes her up, and I says 'Jeeze'! Sharon, What's wrong with that girl? Least he's not getting destructive and violent, eh? Least he's not trigger happy and gonna kill you!' Right?"

"Right."

"But she couldn't see it. And there's Mack, her feller, so happy-go-lucky. You know, couldn't get angry, or in a temper. Like a child. Wouldn't hurt a fly. And if he gets drunk and falls asleep then count yourself lucky, eh."

"Too right. So did she get hitched?"

"Yeah. Finally. But I can see her really getting to him in the end. Nagging on...No. It's all changed up there now Garland. They all got rich now with them big houses. And trailers parked outside all year as status-symbols. And everything bought with cash."

"Oh I know, Shirl. I never believe a fisherman now who says he's poor!"

"Even share-workers in the boats pay 12,000 bucks income tax, my brother says, so you can imagine what they're earning. But it's never enough for 'em...I tell you we'll have to move to Halifax soon, my son, 'cause this place is not what it was and that's a fact...I mean everyone's opinion's different but I couldn't move to Toronto if the world was gonna cave in everywhere else. There's no feeling there, like. No history..."

"Nah. Cheer up, Shirl! Look. Come at me with that Dominion bottle, and I'll hit you on the head, and then we'll get Cal coming running! Just like the good old days, eh!" Garland laughs and Shirley forces a smile. "Just like it used to be here...I got a brother-in-law over in England, Shirl. English, like. And he says it's the same in them bars. Soon as buddy turns over someone else's beer there's a fight."

"Yeah? No, I'm after getting too old to wander, Garland."

"Me and all I guess...Well, reckon I better be getting back to them pussies downtown. But I'll be back in soon, Shirl."

"You know where to find me! See you now Garland."

"Bye." Garland drains his bottle and makes his way out; between tables of men again waiting for the next striptease.

At the door Garland finds an altercation between the bouncer and a drunk trying to gain admittance, and has to squeeze past to get out.

"Look boy! You're not getting in here again tonight. Okay!"

"Just gotta find my glasses, see? Can't see nothing otherwise."

"Look. You never had them with you in the first place!"

"Must have, boy. Had 'em at Tee Cee's so they'll be inside sure? Come on."

"Look. For the last time. You're not coming in. Right?"

"Okay boy. Don't hit me. Just trying to find my glasses."

"No one's hitting you, boy. Now just go home, or back to Tee Cee's."

At last the bouncer manages to close the door. The drunk leans against the wall outside for a minute, fumbles in his jacket pocket, finds his glasses, and follows Garland out into the drizzle of the night...

Eighth Scene

Thursday evening, at a visit to Tee Cee's lounge

'I don't have a drink problem; I drink, I get drunk, I fall down. No problem!' Dr. Mulrooney reads to himself from a varnished piece of imitation tree-trunk nailed above the bar in Tee Cee's lounge earlier that night. Also 'Nautical Science, Departmental Office' on a silver plaque. Dr. Mulrooney and his friends Jane Steenwijk and Terry Wells have wandered into Tee Cee's for a quick drink. *Mulrooney* is a professor of English at the university: late-forties, divorced, born and living in St. John's. *Steenwijk* is a professor of linguistics: mid-forties, widowed, born in South Africa but lived seven years in St. John's. *Wells,* single and early-thirties, has just completed his M.A. in linguistics; born in Vancouver, B.C., he has lived in St. John's five years.

"One Heineken, one India and an Old Stock, please," Mulrooney orders when he has the barmaid's attention. And, "That plaque?" she explains with a grin, "Oh, some of the boys ripped it off from the Fisheries College last Christmas."

Tee Cee's lounge is a new watering hole for Mulrooney's party. Situated in one of the less gentrified areas of residential downtown, Tee Cee's is a neighbourhood bar which does not advertise itself by the canopies and bill-boards and brass knockers and hanging plants of the fancy Water Street clubs and piano bars-cum-discotheques-cum-restaurants such as the Salty Commodore or the Club Paul. It is located at a crossroad; in one direction lies the modernistic City Hall and digital city clock, in another the Anglican Cathedral, Methodist United Church and Roman Catholic Basilica, and in a third the hill which just brought Mulrooney, Steenwijk and Wells up from the street-life and bustle of Water Street. Most of Tee Cee's custom, however, arrives from the fourth direction and the public row housing nearby. From there, Tee Cee's is the place to come for a casual drink or a relaxed night over darts. And next door is the Soong Loong Take Out (Chinese and Canadian Food: Fast Service), so that is convenient too.

The regulars know what they will find at Tee Cee's; and apart from the odd stranger who has lost his way, they recognise the same gangs of drinking buddies. When you walk in, there are the pinball and video machines; and then you can check out who is at the four dart boards and under the spotlights down the steps in the long den area, or what is on the colour television in the far corner, before grabbing a stool at the bar. Then you give your new tape cassette to Tee Cee's daughter to play over the bar stereo and she opens your first bottle of Labatt's Blue and a new pack of Player's, and you tell her all the news. As she fetches Dr. Mulrooney's beer from the fridge, then, she fumbles, still being intent on following the talk and gesticulation between Gord and his elder confidant Stu at the end of the bar.

"What a time! And what's the fucking use? Laid off December 17 and nothing since! What can you do?" Gord pounds the side of the bar with his fist.

"Well you said how you was giving up smoking and drinking when we carried you home other night, so what you got to spend money on anyhow, boy!" Stu laughs and puts his arm round Gord's shoulders. Gord makes as if to punch Stu in the face. "Hey Gord! That's no way to treat y'friends what are trying to help! Go and beat on them! You'll be smashing me glasses next. Or me new fibre-glass kidneys!" They laugh and shake hands, 'black-style.'

Mulrooney listens, pretending to be engrossed in the sign beneath the glass bar top: 'We have a deal with the bank. We promised not to cash cheques or give credit, they promised not to sell beer.' Then he pays for his beers plus a twenty-five-cent tip, and carries the bottles back to the table Steenwijk and Wells have found.

Terry Wells is still sulky and depressed. This was meant to have been the night he showed Jane, his thesis advisor, and her friend Chesley Mulrooney around the newly renovated Salty Commodore tavern. But they had found a queue outside and waited. Then, after ten minutes, now near the front, a drunk had pushed in ahead of them and tried chatting to Terry to smooth over the cracks. Terry had ignored him and lit a cigarette instead. The drunk asked for one. 'Absolutely not. After pushing in!' and Terry gave him a withering stare. Disgruntled, the drunk had left, only to return with his own pack, queue-barge again, and offer the person ahead of Terry a smoke, which had been accepted. 'That other creep gone in yet?' the drunk wondered. 'No. Still here,' Terry sang out. 'And I still think you should wait in line.' 'Watch it feller! You're living on borrowed time!' the drunk had not been amused, and cursed some more. By now Terry felt they would not enjoy the Salty Commodore anyway, so they had cut their losses, left the area and found Tee Cee's up the hill. On their walk, Terry had wished he had handled it differently: told the doorman or stopped a passing police-car. On the other hand, had they not listened and left Terry on the sidewalk with the lout afterwards, that could have been worse! And it would have been Terry breaking a window to get taken into protective custody! Jane had laughed; Terry looked such a college kid, he wasn't big enough to booze in these bars, she said...That had not helped Terry's agitation.

"I must say I'm a trifle surprised," Jane admits as she pours her beer. "I always understood fights here to be arranged for garden-parties, and weddings and funerals and what have you. And all part of this male *macho* ideology that is expected on those occasions. And otherwise I've always found Newfoundland rather a nice place to live. Gentle, humane, little violence directed against strangers."

"Oh, that was nothing, Jane!" Terry reasserts himself. This is 'Quietsville.' In B.C. I got hit in a bar once just 'cause this guy said he didn't like the way I looked. Any excuse over there. 'Specially these slimy bikers' bars. They fight there to see who's gonna become the new bouncer or even owner... Really! There's a career-structure...And it's amazing what people can get up after—like being thrown head first into the grille of a car. And I'd expect that to kill someone, but they do it all the time!" Terry laughs as Jane shudders. "Really. You only need to look at someone there to get into a fight. But here it's so controlled 'cause everyone's too embarrassed. So they don't even need a bouncer like in here, even when they got female bar staff!" Terry shakes his head. "And even in middle class bars in B.C. you get pool cues broken over people's heads. And women too in these really vicious cat fights. Nails and teeth. And pulling hair!"

"Sounds cheap pornography to me!" Jane admonishes as Terry grins.

"No. That comes with the wet T-shirt contests, Jane! And women mud-wrestling. We get that too. Part of the Irish bar scene. Like bucking broncos too. And Paki-bashing." Terry laughs. "I tell you it's really like gang warfare as soon as the bars close back home. People jumping each other and fights in the streets, and guys getting their heads cracked and puking up all over the place!"

"I wouldn't have thought it was something to feel all that proud about, Terry!"

"Well. You gotta understand it, Jane. But I find it funny the police here going on about downtown 'breaking out' 'cause of boozing, or overcrowded bars or something. And it's just nothing. These cops wouldn't survive an hour in B.C.!"

"Oh now come on, Terry! Less of your mainland chauvinism. We have our homegrown varieties of violent pastime here you know," Chesley reminds him. "Like have you tried Norton's? I imagine that would be fascinating for a not-too-gentle evening's fieldwork."

"Yeah, well that's y'local bikers' sub-culture bar, but a friend of mine goes there and he says they're all softies 'til they get tanked up and go mad smashing windows... And also I heard when the police wouldn't allow their Run on the Rock meeting they all went down to Nova Scotia 'cause there's more of these Hell's Angels there, and then they all got badly beaten up by this crowd of cowboys!" Terry scoffs. "They're just another bunch of drunks. See?"

"But I thought Hell's Angels hold all these ceremonies, Terry, and wear special insignia and do all these contract killings with machetes or something?"

"Look. Hold on you two!" Chesley interjects. "You're as bad as the media, escalating things out of all proportion. For a start they aren't Hell's Angels. They're the Pride Purveyors, and what a name that is, to conjure with! And what's all this about 'sub-culture,' Terry, eh? Makes them sound like caricatures. But they're no different to anyone else. Normal Newfoundlanders. And I think it's become something of a unique tradition here. You should listen to Russ Knox, their spokesman, a bit more closely. Like they have local RCMP officers in their Lewisporte and Gander chapters. See my point? It's just the media and then the police getting busy and intervening, like cancelling their get-together, and not letting them sort out their own problems, and then you get trouble."

"Good old Ches! Ever the romantic Newfoundland nationalist!" Jane pats his arm and laughs. "Not quite the image I had of them when I was having a coffee in the Copper Kettle once, and suddenly there's two of them taking chains to each other in the street!"

"Ah! Two warriors sorting out their disagreements. An explosion of leather!" Chesley intones. "And I bet in the blink of an eye eight police cars descended upon them, and immediately made things a lot worse."

"These cops wouldn't have a hope in B.C. with those bikers!" Terry repeats. "I got chatting to one of them in some bar round here one time, typical big thick cop and then I realised the whole bar was full of cops, and he said they arrange it so they all finish shifts together and go out for happy hour! Anyway, he told me about a bar in Mount Pearl where they only go in on odd occasions if they've got sufficient numbers otherwise they get beaten up! And once they're down the floor's so wet there with beer they don't stand a chance of getting up again. And generally, he said, the police won't go in and act as bouncers anymore. And even if people are destroying the place it's up to the management! Now I call that chicken."

"No," Chesley corrects him. "It just means they make more restrictions from outside. Like laws about opening hours, and bar overcrowding, and under-age drinkers, but the restrictions and interference are there all the same. Or else the management hoists prices to keep the so-called 'rowdy' element out. Until someone from the Department of Tourism starts whispering about the money the province is losing, and they slacken off. And then the cycle starts all over again."

"Yeah. But my point is there are still no real fighting bars here, Ches, and these Newfie police couldn't cope if there were... Look, they're either student bars like the Musgrove or the Hive, or else meat-markets like Pat's, or Club Paul, just bourgeois, and could be anywhere in North America, or what I call 'sub-culture bars' like Norton's, or Brad's for the sailors. And still you gets these police prancing about like they're in Hawaii 5-0 or something."

"Yes, well, they are rather a hard-nosed bunch, Terry. But then they're used to being respected and obeyed," Chesley explains. "I remember last time there was a police strike even the students were out demanding they return to work."

"God! You wouldn't get that in B.C. either!"

"Well, like I said, Terry, we do things our own way here. And the same goes for fighting. Nowadays I suppose these small outport bars are the best places for that. And I assure you we Newfoundlanders are not sexist! Women are as likely to be observed taking flight through bar windows as men!" Chesley smirks at Jane's disgust. "I remember as a boy Argentia was famous for beatings of American servicemen. You should hear those now regarded as stalwarts of the community recounting their Saturday night sport of punching out an American from the base! Uh, and then in Lourdes at one time they had a penchant for local murder and intrigue. Those are the two Newfoundland 'havens of violence,' but I suppose if you go into any of these small outport bars with your mainland or townie accent you stand a good chance of being tampered with. And there's your violence first hand!"

As Chesley finishes with a grin, Gord, more inebriated, and having left his stool at the bar, lurches past their table shaking his fist: "Just watch it! If you wanna fight, then fine. 'Cause no-one looks at my face that way! I'd rather die first!" His adversary seems to be imaginary, but Chesley and Terry turn rather ashen and Jane studies the bottom of her beer glass, as Gord thumps an empty beer bottle down on their table, and staggers on out of the bar. The looks of the other regulars that follow him out are rather unimpressed, and they soon resume their conversations.

Jane is the first to recover, on her table. "That was pleasant! Terry. Wouldn't the Hive have been safer? It's only pure devilment takes me to any of these other bars these days. And the stares if you're a woman... I should've known."

"Maybe. But this was nearer. And anyway, the Hive isn't even all that innocent. There was a fight there last week. These drunks no one knew came in on a pub crawl and were bugging Vivien Lawrence—you know his dad's in the Philosophy Department—and he'd just gotten beaten up and put in hospital by this gang of kids round by where he lives, so he was through with being bugged and laid into these drunks. And then in the end we threw them out," Terry concludes with satisfaction.

"Aha! So the St. John's CFA Club-cum-*nouveaux riches* stakes out its territory, eh!" Chesley is sarcastic.

"Hey! That's not fair, Ches. And you know. Normally it's your Derek Linehan or Crystal Kane causing the bother. And you know they're troublemakers," Terry protests. "Last time it was Derek arguing with the barmaid over his change and threatening to 'take the face off her,' I think it was, then he's shoving everybody and Crystal's pulling the singer off the stage 'cause she doesn't like him or something. And then suddenly they're all smiles and innocence again."

"These are the two we saw in that play at the LSPU?"

"Yeah. They claim to be actors."

"Well they weren't *that* bad, but what you describe sounds more like immature desire for attention. Adolescent sexual inadequacy or something."

Terry laughs. "Well I don't think I'll tell Derek that, Jane, or I'll get knocked into next week! I remember them gate-crashing a party at Jock Fleming's—no one ever actually invites them—and Derek had the usual Portuguese in tow, no English, straight off the boat, doesn't know what's happening, and they started trashing the place. So Jock laid into 'em 'cause he's from a Scottish brawling background himself, and knocked Derek down, then Crystal went even more ape 'cause she *can* fight... Anyway in the end someone offered to drive them home but they got so abusive in the car he told them to get out. But they refused and started laying into this guy driving them."

Jane laughs. "Oh come on Terry. This must be a joke."

"No really! They started biting him and they all ended up scrapping on the sidewalk. 'Til the guy drove off and left them there... and I think in the end he managed to get Crystal charged with assault and fined!... So, still wanna go to the Hive, Jane?"

"Okay, Terry." Chesley is defensive. This culture does invite a certain sort of person to do quips and party tricks and I agree Derek Linehan and Crystal Kane probably fall into that category. They come from a street-brawling background after all, and they're used to making violent gestures in public that might seem antisocial... And I think one of those Linehan boys has the dubious distinction of being the youngest inmate to attend on Her Majesty's pleasure at Quidi Vidi. But still, I wouldn't call it mere destructiveness. Whatever's been written in ignorance, we are not a culture out to destroy ourselves. There's far too much admirable intellect here for that... There isn't violence for its own sake... "

Further discussion is suddenly cut short by a series of shouts emanating from a group of lads who, having left their darts game, cluster around an ice-hockey game begun on TV.

"Hey! Hey! I told you boy! The Nordiques are playing with real balls now! You just watch Dale Hunter go!"

"Yeah, if the Flyers don't punch his face in first! They're just trying to pick fights. Whole lot of them!"

"These Nordiques just need a few shotguns in their pants and then shoot any Flyer who comes too close!"

"Hey! Ref's given a penalty for *that!* Crap! That was no deliberate elbow y'meatball!"

"Jeeze! Blind fat pig ref!"

"And look at him acting!... Get a walking stick y'weed!"

"Pussy! Wimp!"

"Hey! A fight! Look at them two slugging it out then, boys!"

"Ha! Look at Werbinek go. He's always at it."

"Wooo! There goes his helmet. Arsehole!"

"Racket, racket, racket, Look at them go!"

Finally, the two fighters, losing their balance on the ice, are jumped upon, separated and restrained by the three referees, and go to cool off for five minutes in the penalty box. The Tee Cee's spectators remain excitedly on the edge of their chairs.

Watching from her table, Jane is not amused. "God! It's disgusting. That lot's just out for blood. And I think it should be stopped. Kids losing eyes from skates you hear, and severing arteries. It's as bad as boxing!"

"I thought you were the one considering forking out fifteen dollars to go and watch Marvin Hagler on close-circuit TV at the stadium a while back Jane?" Chesley reminds her.

"Only for the occasion, Ches... Anyway I didn't, did I? I get feelings of guilt if I enjoy that sort of thing."

Chesley laughs. "Ah yes. Of course. The Steenwijk anal guilt complex! Was that Gretzky fighting down there, Terry. Did you see?"

"No. He's not playing in this one. And he never fights. And if he did they'd all jump in to stop it. Save that perfect face... But it looks like Quebec general hospital's gonna get some business tonight if they carry on like that! Phew! Some fight. I knew Philadelphia had a reputation for being a violent team a few years back, but I thought they'd changed. But it looks like they still turn on the rough stuff when they have to. I guess you still gotta accept violence as part of the game, eh Ches?"

"Did you play it at school, Terry?" Jane wonders, still estranged.

"Not really. I tried it once, but I spent most of the time on the bench. And then the few minutes I was on the ice I got hit, and hard, so I took up badminton instead. But I have refereed some senior hockey and got jumped on after the game by disgruntled losers more than once! That's why they're thinking of protective gear for refs actually... And you'd be surprised how many fights take place off the ice afterwards when the game's all over. Really!"

"I wouldn't be a bit surprised, frankly Terry! And I suppose you're all gung-ho about this hockey violence as well, Ches?"

"Well, rugby was always my spectator sport. 'A hooligan's game played by gentlemen,' as they say. As opposed to football—or soccer, as they seem to call it now—which is 'a gentleman's game played by hooligans'! But if you want to see a really exciting and partisan hockey game here, Jane, then go to the stadium when the Orangemen are playing the Saints!" The very prospect excites Chesley. "I mean what you just saw was nothing. Not really 'Newfoundland' at all. The mainland is still really too distant and flimsy a sort of thing to get too excited about. But you watch when there are some local religious differences involved and everyone goes wild! Even the nuns and priests watching. Now there's a fine St. John's spectacle! I remember when we first began school hockey here, back in the forties, and suddenly the Protestants weren't just the kids who threw snowballs at you on your way to school, but the ones you could thrash at hockey! Yes! Fine fun then, for sure."

"My little brother's still a hockey nut back west, Ches," Terry enthuses. "You know. Sort who pays hundred-ninety bucks for two tickets to the B.C. Canucks. Now he *did* play school hockey, and I remember once the puck hit him in the face—quite serious, really; think he needed a couple of stitches—so he comes home and Mom of course just about took off through the roof. I mean he was all bruised and swollen, looking like something out of *Rocky*. Like he's just done ten rounds with Hagler himself. But I dunno. I think hockey was more skilled before. Now they've got that new stick, and it's become such a spectator sport, they just about encourage fights now just because that's what the public wants to see."

"I think that's probably the case in rugger too, Terry," Ches agrees. "You do hear of some despicable offences nowadays, that aren't part of the game at all. Just players devoid of skill and out for a fight. Tearing opponents' ears off in the scrum given half a chance."

"Well I find this discussion all very boring and rather vulgar. I think you're all as bad as each other and I want to go," Jane concludes. "So could we drink up? Move on to the Hive please?"

Terry laughs and gulps down the last of his beer. "At least we aren't into wrestling here, Jane, and all those fake bags of blood. Like in Sudbury or these other single-industry, working-class towns. That's the pits."

Chesley also downs his beer and they follow Jane out of the pub, still chatting on the way. "And did you read that article in *Newsweek* about European football supporters killing each other at that game...?"

On the sidewalk outside they find Gord leaning back against a parked car near some friends. He is still drunk, and, it seems, in menacing mood. For as they pass, Gord suddenly hits the man next to him, and knocks him to the ground with a thump: "And don't ever do that to me again! Right?" he shouts, kicking the downed man, then bending over and punching him again.

Chesley, Jane and Terry stiffen but pretend not to have noticed, and keep walking. Some cars, passing in the street, slow down but none stop. Then, Stu emerges from Tee Cee's and convinces Gord to stop punching his man, and coaxes him back inside for another drink instead.

Meanwhile, up the street, Chesley, Jane and Terry still have not turned round. Reaching safety and friends in the Hive, they agree, will be soon enough for the next post-mortem...

Ninth Scene

Friday morning, Open House at the Detoxification Centre

"My dear! I don't feel safe downtown now! Time was, people'd stand on the wharves and come up and say, 'How are you, boy?' and be after inviting you home and all this. Proper t'ing. But my dear: it's some different these past ten or twelve years. I'd not go near the place now! All those bars, and no shops, and all these people wandering round on drugs or something. And no one saying hello. I'm scared to go there now," Bridie takes a breath and Margo agrees.

"Yeah, yeah. It's got violent. And Keith said it's the problem of the '80s, drugs and all this, on Answer Line."

It is the following morning, and Open House at Brady House Detoxification Centre, in the old 'West End.' Living up the street for so long, Bridie O'Brien welcomes an opportunity to come inside and see if all she has heard about the goings-on are true. Just in case, she has brought Margo along. *Bridie* is in her mid-sixties; a housewife and grandmother, she has always lived in St. John's, where she was born, although her children have now moved to Mount Pearl. *Margo Halleran* is early-sixties; a widow, she was born and still lives in the 'West End' although her children now live and work on the mainland. Brady House was once Margo's school—St. Kate's—before the girls joined the boys at Bishop Aloysius. And the refectory where she and Bridie now sit awaiting the talk 'Drug Abuse in St. John's' used to be her classroom. How different it all seems.

Brady House is a large old building now run by the Sisters of the Beatitudes General Hospital as a twenty-four-hour residential unit for 'detoxing' in a non-medical way, 'persons in alcohol- or drug-induced states of discomfiture.' About twenty-five residents may be accommodated, with two members of staff always present; one is gatekeeper in the office by the door downstairs, and one patrols the dormitories and television room, checking and chatting. For 'through empathy and low-key interaction, and discussion about treatment resources, detoxification is hoped to be married to rehabilitation.'

This morning, the house director, Geoff Flynn, is also present, for a busy day may be expected. *Geoff,* late-forties, single, born in Dublin and an ex-seminarian, has lived in St. John's twenty years and directed Brady House for over ten. First on his day's agenda had been the lecture by Corporal Duffy of the RCMP Narcotics Division. But the *Corporal,* in his late-thirties and married, born in Halifax and lived in St. John's ten years, was pre-empted by the early arrival of the reporters from VOCQ Radio and *The Evening Telegram.* So while Geoff was interviewed, his assistant staff member showed the lecture audience around the house: the kitchens and bathrooms and the rec rooms all clean and, for the benefit of open day perhaps, free of residents.

The audience is a small one. There are the nurses allowed half-an-hour away from their wards at the Sisters, and some ladies from the Sisters' auxiliary—volunteers and fund-raisers come to see the workings of the hospital extension service, and then Bridie and Margo and one or two more. The tour complete, the audience has spaced itself out on the chairs put in neat rows in the refectory. Reading the pamphlets provided, Bridie and Margo are having a quick chat before the talk begins.

"And here you are: 'People who abuse drugs often end up with serious problems. They may...get sick, have accidents, build up tolerance, get hooked, commit crimes, be arrested, become violent, go to jail and lose friends,' " Bridie reads out from 'Drugs and You.'

"Yeah, yeah it's a terrible way of life, girl...Sure there's tremendous statistics, Keith said on the radio. And it's not like we're trying to be Gabriels or anything, but this oil boom will make it worse because young people think it's 'smart and sophisticated,' was how he said it."

"My daughter Mary says it's all they have at parties now is drugs. Not like the old Screech bottle to go round thirty of us! Remember? And she said she just didn't know what she was smelling in her Janice's room, but it wasn't cigarettes. And she had to wash the curtains to be rid of it...And the way those girls were dancing! She said it was so embarrassing, she could never do it. And they must have been stoned, she said. And— "

"My dear! You know Doctor Hare? Well it was in the *Telegram.* His brother was arrested for drugs, and released on $5000 bail, it said. And maybe he was linked to a big Montreal gang!"

"There! I told you I wondered where he was so rich from, after his shop was always so empty. And them with that big house and car...And our Mary said the Mounties told them at school to cut down on Janice's pocket money, so if she bought a package of cigarettes, then that was all she could afford. 'Cause it's from them they get into drug-addicts. But what can you do with Janice coming up for seventeen?"

Margo nods. "And if you don't give it them then they're likely to go and steal it from you. I mean all these young people are just crazy for money."

"My Lord! And you're desperate, they say, when you're addicted. And I heard you don't stagger about like with beer, so if you're driving then the police don't know if you're impaired or no. So, like Keith was saying, they should be allowed to do compulsory blood-tests on these folk, so they don't go killing innocent people."

"Well I reckon, for me like, the Mounties should have every power to prevent any slaughter in this nation. I mean drugs need stern steps. And surely God, who else can you trust if it's not the Mounties?"

"For sure girl. They protect us after all, so you got to trust them."

"And I heard said they're the finest police force...But I don't know. I hope and pray to God they stop these drugs. And use all the laws against them! I do so...And what an awful age kids start at, Keith said, age ten!"

"Some mad fashion... "

The room goes quiet as Geoff Flynn leads in Corporal Duffy, down the central aisle to the table at the front. "Well, thank you for coming and taking the time and interest, ladies," Geoff begins, "uh, and gentlemen!" He swaps nods and smiles with the *Telegram* photographer standing at the back, whom the ladies also turn to inspect.

"Before I hand you over to our speaker, Corporal Duffy, let me say one or two things about Brady House Detoxification Unit. As our brochure explains, the misuse of drugs became a major national issue in the 1960s, and alcohol abuse is one of this century's major health hazards—maybe the worst. Detoxification is a process we give someone to get a minimally acceptable level of functioning, after an alcoholic or other drug-induced state. If a person uses chemicals, and these cause a problem in his life, and he still uses them, then we call that 'abuse'...Now a little about this House. John Brady was an Irishman in the last century here, who started as a heavy drinker. He and buddies would buy drink together, and then look after each other when they'd had a skinful. But John became disenchanted when his so-called buddies walked out on him once when he was drunk, and he swore from then on to help other poor alkies. Then he had spiritual succour, and he had a transformation, and locked heavy chains around himself as penance. And that was how they found him when he died. And now he's being beatified: made into a saint. So Brady House has a lot to live up to!...We began here July 1970, and rule number one is of course 'No drugs and no alcohol in the House.' For detoxing from alcohol, one week is really necessary, and longer for drugs. But it's hard for them to just pick themselves up out of their society...You can preach 'til you're black and blue in the face, but afterwards most return back to the environment they left, where everyone drinks or is stoned, like in boarding houses. So we can't expect them not to start in again right away...We have about ten regulars who keep returning, like one man the corporal probably also knows who signed himself in here seventy-four times in sixty-four days!"—the corporal nods— "sometimes more than once a day. That's abusing *us* as well as him, so we had to stop him. Our recidivism rate, by the way, is 87 percent, which is not too bad; and not nearly as bad as the Ontario House rate of 90 percent...We get people in from eighty-eight down to eighteen. Below that we need their parents' permission for them to stay, but we often suggest that, anyhow, for the kids, as a shock treatment. Our aim is to provide these people with a chance to get sober, and sort of assess their lifestyle. Friends refer men here, or family or clergymen do. Or the men themselves. And sometimes the police bring us inebriates...Of course any violent or criminal offenders go to the lock-up. But ladies! This service is just band-aid help really. It doesn't stop the problem...And we can't even advertise ourselves or we would be swamped. We just spread by word of mouth round town...Now I know it's hard to talk about abuse without seeming holier than thou. And better minds than mine will be thinking about this still in twenty or fifty years time. And I'm just a social drinker myself, so no one even listens to me around Brady House!" Geoff laughs, "No, but seriously, ladies, this talk is to ask you to think, not reach any final decision...But remember, ladies, these horrors go on! We're all created, so we have to believe in creation and one creator, but the atrocities are out there, worsening, and I don't know what to do about them...It's the number one problem and it drives me nuts because no one realises it—the technocrats—or if they do they don't do a lot about it!... Anyway, enough from me. Let me pass you on to Corporal Duffy. Always interesting to hear, and to examine his drug-kit." Geoff dismissively indicates a large brown leather suitcase that Corporal Duffy lifts onto the table before him as he stands to speak:

"Thank you Geoff... You know *I'm* not even a sociable drinker myself. And never have been. A glass of wine at Christmas and I feel tipsy!" The corporal has a prim, trimmed moustache; it becomes a little sparse when stretched into a smile, like now, but he does not smile often.

"The possession, trafficking, and importing of cannabis, heroin, and cocaine are criminal acts according to the Narcotic Control Act. The possession, trafficking, and importing of LSD, PCP, and barbiturates is a crime under the Food and Drug Act... Good afternoon, ladies. My name is Corporal Duffy, from the St. John's Federal Narcotics Section of the RCMP. We, eleven men and three women, are after nationally organised drug rings. And we also do some street-level investigations—that's what there is always a public outcry for, even though these operations are not the most beneficial. Last spring, we had twenty-six street targets in Mount Pearl, took seventeen of them, seized $2,000, and it cost us $26,000... I'm over the hill now, but until two years ago, I worked undercover. I spent seven years at it and I bought every kind of drug here in St. John's. I floated around at night, had informants, wore disguises—hair down my back like a bikeganger!" The ladies laugh. "But after seven years you get to be recognised! So they brought in some new operators from outside—and now I do presentations like this... Now, we try hard, and we take exception when people say we do nothing. We recently followed up a St. John's lead and seized forty-four pounds of marihuana getting off a Toronto bus. We made five arrests and now the head man is serving five years... He'd never worked a day. Never paid any income tax, owned four cars—Cadillacs—had a summer house, and a big one, and ate steak every day till we interrupted his little game!... He was turning over $50,000 a month, tax free. A muck-raker drug-addict, living the life of Reilly till we stopped him!"

His audience tut-tuts in disgust.

"Now, cocaine, or 'coke' or 'snow' or 'flake,' comes from South America. The natives there chew it and get high... But Indians listen to you more than whites do, and are changing their drug habits and are better to work with. But it's the Cubans. They run guns to revolutionary areas, armies pop up everywhere and drugs leave in return, for Miami, and then cash comes back for more arms. It's the same in South-East Asia:

communist governments in drug-running...Newfoundland is the only province this year where we found pure 'coke.' One kilo of pure 'coke' has a street value of $1 million here, $600,000 in Toronto or Montreal. Prostitutes bring it in when they've done working other provinces and move here. So 'coke' is becoming big here, hash is readily available, and in ten years I bet there'll be heroin addiction here too...Now. Amphetamines—'speed,' 'bennies,' 'whites,' whatever you want to call them—are controlled by motorcycle gangs in Ontario and Montreal. Pretty rough places where you have to be bad people to be known by the police! 'Speed' makes you high—go, go, go—and unbalanced and dangerous and thin, with no appetite, and you flip out...LSD, lysergic acid diethylamide, to give it its full name, a shot of 'acid' for short, makes you hallucinate, and you can be up for four or five days if you pop four or five hits at once. And they carry them round in aspirin boxes!...PCP, 'angel dust', makes you very violent...Heroin addicts are easiest to deal with, because they go all relaxed, and dream up UFOs sightings on Water Street!...The commonest drug in St. John's is hashish, at $225 to $300 an ounce. We busted a red-hash gang here last year, so this year it's black about...Parents often wonder how kids can afford hash, but like I always explain at PTA meetings, they don't need any cash. Johnnie goes to a trafficker and gets $250 worth on $300 credit. Then he goes and splits them into twenty dimes of hash for $25 each. So if he sells them all he could make $500. Or he may sell fifteen, break even, and smoke five himself. Or get hooked and get behind in his debts and get beaten up. There's one over in the Medical Centre now getting his face reconstructed. Or he commits a crime to pay his man—break-and-enter, or theft of a stereo...Or his parents give him $20 for jeans and he buys drugs, then steals the jeans. So mothers should always ask to see the receipt of things their kids buy. We talk to kids, tell them it's bad, and they say 'No. It's good.' Scare tactics fail, so now we are hitting them with the legal angle: they can go to jail—for a long time!...But remember: we're dealing with grade six and up. And there's lots on the go. Last week in the Avalon Mall I saw three sales. But it was my day off, and I didn't feel like getting involved, and I was by myself. But you watch, ladies, next time you pass the amusement arcade, and all the kids going to the washroom together. And there's bars and places you can guarantee it, day or night."

"But my sister owns an arcade!" Margo cries. "And if she knew there were drugs there she's sure to put a match to the place! Oh Lord!...But where would an eleven-year-old get $200, Sir?"

"He wouldn't need any. He comes from a one-parent family, so his mom's in clover and it's us who are paying, Ma'am."

"Shocking!"

"Another regular move is dealing out of cars. Through the windows. Unless they know you, they're too cautious to approach you on foot. And as soon as you get out, they know it's the 'heat' and they run. Some fast!...But you can arrest nine at a time on the streets and they just come wave after wave: you won't stop the problem...But the street-traffickers and couriers are small feed. It's the central people, the suppliers we want. We have an investigation ongoing now and they're already on the police system, but it's organised here like the Mafia...Each gang takes part of the city, and then they have little wars between them. So everyone who buys drugs is assisting organised crime...Drugs mean more violence in the city. No doubt. It's the easiest way to 'lose' money. Definitely. Eighty percent of armed robberies are drug-backed or organised, or caused because people need money because the heat is on them. You get $13,000 stolen from Colonials, Topsail Road, and a few days later you find forty-four pounds of hash at the house you traced the get-away car to, just bought on the mainland, and the money's gone...Trafficking can get you, maximum, life. If you're caught with sales and baggies, and bags of money, and what we call a 'scoresheet': 'Bill: $20,; Ed: $50,' I'd give you a run on a Section 4:2, anyway, and a good run, and I'd probably get you...But if you're eighteen or nineteen or twenty, and you can plead it's a first offence, then you'll just get a slap on the wrist. Most judges here are just old weeps. No backbone; they're too far above to realise. So we set dates to get a good judge if we can. And we're careful not to bring them before just any...But we have one judge down there who operates very differently: Judge Whelan Dindale. Did you ever watch *McCormick* on TV? Well, Judge Dindale works like that. Drop into the court-house one time and see how he stings 'em. He can latch onto them and really make them dangle!" Duffy smiles. "But that headman with the Cadillacs I told you about: sentenced to fifty-seven months, he'll serve eighteen! Nine if he gets a job offer. Like some patsy. That was Judge Croft."

Geoff shakes his head. "And all those lives he's destroying!"

"Cannabis is in every nook and cranny of this city. I've seen twelve foot high marihuana plants here. In fact, birdseed is marihuana; just sterilised so you can't plant it. Maybe that's what gets 'em to sing'— "

"Mother of God!" there is a cry, "in my kitchen!"

"—Every day, mothers are handing over children to us. And neighbours call and say someone buried something in the yard next door under some leaves, and it'll be a bag of weed. So don't be scared to give evidence in court, ladies. It's easy…Though it can be really annoying. We hand over boys to the lawyers, and we know they're guilty as sin, and then the lawyers get them off on some technicality, and they're away and laughing. Even if they're real dangers to society…I've had a few cases thrown out on incredible technicalities. But that's the administrative point of view for you. The best thing I heard was from an officer in Toronto. He saw a judge there say 'Right. You lawyers have got thirty seconds each to state your case, and nothing more!' Now that's the way to go! No word-twisting then!…And doctors too. The way some of them give out medication to whack patients through, you'd think they had shares in the pharmacists!'…And from Valium and Librium they get into acid, and that makes them schizophrenic, and then it's spending time in the Oakleys. That is, when the doctors aren't smuggling it in themselves like old Dr. Wirnell down the southern shore, burying hauls of marihuana off his private yacht, till we put a stop to his little game!"

"That's right! Bridie whispers to Margo. "I blame these doctors and psychiatrists for doing more harm than good. A friend of Mary's began on five pills a day, and now she's up to seventy-five!"

"Lord, girl, and then they need some looking after, for sure. When they're dependent…And remember how they said that Liberal, Pius Joyce, was part of that set-up too!"

"Implicated, my dear. Shocking! No wonder he and that woman took off for Canada pretty quick, 'til the waters calmed. Shocking!"

"Well, ladies," Duffy concludes, "that's about all I have to say. If you'd like to come forward, I can show you my case of samples. And please help yourselves to those pamphlets on LSD, methaqualone, phenyclidine and the rest…And if you want to know anything further, ladies, that I am at liberty to tell you, just call the RCMP and mention my name. Normally of course, the police hate talking over the phone, 'cause we have to be careful, obviously, who we say what to: no we don't want to give out information out of the blue to the wrong people, but now I've met you…"

He stands easy as the women look to their friends and then, giggling, approach his drug-kit…

Tenth Scene

Friday lunchtime, at the General Hospital, Room 414

Shortly after the lecture, the Sisters' hospital staff have to return to their ward duties. Most of them are student nurses learning the ropes, but there is also Ms. Pringle, who has been physiotherapist at the Sisters for a number of years now.

The Sisters of the Beatitudes General Hospital is an old building, variously extended since the 1920s. It oversees the downtown, the docks, and the Southside Hills, and Pitts Memorial Drive—the arterial road which leads out of the downtown towards the burgeoning suburbs and then the Trans-Canada Highway.

Many of Ms. Pringle's patients are to be found up on Medicine Four. This is a mixed ward; there are the stroke victims learning to walk, and the diabetics, and the heart patients undergoing stress tests after angina attacks or stints in Intensive Care, and the senile or chronically ill awaiting beds in over-full nursing homes. The air is thick and warm, and the furniture standardised and functional: floor tiles and linoleum for easy mopping, vinyl-covered mattresses in case of incontinence, and sixty-three tube-metal beds on wheels, for easy manoeuvring by rushed staff.

In room 414 there are four beds: it is a 'public' room. (semi-private rooms, with only two beds are $30 extra per day, and private rooms $40). Two beds are nearer the windows, and two the door and washroom, each separable by curtains. Each bed also has its mobile meal-table and side-table, and telephone socket, and wall bracket for mini colour TV and earphone (if rented).

Ms. Pringle has four patients in room 414. There is *Edgar Green:* late-fifties, married, a retired shopkeeper born in St. John's and now living in Topsail, and *Max Dawe:* early-fifties, a widower, and currently unemployed cook, born in St. John's now living in Outer Cove; and *Gerald Hunt:* early-sixties and married, a retired docker, born and living in St. John's; and *Bramwell Lester:* early-sixties, a widower and a retired service-station owner, born and living in Conception Harbour. Coincidentally, Bramwell's married daughter, Clarice, is also a patient of Ms. Pringle's and in for tests in a neighbouring room. All are by and large on the mend, although Ms. Pringle sometimes notices impatience when rates of recovery slow and doctors' tests are irregular. In other moods they seem to have a fine time and this appears to be the case today; for as Ms Pringle returns and makes a circuit of the ward, past the cleaners, in green, mopping the floors, and the kitchen staff, in white, carrying the used lunch trays to a dumb-waiter, and the self-assured doctors and their students pinching chocolates from the patients' 'thank-you' box on the counter by the nurses' station, and the nurses checking their files and medicines, through the open door of room 414, Edgar and Bramwell and daughter Clarice can be heard playing a noisy game of cards.

"There, you old bugger boots! Ha! Woman power!" Clarice crows out another victory and marks the round down, as Bramwell smiles and spits out his chewed black wad of tobacco into the bin at his side.

"Thought you were gonna give up on that stuff, Father! Look at all y'fruit." Clarice nods at apples and oranges being kept cool at present on the window ledge between the inner and outer panes.

Bramwell changes the subject. "Hey! Shut the door someone! There's Reverend Bill on his rounds!"

Clarice laughs. "No chance Father! And you'll still be on his pastoral list and won't he have something to say about what you put down for 'Religion,' eh!" Bramwell grins at Edgar as Clarice goes on. "They asked him in Admissions, Mr. Green, and he says how he hadn't decided, so they put down 'None.' And there's Reverend Carnell a family friend! And he's always round our place for a little supper and off his collar comes and he isn't 'Reverend' then! Just 'Bill' then."

"Hey! There goes the Coast Guard boat out again," Gerald reports. In socks and pyjamas, he is standing at the window, keeping an eye on all the familiar territory. "Cranes still loading them Japanese ships too. And I said they'd get about sixteen trailers of caplin a-piece, didn't I!" Gerald raised five sons working the docks, and you can still make good bucks at it. One of his sons is there now and he made $60 an hour working New Year's Day. And those oil companies can afford it. But then it's just hard luck when there's no work and you get laid off unless you have seniority. But then that's what life's all about, Gerald says, changes and disappointments. "And the whole visibility's better now. Even see the Newfoundland Hotel."

"Who wants to?" Edgar calls, and Bramwell chuckles. "And I know! I used to live a gunshot from it, boy, remember. Just about as far as a rifle'd shoot... Remember all them wooden wharves for the schooners back then? Not like now, eh Ger?"

"No boy! The war and them big ships soon changed all that. And them deep piles they sank for foundations."

"Whole place is gone cracked now, if you ask me! All them new buildings and four-lane highways, and nowhere to walk or park!" Edgar grumbles and Bramwell grins a 'here we go again' to Clarice. "They should plant the whole place over with grass again so you can breathe proper, if you ask me. It's all bang-bang here now. They're changing it all beyond recognition, boy." Born in the downtown, Edgar used to run a second-hand furniture and appliances shop; fifteen hours a day, but he enjoyed it. Always throwing in the odd chair, or whatever, free; it cost him nothing and kept his name good. But now, after twenty-three years he's had enough. And if he's going to die soon of his heart then best to set his wife up properly in a nice house out of town first. Get her settled because she's done good by him for thirty years.

"Where's Mr. Dawe, Father?" Clarice tries to bring Edgar back to the present. "Moved wards? Not seen him today."

"No, girl. Or they'd 've soon moved in someone else some quick! They just wheeled him out for more tests. Still flat on his back on a stretcher. Jeeze, that old trout must have a pair of sore buns on him!" Bramwell laughs, and nods at Max's crumpled blankets hanging over the foot of the bed and nearly obscuring the name-tag: Max Dawe, 52, patient #B0001062. Religion: RC. Outer Cove. Patient of Dr. Norris.

Max is feeling under the weather. His youngest son has just died. His baby, the one he did everything for. He fell off some construction scaffolding at the Court House, so now Max is planning to sue for all he can. Not blood-money, but someone is responsible and they must be blamed before someone else gets killed.

"Well these nurses must be some busy today at something," Edgar starts in again, not to be deflected, " 'cause that pail of water's been there all day and I'm just waiting for someone to spill it."

"You should try the Medical Centre, Mr. Green, if you think this is bad. So few nurses there, they're rushed off their feet!... And corridors the size of this room so they say it's impossible to find anyone. Even the doctors can't!"

"Right. You can't have everything, Edgar." Bramwell joins his daughter's defence. "I mean this hospital may be old and all that, so you need extra blankets at night for the drafts and all, but 'least it's friendly. And homely. And you can't have everything boy, eh!... And look at these beds, ends going up and down and all. I reckon they must be worth a bit."

"That's it, Father. Old or new. No mod-cons—like micro-waves, and all those up-to-date thermometers—but 'ne'er the twain shall meet'. And we may not have a television lounge on every floor but then you got Mr. Hunt's little colour one over there."

"Yes girl!" Gerald responds from the window. "That gets us through the weekends all right when it gets a bit dead." Gerald's portable radio-TV above his bed is rather against hospital regulations—he should be hiring the standard one—but no one's said anything so far, and Edgar told him if they did he could take them to court and win. He's paying for this room after all. "And then we always got my gillbuster too." Gerald indicates his stereo cassette-player on his side-table.

" 'Ghetto-blaster,' Mr. Hunt," Clarice corrects him and laughs, as she adds up the final scores from their umpteen rounds of Scat.

" 'Gillbuster' my nephew calls it," Gerald is adamant, "or 'Gill-o-blaster,' maybe, but I guess you can call 'em what you like, long as people know."

"Ha! I won! Boot's on the other foot now, Father!" Clarice announces. With Edgar a close second and her father nowhere, she is delighted.

The men start moving back to their beds as two nurses enter wheeling a stretcher between them with Max Dawe lying on it.

"Hey! Max boy! How you doing, me old son?"

"Fine, boy." Max waves a salute to the room, before the nurses draw the curtains around his bed and manoeuvre him back onto it.

"I'll see you later, Father," Clarice gets up and departs for her own room across the corridor.

"Right'ho, girl," Bramwell waves her away, already looking forward to Max's news.

Max soon emerges, propped up on pillows on his bed, and holds court as the nurses withdraw. "What did I predict, boys? I'm out after I see Dr. Badcock! And I feel fighting fit... Like I said, all you need to get well is determination, right, and I got lots of that. And of course your doctor's faith in you. And faith in God, and faith in yourself and all."

"And them iron tablets, Max!" Bramwell jokes.

"Well I got faith in the Lord Above, but I also reckon on another operation before I get out 'cause of Murphy's law!" Gerald adds and laughs. "No. That's a sin. All these sick folks about, I feel more like some kid getting off school! And keeping an eye on everything from his look-out!"

"So you all gimme a call when you're out too, and we'll have a time together and solve the world's problems, eh!"

"Mr. Dawe?" Max is interrupted as a nurse pops her head 'round the door, "Dr. Badcock said you can go home now. Just call in a couple of days, say Tuesday, for your results. Okay?"

"Uh...Could I stay 'til tomorrow, please nurse? Organise my daughter to fetch me?"

"Well...All right. Tomorrow morning, Mr. Dawe." She goes.

"Shall I call Will's again, Max? Get Bernice on?"

Bramwell rents a telephone to keep in touch with friends and their business, and has called the fish-and-chips cafe for Max's daughter before.

"Thanks," Max mumbles, rather deflated all of a sudden at the thought of really leaving.

"She's busy. Must have a customer. I'll try again after a bit."

"Well, I guess I'll stay inside today after all. Warmer...Funny. You crave to walk out, and then you're allowed to and then you don't want to. When you got the privilege, like."

"Well, that's the human condition, Max," Bramwell philosophises. "It's only human, eh."

"Right, it's logical," Gerald agrees. "Bet you'll be walking up them Southside Hills by tomorrow afternoon then, Max. You and the dog, eh?...How 'bout sending us down a brace of rabbits then, Max, or just some paws, and we'll get the boys in the kitchen to prepare 'em for us, eh!"

"They'll soon be carrying me back in here, boy, if I gets to go rabbiting so soon, I tell you!" Max laughs. "And I told you it's different staff down in the kitchen from when I was there, mostly, and most of 'em dunno the arse-end of a rabbit from the ears. Don't even know who runs it now that Gord Cleal's gone." Max's twenty-six years and two months in the hospital kitchens is recognised, nevertheless, by a numerously signed, get-well card on his table.

"Cooking's still good, Max. You polish off what they send up at any rate!" Gerald reminds him and laughs. "I'd love to see 'em cooking for a thousand down there, and all."

"Right! More like some hotel," Bramwell agrees. "Good food. And juice whenever you want. And all y'medications... And best part is no whopping bill at the end, like!"

"Well, I tell you I can still smell chlorine in that water they send up," Edgar moans again. "And like I said, I don't call fish chowder and then beef stew a dinner! Not for me. That's two meals, not one."

A young student nurse enters, hands shyly clasped before her. "Mr. Dawe?"

"There's no 'Misters' in here, lovely!... It's all right. I'm Dawe. And this is Hunt, Lester and Green, eh," Max indicates.

"Speak for yourself, Max Dawe! I may not look it but I'm not short of a dollar or two so I'll be 'Mr. Green,' thank you. Don't always judge a book by a cover!"

They laugh at Edgar rising to the bait.

"Mr. Dawe. I'll be coming in to shave you tomorrow if you want, before you go?"

"Okay. But don't be late, mind." Max smiles at the girl and she skips out.

"Nice young thing for you there, Max!" Bramwell laughs. "Though I dunno what you could do with her, God forgive the thought. 'Cept maybe pretend she's a picture to hang on the wall!"

"Don't you believe it, boy!" Max scoffs at the others' grins. Lots of women round this hospital I could've brought back to this bed with me tonight, you know, Bramwell!"

"Dirty old man!... Nice maybe, but still a dirty old man!... Then you really would wake up dead."

"Mr. Lester and Mr. Hunt," Ms. Pringle announces from the door, "I shall have the slide show on the valves of the heart, which I promised you, ready shortly. Some other patients are just finishing with the television."

"Thank you, nurse." Bramwell smiles as she disappears again.

"I heard they had a TV and video stolen from the women's ward here last week!" Gerald reports, shocked. "Guess it's hard when you don't know people and the rooms are open, eh?"

"Nah! Nothing's safe now," Edgar feels. "It's getting so they even rob you in hospital. Or going to church! And I heard they robbed a church safe in Mount Pearl... It's 'cause traditionally your church was everything, right, but people aren't part of a church morality anymore so you get all these robberies and people getting more greedy... Greed is the world problem now, boys. Yes Sir! And if I owned a fastfood place, or a service station like you, Bramwell, I'd have three German shepherds right off the bat. Or else guns, so if there was ever any trouble I'd be ready."

"Nah. Them's all put-up jobs, Edgar. It's obvious. Local inside jobs. Easier than handing money over the counter!" Bramwell owned a service-station for eleven years. But then he had to sell it when he stopped, three years ago, because the only son who was big enough to take it over insisted on keeping his longliner and going inshore-fishing like his grandfather.

"No, but these armed robberies are something else altogether!" Edgar insists. "This isn't your snatch and grab with a stick or something. This is new. And I was just waiting for the day some young feller'd walk in around 5:30 just as I was closing up, toting some sawn-off shotgun and saying, 'Money or I'll shoot,' and I'd give him the lot! I mean I was army-trained, eh. I could run up Signal Hill before I got this heart, so I could take four or five of 'em, and I had my iron piping ready, and I was half wishing they'd try me, like, and I'd soon hurt 'em, scare 'em off. And there's the police telling you 'bout sonic alarms and not staying open late, and not keeping more than $600 float, and then deposit it at the bank when you got more 'n $1500, but at different times every time! I mean Jeeze! It's not worth it. And there's the police on the go all night and it's still not safe and you get molested or robbed or violence as soon as you step outside. I tell you, boys, it's lucky we're in here. It's a world gone mad out there today," Edgar concludes, nodding towards the window.

"All I know is, time was you never thought to lock a door, day nor night. Now, wife and me do it even if we're home nights! Can't trust no one in town now."

"You can't Gerald!... And mark my words, we'll see a lot more of that here in the next few years, all this oil business and foreigners coming in. I dunno what's coming of the world. You get trouble spots all over, like Lebanon, and then they let them come into here and carry on, like all these Armenians, and what have you, fighting in Toronto." Edgar shakes his head and glowers. "I reckon a Christian government should take a stand before all kinds of ungodly things happen out there, and chaos. God's words!"

Bramwell chuckles: "God forgive me but I can't see why anyone from outside'd want to come into here anyhow. Into this Newf weather!"

"Right!" Gerald grins, glad for a lighter note. "I always say John Cabot should've got ten years not ten pounds for discovering this place!...And I reckon God's blessing would've been if Gilbert had got shipwrecked off Bonavista. Or gone to Halifax at least! Eh?" He laughs.

"No, come on Edgar, you can't call what we got armed robbery. Like of a bank. This is just Newfie hit-and-run artists," Max suggests. "Some guy on the street, boozed up, three sheets to the wind, but got nothing in his pocket for another on his way home, so it pops in his head to go rob a hundred bucks and that's it...And a lot of this thieving and shoplifting and what have you is looking for food, I heard. And clothes. And if you can't get a job and you're running round with an empty pocket, I guess you'll go to drastic measures to survive."

"But it was never like this in the Depression, Max," Edgar counters. "And God help us if it had've been!"

"Well, now I remember, as a young feller, buddy breaking in and stealing fish in Conception Harbour and Father wouldn't press charges or take him to court 'cause he said it was just for hunger's sake."

"All well and good, Bramwell," Edgar is undaunted. "But to my mind, even them on welfare now do well! They get their rent paid, and then still $400 to spend, or something, on top of that. And if they still can't survive without thieving then they never will...And you can't say it's alcohol neither, Max, 'cause they had that here long before there's been this crime-wave over the past few years...Nah, to my mind, it's idle hands, and young people with no hope of owning anything 'cause they don't start saving. And then like they say, poverty comes in one window, and love goes out the other. And then they rob from the poor, and that's a sin. Right Bramwell?"

"It's the way of the world, Edgar my old son...It's the same the world over and now it's come here and we gotta accept it and get used to it...Look, we're okay in here, aren't we? Never better.

"Yeah. But to my mind change is coming too fast, Bramwell. And all this interest in money...I mean, okay. A buck is a buck. But we used to know how to earn 'em and save 'em as well as spend them, eh? But now they go through their welfare and then their parents' pensions I guess, I dunno, and then there's nothing. So they see all over the TV and the papers how everyone's doing armed robberies and getting away, and you get a craze of people copying."

"Yeah, but Edgar. What about parents desperate for giving their kids same as what others got and they can't? Now, I feel sorry for 'em. And I reckon it's an immoral act for Premier Peckford and them in government to cut down on jobs and all, 'cause now it's even more of a class thing. Some on forty-fifty thousand and others got none. And it's all very well for us all snug and cosy in here," Max reminds them.

"Well I read in the *Telegram* as how the police always know who to pick up 'cause it's a handful of people doing all these robberies. Like buddy in court for 126 break-and-enters, and 20 in Shea Heights in ten days. That takes some doing! Sheesh!" Gerald is impressed despite all.

Edgar is not, and so Max continues his explanation: "Look. As soon as you get twenty houses together and a community you're gonna get robberies. And in a city you got more people, more bills and mortgages and economic pressure and what have you, more unemployment, more social problems. You get your Arts and Culture Centre, and more violent crime—I guess you call it, if you wanna call it one thing. And St. John's isn't bad compared to other places."

"Then why don't we go round robbing off each other in here, then, Max?...More than twenty of us here!"

"Okay, Edgar. I'm not saying there isn't less of a community feeling out there, than since the thirties, say. Smaller city then. Not like now. Shea Heights, Mount Pearl. You can be in and out of St. John's and get home before anyone knows you left. And it's not like there's only two roads to go so it's easy to catch 'em. And easy to see who's suddenly got better off. I admit it's changed. I mean there was only groceries to steal in the thirties anyhow, but I reckon a city's gotta expand and it'll happen if you want it or you don't. And if you're paranoid then move out to the suburbs or the outskirts. Like I did. Make home where you're at...Or stay in here!" Max laughs.

"Oh I did, boy!" Edgar retorts. "Me and the wife soon got out to Topsail and away from all the violence and God knows what."

"Only petty crime. I reckon St. John's is still a pretty good place to raise a family. Still works the same way, so you can know people who work different parts of town. And with any luck it'll still be more expensive bringing oil ashore than buying y'barrels of crude from Alberta, so they never will, and St. John's'll still be St. John's in fifty-years time!"

"Right Max!" Gerald agrees, but mistakes the point: "We're the generation who came too soon. I mean oil and that's still a big 'if' I grant you, but maybe some easy prosperity's gonna come to this next generation and then our grandchildren. And that'll be first time and all, after the hard times we had, eh!...Sheesh! Best thing's happened to us yet was the war. That were a godsend to my mind...Better than getting up and bidding for a crust of bread for breakfast!"

"Sounds like you wanna go get y'self killed fighting 'for king and country' again, Gerald! English all buddy-buddy when they want us to fight Nazis, and now won't even buy our fish... Sure think I'll stay in here, thank you very much... And they can kill you off easy enough out there nowadays, without any war, mind!" Remembering his son, Max sinks into depression again.

" 'Fight for'—bullshit! It was 'fight for three meals a day' more like, and a pair of pants so you weren't going round bare-arsed, living off ten cents a day," Gerald explains himself. "Like our fathers and forefathers fought for."

"Mr. Hunt?" Another nurse enters and interrupts.

"He left!" Gerald laughs. "No. Over here, nurse."

"Time for another blood sample, Mr. Hunt." She syringes three test-tubes of blood from his left forearm, and then leaves him pressing cotton wool to the perforation.

"He was after holding onto the other nurse's hand yesterday, nurse!"

She laughs. "Well, Mr. Lester. You have to ask after all. You'll never get anywhere if you just wait."

"But didn't anyone ever ask you, nurse?"

"I wouldn't quite say that, Mr. Lester!"

"So you like a helping hand sometimes! When you're busy." She colours slightly as she walks out. "That's enough of your flannel Mr. Lester, or you'll have me even more beat out." The men laugh.

Bramwell presses his advantage. "Hey boys! What do you say we get a '999' emergency going for this room tonight. See 'em all on the run. Max's last night after all, so he could probably do with a stress test!"

"Yeah and we had too much peace today, Max, with you out with them young nurses all day!" Gerald laughs. "So let's have a singsong, and Bramwell'll play his keyboards again... Hey, remember what a shock Dr. Badcock had last time when he came in and us all singing! Thought we was all drunk, and that soon made him leave sharpish, eh!" With Bramwell playing the Kawasaki electric piano he keeps under his bed, that had been a fine old time. Even Max is cheered by the thought.

"And get in some champagne and all," Bramwell suggests. "Nothing too ritzy but you can't live by bread alone, eh? And like they say, y'never too old to party. Specially for a last night."

"And I told the wife not to come today, so we could get going after supper, sharpish." Edgar is excited too. "She wanted to and she were some upset, but I mean it's foolish. She comes in all the way in four-wheel drive and she's ruining the pick-up, eh."

"My wife'd not be bad in here tonight! Least ways when she's snoring 'cause she sounds like something from one of them films, *The Deep*, and that, she'd be sure to scare 'em nurses off!" The boys laugh at Gerald's plan.

... "You know boys I'm after writing a book about this place. My experiences. When all you lot are gone off home, and it's the 'Edgar Green Room' or something!" Edgar picks up a notebook.

"Nah. Won't leave you, Ed!"

"Yeah, you will, Bramwell! You baymen can't get too soft lying in bed. You can't take the bayman out of the bay for too long, eh! You'll all be gone... But you're all in the book. Just first names. And it's not horrible 'bout anyone. It's like a comic strip. Like I had a set-to with a doctor and it's in there as a funny incident. Him saying how this won't hurt, and me saying he's right; won't hurt him a bit!" Edgar chuckles. "And I got all these suggestions of improvement in it too, like when I was in Intensive Care I gave 'em 120 suggestions. Like against women working up there when they're about eight months pregnant 'cause they're useless, and it's stupid. And how student doctors don't care and I seen 'em just standing there watching buddy die of short breath and me shouting 'do something' and them 'are you a doctor?' all saucy like. Just 'cause some doctor sends 'em to a room 'cause he's busy. See. Suggestions about administration here."

"Well. Only certain thing I guess is we're gonna all die sometime!" Bramwell finds his *Readers' Digest* and his bookmark.

"Is that what you been writing every day then, Edgar?"

"Yes, Max, and should be published December sometime... Guess it takes all kinds to make a world."

"And we got 'em all in this room, boy! Sure have." They laugh with Bramwell.

"And almost as good as money is friends!"

"But don't you be complaining too loudly, Edgar boy, or they'll be wheeling you back in, to the psychiatry ward next!" Gerald jokes and Max and Bramwell laugh.

"Well, wake me when the fun starts." Max closes his eyes. Bramwell and Edgar seem to be settling down for a good read; Gerald still keeping watch at the window. Time for a little snooze...

Last Scene

Friday afternoon, at work in the Occupational Therapy Department

The psychiatry ward is on the floor above Medicine Four. While the Oakleys Hospital remains the city's main psychiatric facility, the Sisters still cares for those not so endemically or criminally disturbed.

Up on the fifth floor, the atmosphere is not quite like that of the rest of the hospital. Nurses are still chatting and scribbling at their stations, but patients are dressed, smoking, watching television, playing cards in the cafeteria, and not confined to bed unless heavily sedated. Many wander the ward's corridors, padding along in their slippers, slowly, earnestly, and pre-occupied, sometimes with a nurse or two in tow. The plastic name-tags on their wrists give them away but volunteers and patients from the rest of the hospital still tend to leave the ward alone: with psychiatrists, visitors and occupational therapists wandering around in civilian garb too, the place is too confusing.

The occupational therapy office-cum-craftsroom is almost directly above room 414. The office is small and cluttered; kettles, files, film projector, pamphlets, therapeutic aids, and reality-orientation charts on the walls: "Today is__________, The weather is__________, The season is____________,' ready for patients to slot in answers.

'Reality-Orientation is a program designed to assist patients to focus in on their environment at the present time, and to sift out the inner turmoil uppermost within,' therapist *Mirium Hagentasch* is writing at her desk: early-thirties and still single, she was born in Montreal, but has lived in St. John's for nearly seven years now. She thinks a moment, then continues: 'R-O is attempted through two ways: twenty-four hour R-O, and R-O classes for life skills, creative expression, relaxation therapy and home management (theory and practice).'

Today, Mirium was engaged in a home management practical with patients Mary Downey and Brian Power. Then she wrote the reports on their progress, before returning to her manual for new occupational therapy (O.T.) clerks. Mirium has two such assistants at present. Bright girls, they are becoming quite experienced. There is *Rosemary Piper:* early-twenties, single, born in Toronto and lived in St. John's almost a year, and *Laura Dumont:* early-twenties, single, born in Montreal and lived in St. John's a year. As Mirium writes they can be heard working in the craftsroom through the adjoining door, tidying up after the cookery demonstrations and facing a mountain of charred pans and dirty dishes. Laura is meant to be washing and Rosemary drying but as the latter part of the afternoon approaches it is an effort not to gaze out of the window at the city and chat.

" 'Must meet lots of crazies in that hospital, girl!' That's what my landlady said to me last night!" Rosemary reports, accepting another wet plate.

"Well, they all go on about 'retards', don't they?" Laura agrees, "and how mental illness is a joke, and loonies are funny or comic."

"Yeah. And have them out in the community? Not a chance! 'Oh, y'crazies need constant care and attention by doctors who know, or else they kill people and fight and set fire to things!' God! All these people think mental illness means zombies and electric shock treatment for the communally insane, eh!...No it's a different culture here. It's like they're still scared of the yellow peril or something...At least the nurses seem okay. Quite gentle. I guess it's so close-knit they know the patients' home and family and the rest."

"Right. Parochial! And you should tell your landlady how criminal violence is no more frequent among the psychiatric patients than anybody else. And in fact it's her next-door neighbour who's more likely to commit the crime!"

"Like these kids getting sexually assaulted not by strangers or guys with histories of illness or violence but their own relatives and parents' friends."

Laura leans against the basin. "You know I feel horrible criticising Newfoundland culture all the time. Feel like some colonial élite and the rest."

"Like, 'Oh, not another CFA meeting a culture of poverty, or a minority, for the first time.' "

"Right. But I dunno. All this Newfoundlandia stuff is so small-minded. I feel so isolated. Cut-off from Toronto and Montreal and the centre of things. I mean I found it exciting at first. And stimulating. And you wanna sort of come and help them. Do your bit, but it's like if you stay too long you end up with a mental breakdown y'self or something. And that's not much help, is it!" They laugh.

"Right. The place does nothing for me now," Rosemary agrees as Laura dips her hands once more into the soapy water. "I mean I was quite into the place and the people at the start, but sometimes, I think I should never have come."

"I know what you mean. Newfoundland heritage coming out y'ears! God! 'Gag me with a spoon'." They laugh at a favourite current expression Laura brought back with her from California. "Did you know about Newfoundland before you came, Rosemary?"

"Never thought about it. And my mother was really worried. Kept on about no marital prospects over here! And how they were all inbred from the outports, full of genetic diseases and incest so you never knew how they were gonna behave. Then it was them being anti-intellectual, 'cause she read how 49 percent of those born here in 1963, when my sister was, left school before they were fifteen and can't fill in tax returns and write. Think it was 49 percent. Something incredible anyhow."

"Sure, d'are some stunned, girl!" Laura mimics and they laugh. "Mind you some of them develop amazing memories to compensate."

"Anyhow, Mom didn't stop for weeks. Next it was how Newfs were all on welfare and all welfare families produce is more kids."

"And the extent of their aesthetic sense is to go round painting rocks green, instead of growing lawns, right."

"Then when she knew I was definitely going she got me a write-up in our local newspaper. Like 'Girl braves Third World,' " Rosemary laughs. "Mind you, one thing I do find pathetic is people here expecting wage parity with the mainland. Like the telephone strikers. Who the hell do they think they are? Eh? I mean you get paid what the province can afford. Right? It's crazy. And look at them! Inefficient. Slipshod. And look at us. We'd be on a few thousand more if we'd stayed home." Rosemary shakes her head and gives up.

"Fair enough. Sure. But don't you still find it obscene, men getting paid by the telephone company more than women for the same work? I do." Laura gives her dish cloth a despairing shake.

"Oh sure. But one minute Newfs want wage parity and hand-outs from Ottawa, and next minute they're complaining when someone does get a half-decent salary like the teachers...Like d'you ever hear that open-line show on VOCQ Radio?"

"Keith's Answer Line?" Laura hands Rosemary the pot she has finally scrubbed clean of burnt baked beans.

"Right. It's garbage, but they always have it in for the teachers. And then against abortion and in favour of birching and the rest. God! That show's a real education in itself!"

"I guess it's all part of this obedience syndrome they have here. You know: 'Obey your betters' and 'Obey royalty' and 'Obey your premier and your MP'—even if he's a sleazebag with a criminal record and all he wants is a new car and more freebies all the time..."

"And always switching parties when it suits them. You're right Laura. They're scumbag crooks. Certainly wouldn't get my vote or respect...specially not if they forced me to keep living in some ugly, fire-trap of a box-house downtown, and then insist it's not inner-city death and a slum but a 'heritage area' or something!" Rosemary waves her towel towards the window and laughs. "They're also always on about how us 'CFAs' should go home if we don't like it here, eh, on Answer Line, and I just think 'Hicks! Eat y'heart out buddy' when they phone in. I mean you don't want to degrade yourself by answering all this defensive trash."

"I blame the denominational schooling, myself, Rosemary."

"Oh sure. Government-funded witch doctors saying: 'Obey! Question nothing.' "

"Never offer any feedback, even if you see something wrong."

"Instead of school making you able to think for yourself; and a bit independent. And responsible. So schools and families decide everything 'til kids are eighteen or something, less I guess, and then they're so used to obeying they just go and elect parent-figures for politicians and leave all governing up to them. It's like a general mentality."

"Right. 'The church and the government know best. Just stay dependent.' Then they feed you the line about Newfoundland culture being a fundamental force that you can't change fast, or put pressure on. Like culture is some sacred cow! Rot! Sounds like the same arguments they use about women having clitoridectomies in Sudan. 'It's tradition.' And 'women want it so they can become respectable adults.' "

"Yeah. So just change their traditions. Show them other ways."

"It's rot. Right. Why should any woman lose her sexual pleasure or inclination! Get some social workers over there. I mean it's just the same as abortion. Like they say, 'If men could get pregnant, abortion would be a sacrament.' " Rosemary laughs. "And I reckon people can always escape from their cultures, or change them if they really want."

"Mirium is, isn't she?" Laura agrees. "I mean she revolted when her culture said women couldn't be independent and had to marry at twenty-one or something... "

"Kids by twenty-five. Right. But it seems hard to get them radical or activist around here. Or advanced and respecting gays or women or the developmentally delayed. So they're even afraid of people in wheelchairs. Oh, I must show you this pamphlet we had at the women's group last night. 'A Voter's Guide for Women' it was called. You know in sixty years of voting in Newfoundland, they've only elected five women to the House of Assembly!"

"Is that right! That's bad."

"And they've never elected a woman federal representative from here. Then there's also a bit on rape in it. Like how one in every five women gets sexually assaulted. But out of every ten cases reported to the police, only seven get investigated, and only about three ever lead to arrests, I think it was. Never mind convictions."

"Is that right?"

"Yeah. 'Course not much point some of these women reporting it I guess 'cause there's nowhere to run to escape. Only two shelters for the whole island. And that's when you get the suicides, like Mirium told us of those kids in Conception Bay last year."

"Reminds me of that RCMP officer at that talk on rape we went to at the women's centre. Remember?"

"Sure," Rosemary shivers. "Gave us all the gory details didn't he. For their shock value. Scare the girls about the nasty, macho world out there."

"Well weren't those leaflets he handed out—'Lady Beware,' or something—weren't they all about 'don't hitch-hike and don't do something else. And be careful babysitting. And be careful in public places at night. And be careful in your car.' "

"In fact 'be careful whenever you little ladies leave your homes, and better still, don't! Just be a good housewife.' Yeah! Right!"

"And any woman caught out in the streets deserves what she gets 'cause she must be 'on the game' anyway."

"That's right, Laura. And maybe that's why you don't see prostitutes around here, 'cause all these women are all so obedient to the coppers!" Rosemary sneers.

"But you do get some 'ladies of the night' on Water Street."

"Yeah?" Rosemary didn't know.

"Apparently their husbands act as their pimps. They go out for a few hours, get enough cash for Bingo. All go to Bingo together and then the wives are out again after!"

"You're kidding!"

"I kid you not!..."

"Oh wild! Not so folksy then! And I didn't really tell you about our 'Take Back the Night' march did I, but some men in cars rolled down their windows and called us all 'sluts'!"

"Is that right? No you didn't. That's horrible!" Laura is dismayed.

"Oh, that's just from your typical slumland male," Rosemary explains. "You know. Rapes his sister-in-law at eleven. Fourteen if she's lucky. Large Catholic family. Read on from there."

"Yuck! Well, how was the march apart from that?"

"Oh great! We had about 110 or 120 women, eh, despite the rain, and the atmosphere was just great. We met at Bannerman Park, then went to the Playpen on Harvey Road and chanted 'This shop sells porn'—well some of us chanted. Some of the girls don't like chanting in the street, but that's okay too. There were enough vociferous ones. Then after that we thought there could be trouble so we had a police escort down Long's Hill. Just one cop-car, lights flashing, and the cops smiled at us from inside. Then we ended up outside City Hall... I mean I reckon most people realise all you want is fair play. And if men can walk the streets at night in safety then I want to."

"For sure! Sounds a good time."

"Really, Laura. You should come next time. And you find who are the real supporters, not just your professional feminists. I mean some of the real man-haters cried off. But that's fine by me with them lot."

"Maybe you'd get more local women if you went round the malls?... Could I come along to one of your women's group meetings sometime? See what they're like."

"Oh sure! It's fun. Even though it does get a bit frustrating at times. Like at the moment there's this one girl, Donna Cooney, who's sending us all batty. I mean we aren't all academics, eh, but this one girl is awful. She's so naïve and badly informed. But she talks loudest and dominates the conversation. So some people aren't going just 'cause of her!"

"Sounds rather obnoxious," Laura agrees, soaping a cup.

"Like last night we got into alternatives to the family, and wife-battering, and she goes on this long spiel and ends up saying 'it must be a social and cultural thing,' right! I mean wow! So there's Mirium holding her head in her hands, and me looking down trying not to laugh and there's Donna just deaf and not self conscious at all!"

"She doesn't sound right for it."

"No. And it's not supportive for her either. I mean, it's good to have people at different levels of awareness, so you're not just preaching to the converted all the time, but still..."

"What do you say to her?"

"Well, it's hard. I mean you don't wanna go back a few years and discuss everything all over again, so we just tell her 'Yes, the family can be supportive, but more often than not it fails.' Things like that. Anyway, last night we also read this interesting article on speech-patterns and how women are taught to sound less confident and apologise more and always sound like they're talking to a superior, so men end up not listening. Like those in power."

"Money talks?" Laura suggests.

"Right. And like women having to put initials on letters not their names or theirs aren't taken seriously."

"Reminds me of that guy from the x-ray department we had a meal with one time in the cafeteria."

"Oh yes. Acting devil's advocate," he called it didn't he! Sexist, chauvinist creep. 'If girls got the qualifications, they could end up in science just like d' boys.' And the rest."

"I remember watching you just fighting for control," Laura laughs.

"Me! I just wanted to punch him out. The little shit. And what else was it? Oh yeah. 'What's all d' beef about? Girls go out and work as teachers and nurses already don't they? So you girls aren't gonna change d' world, you know.' Huh! Just watch, baby!"

"Mind you, with his sort next thing you know he's sending you obscene phone calls. Remember mine, Rosie!"

"Sure! God that was bad."

"I was a nervous wreck! On tranquilizers at the end before I left Elizabeth Avenue! Remember?"

"See! Some loony chauvinist against you having a good paying job just 'cause you're a woman. And did they definitely find out in the end it was someone in the Medical Centre?"

"No. But it must've been. How else would he know when I left work and got home?"

"Seems to me any man around the city could do that. Christ, Laura!

Women suffer from prejudice all through history. And violence. And then we mugs blithely come to Newfoundland for more harassment! Tell me. Who's the crazy ones, eh!"

Laura laughs. "That's true. And I told you I had to give up running round Quidi Vidi Lake after these two men attacked me? Last time I ran it was just getting dark, and these two ducks took off in front of me and I nearly died." Rosemary laughs and Laura has to join in. "It's funny now, but you know at the time it was really spooky. Nearly scared me to death!"

"I remember. God I'd 've been terrified. You should always get people to call you to check you get home safe... God, where are you finding all these plates?" Rosemary complains as Laura discovers more in the soapy water.

"Nearly through now, my dear... I guess we all have gruesome stories to tell. Like have you met that new girl in here? Tracey? She was raped by her boyfriend, blotto drunk, of course, when she was babysitting and told him she didn't want to. So he just goes and pulls a knife on her. There's your macho male for you! Or else he stands around and says it's none of his business if he sees another boy beating on a girl!"

"Yucko! Or like that friend of Mary Downey, in here visiting last week. Remember him, Rosemary? He had weird ideas of privacy and public responsibility. What was it he was on about? Oh yeah, how it's worse to rape a girl than murder her 'cause what sort of a life would she have after that so she may as well go and kill herself. Remember?"

"Yep. Said he'd rather come across a murdered woman than a raped one 'cause a raped one would never recover anyhow. Christ! Weirdo. Good socialisation eh! We should never have left our sheltered homes, Laura!"

"Right! Can you imagine that! It's so warped."

"Yeah, but when you think about it, all this violence against women is just part of a wider ideology. I mean a sort of war mentality in society, so it's legitimate to use violence sometimes, and okay for boys to brutalise themselves by playing with guns."

"Right. Like *Soldier of Fortune Magazine* and all these gun-freaks into urban war games. And then you get your macho Newf who'll shoot anything so long as it's big enough and stands still," Laura laughs.

"It's so puerile. And you'd think people would've found other outlets by now or ways of being creative and expressing themselves without stooping to fighting. It's like education hasn't given people any more foresight at all."

"Right. They just want American extremism as a role model and all their romance with violence."

"Power and militarism making violence into a viable policy and something to win at and get off on. So black and white!... 'Course, if you listen to these 'professional Newfs' it's always the mainlanders' fault. Or else the townies' if they're from round the bay. I mean they go on about all this rape and violence as brought in from outside. And the collapse of traditional culture just 'cause us outsiders have imposed an 'alien matrix' on top, or some such twaddle! What garbage, eh! Never blame themselves."

"Yeah. That's just rot."

" 'Us, violent? Never m'dear,' " Rosemary mimics. " 'It's them Indians you'll be wanting. Or them Canadians. Not us'!" They laugh. "Oh yes, Laura. Another good one I heard on Answer Line was buddy saying men commit sex crimes 'just 'cause women tease them and drive them to it by wandering round in skimpy clothes. And it's all just to attract men's attention, so society has to accept it if some of them happen to get raped'! Well, my son! Is that cracked or wha' b'y!" They laugh. "Then he's on about the injustice of men going to jail on a women's word and she gets off scot-free."

"Iran, here we come!"

"Yeah, really."

"Well, my dear, that's the last of the dishes." Laura hands Rosemary a final scoured saucepan, pulls out the plug and dries the soap from her hands on a towel.

"Good, there were more than there seemed when they were cooking. Must be 4:30 by now. Must be."

"Yep, 4:34 to be exact." Laura straps her watch back on. "Great. Let's split." Rosemary finishes the pan and hangs up her dishcloth. "Let's go and offer that dishy doctor friend of yours a ride home. And see if we still get these cruising macho cretins hooting at us with a man in the car too."

"So we should proposition him? Derek you mean? Okay. Though I don't know him that well." Laura is a bit dubious.

"Soon will my dear. Sure. Why not? Women's lib. at its best!" Laughing they pass through to the office to say 'Bye' to Mirium and go...

Part II

An Analytical Interpretation of 'Violence'

"Dear Sir." (...) "yours faithfully"; one cannot despise these phrases laid like Roman roads across the tumult of our lives, since they compel us to walk in step like civilised peopled with the slow and measured tread of policemen though one may be humming any nonsense under one's breath at the same time— "Hark, hark, the dogs do bark." "Come away, come away, death." "Let me not to the marriage of true minds." and so on.

Virginia Woolf
The Waves

Indeed, in any complex society such as ours, there are almost as many distinguishable 'systems of customary rules and conventions' as there are individuals.

Edmund Leach
Custom, Law, and Terrorist Violence

Analytical Interpretation

Journeying around the city of St. John's, we have encountered the multifarious discussions dealing with 'violence' which I recorded my acquaintances regularly rehearsing, the habitual conversations popular during my fieldwork. In this part of the book, I want to treat those same discussions more analytically, and examine more precisely the use made of the catchword 'violence.'

Raymond Williams has called 'violence' a *keyword.*[26] He selects it as one of a class of words which force themselves on one's attention as invariably entering general discussions of modern society; and he identifies eight denotative senses: 'violence' as unruly behaviour, as vehement conduct, as an infringement of property or dignity, as use of physical force, as physical assault, and as threat or dramatic portrayal of the above. In 'violence,' Williams finds a word which significantly reflects present ideas and values.

The modern society in which 'violence' finds such currency, Leach would describe as incorporating within the matrix of a single political domain a very high degree of normative pluralism. In such a society, hero, prophet, madman and criminal become totally confused, and there is politicised competition for irresolvably contrasting and conflicting utopian values.[27] This portrayal may be glossed as society which fears for the safety of its identities—national, community and individual—and the sanctity of its conceptual boundaries; and when it is realised that despite tacit agreement over customary rules which the notion of their society had led members to expect, social boundaries of consensus are far from extensive, and general rules of the game far from universally shared or applauded, the response is outrage and indignation. Furthermore, the response (such as recorded by Cohen on the level of community[28]) is a vigorous reassertion of identity and a restating of the boundaries which it is feared are threatened by encroachment; a reaffirmation before irreversible damage is done.[29]

'Violence' may be found to appear repeatedly, then, as the cliché of a Leachian "runaway world."[30] If 'mannered society' is the catchphrase of a confident and inward-looking Jane Austen-like social commentary, a commentary on games of etiquette played with granite-bounded identities, then 'violent society' may be the catchphrase of commentary constantly fearful for social identities, a nervous scrutiny of threatened boundaries without. Moreover, 'violence' accompanies that modern society wherein it is no longer Wickhamite manners which 'maketh man' but the calculated violating of hallowed custom. One exercises fear for one's own territory—political, psychic, physical and moral—by committing violence upon others; part of what McLuhan has called a quest for the meaningful,[31] a quest for one's own Warholian quarter hour of eccentricity. In the modern embracing of 'violence' is to be found not just the deviance of the criminal and the crazy but also claims to the heroic and the divine. In Renek's words 'violence' is a shorthand in which to read the "dementia of the times."[32]

However, as Devereux reminds us: "Si bis faciunt idem, non est idem (If two people do the same thing, it is not the same thing)."[33] In a shorthand or a catchword there is a tension between sameness and difference, between, as in my quotation from Virgina Woolf, similarity and idiosyncrasy. It is this tension which I wish to explore. That is, I am not so much interested in an emphasis on the omnipresence of 'violence,' in 'violence' as a macrosocietal stereotype, as in an exploration of where such a cliché leads in terms of the niceties of particular expression, and in the whole gamut of its uses. I am less interested in the question "why is 'violence' so universal?" than "what may individuals habitually coming together and talking violence with each other tell us about how people knit themselves together to constitute society?"; at least, I shall only approach the first question via the second. For I shall argue that through an examination of talking violence, the institution of language can be seen serving as a vehicle for the creation of diverse meanings and identities, as in my quotation from Leach. Rather than a merely coercive instrument of social structural replication and a monolithic entity of univocal enactment, language may be revealed as hosting a multitude of voices in situational agreements and oppositions, overlapping, colliding and contradicting. I want to view society, in fact, as constituted by multiple agreements and disagreements over preferred verbal usage.

The design in what follows is of a central argument (in ordinary print) interleaved with detailed illustrations (in italics) in which I refer back to one or more of the above conversations. I shall start by arguing, (a), that individuals personalise cultural institutions when they use them, and the latter become created parts of egocentric worlds of meaning; and I shall illustrate this by reviewing the scene in the kitchen of the Lightship halfway house and that in room 414 of the Sisters hospital. Then I argue, (b), that the same is true for language: used in the context of their own lives, individuals breathe life into the institution in manifold ways, and through their preferences of verbal association produce a diversity of meanings when they speak, even through the same fund of words; and I illustrate this by a review of our scene where Leo Normore is chauffeured downtown in search of work, and then that where the occupational therapist clerks discuss their life and work at the hospital. Next I argue, (c), that linguistic usage is inherently oppositional, and even in the same setting, using a seemingly common language in a diversity of ways, speakers are to be found meeting with some and differing from others. I say that agreement and disagreement over the proprieties of ways of speaking are inextricably bound together, and that it is by these means that individuals come together in larger groups and affirm common identities in opposition to those of outsiders. It is through an interplay of verbal agreement and contrast that individuals relate to each other in society; and as illustration I return to our party of carousing academics. But such group belonging ought still to be seen, (d), as of variable closeness, and the agreement over ways of speaking owned by individuals in one group may be more tenuous than that in another; and as example I offer a comparison between our conversationalists in the Salon Paris nightclub and those in Tee Cee's lounge. Moreover, (e), such agreements between speakers are also situational, I argue, and as illustration I compare the different ways in which Judge Hussey found it legitimate to speak when we met him first at his criminology lectern and second at his Provincial Court bench. In fact, (f) in any one situation I say one may identify a number of agreements by which individual speakers are linked in different ways—from the proprieties of simple verbal associations shared by many to more complex associations shared by the few; and taking our remaining scenes as illustration, that in Milligan's Irish pub and that in Brady House Detoxification Centre, I suggest a sliding-scale of more and less inclusive societal boundaries and belongings, a diversity of social identities, in use at the same time: an image of modern urban society as a complex meeting of verbal samenesses and differences.

An idea of society as composed of an interplay of relations of sameness and difference has, of course, a long history. To recall just two expositions, Bateson described peripheral and centripetal integrations, the first a matter of links of behavioural symmetry and the second of complementary difference, while Durkheim conceived of mechanical and organic solidarities: society founded upon likeness contrasting with society as a meeting of dissimilarities. What both share is a recognition of the constituting capacity of an interplay of these complementary but opposing tendencies in societies at any one time.[34] My own idea is that such constitutive factors may also be revealed in the realm of verbal usage: that society may be seen to be constituted by an interplay of verbal sameness and difference. That is, I shall say it is through overlapping preferences of verbal association that individuals align themselves in conversational groups, groups which encompass verbal agreements of varying fashion and degree; and it is an aggregation of these groups of which society can then be found to be composed.

My argument will present a biased image, then. It will privilege the verbal in the linguistic, the linguistic in the behavioural, the individual in the societal and the constructional in the cultural. But these are my interests—interests which informed my attempts to reconstruct others' expressions of meaning in conversation, and interests which will inform my analysis too; and interest is an apposite term, combining as it can curiosity and concern, with the partisan: only in an absence of interest is there an absence of bias. Hence I state my bias at the outset. I treat the individual as a given. Moreover, he (or she) is the key purposive entity in the social universe. He is the source of social energy, responsible for the making of experience through an active and possibly idiosyncratic interpretation of what he perceives, and a creative imparting of meaning to it. It is the individual who draws up courses of action for himself by building models of information and hypothesising in terms of them. Thus individual behaviour is always mediated by perception, and it is to individual cognition that one must look for a definition of the classes and structures of events, and for their evaluative and affective mapping in a meaningful universe. It is individuals' personal cognitive constructs which mould their worlds, and it is the individual who acts on intentions and takes initiatives for the gaining of value and significance inside them, and for the fulfilling of expectations of order and form, objects and people, old and new.[35] Initially, individuals stand alone in the societal crowd; I am interested in the ways and the extent to which speakers meeting each other in conversational exchange may be described as achieving communion, as sharing meanings with each other.

My bias is a simplification, perhaps. If so, I would argue it is only to the extent of fulfilling what Gluckman and Devons have termed the anthropological "duty of abstention."[36] In the broad harmony of different anthropological styles, each point of view takes from the complexity of social reality certain simplified facts and variables in order to isolate essential features of a social phenomenon; mine is the relating of individual to individual and hence to society: a building up of society from building blocks of individuals' face-to-face verbal interactions.

My anthropological style has a biography which ought to be mentioned. The biases derive from an earlier study based in the small farming village of 'Wanet,' in northern England's Yorkshire Dales where I explored individual constructions of meaning and the meeting of these in conversation. My specific focus was upon seven individuals who were long-term neighbours. I argued that to really understand what they said one had to look at their words in terms of individual speakers' cognitive contexts—longer strings of regular word-associations from which these words and phrases were abstracted when individuals spoke. These cognitive contexts which individuals brought to conversations were disinterred when my analysis revealed the interconnectedness of individuals' utterances over time—their repeated aggregation of phrase with phrase. I found that for each individual I could isolate a number of closed loops of thought; I could map out several often mutually exclusive, cognitive worlds, which I called *worldviews,* in terms of which individuals were interpreting behaviour, constructing meaning, and, moreover, perceiving their own identities. For a different persona fitted each loop of thought, and I suggested that the character of each individual, far from being a single, integrated and consistent whole, was better described as a loose aggregation of a number of different *personae* which the individual manifested in different moments.

The study then followed these seven individuals (with their numerous personae) through conversational interaction, and I argued that these habitually took the form of an exchange of phrases and catchwords routinely rebounding off one another: the exchanges with different neighbours were each phraseologically formulaic. That is, these individuals would meet and repeatedly appraise certain common symbolic objects with each other, and over time, each had come to regard the behaviour of the others in relation to these shared symbolic forms as expectable and appropriate. Each had come to construe these routine meetings as apt and legitimate.

However, I suggested that the exchanges were being differently interpreted by different participants, interpretations often so different as to be incompatible. For each participant was approaching the common symbols in terms of different personae and different worldviews, relating to the formulae of the interaction to different cognitive sets of word-associations, different personal lexicons. And furthermore, intent upon their own performances, expressing their own meanings and fulfilling their own expectations, these diverse construings did not become apparent. After conversing, as during and before, individuals' different cognitive contexts remained apart, and often at odds. Even though these close neighbours habitually related to each other as significant others, and engaged in daily, collective discussions over common objects, still I argued that precisely the same set of verbal signifiers was being used in often contradictory ways, as home to very different evaluations and bases of normative judgement.

Thus, I concluded in my study that far from being shared, and a common denominator of macrosocial proportions, meanings in a society could be highly idiosyncratic and inconsistent. Interaction did not of itself determine a consensual use of words. Instead there was a tension to be recognised between a common linguistic surface and underlying meanings. For, as within the single person, so within the seeming singularity of a cultural form, such as a negotiated medium of exchange, may be uncovered a miscellany of contradictory identities.

I took issue, then, with those who would decentre the individual from analysis, and deprive him of his central role in the creation of meaning in favour of the social fact of a collective grammar coercively speaking through him; for I felt these individuals in Wanet were to be seen confronting themselves with people and events of their own definition. I came to argue for more of an acceptance of the distorted in social interaction. Tacit contracts of family, of neighbourhood, of acquaintance, are matters of form which need not negate individual idiosyncrasy and creativeness in the use of language, the defining of order, the judging of identity, the deciding for action and the pronouncing of legitimacy: a commonality of meaning is something that may or may not be achieved as people interact, while casual and habitual talking-relationships may merely serve to fulfil private expectations.

Hence, I arrived at a notion of society as involving less integration and homogeneity than the aggregation of diverse personae and worldviews; and often amounting to a chaotic relativism, as constructions of meaning continue to meet and influence one another in all manner of non-prescribable, tangential and random ways. This was not an impoverished notion, I felt, but one which, in treating sharing, negotiation and conformity as problematic, recognised and emphasised that social life, the relating of individual to society, may entail a continual muddling through.[37]

For the present study I wanted to alter my focus and begin not with specific individual speakers but with what many seemed to share, the catchword 'violence,' and through its broad currency examine the word's life in use; explore what may be the tension between a singularity of verbal form and a diversity of meaning. However, I would still emphasise individual intentionality and 'in order to' motivations, playing down 'because motivations' and exterior determinings, and the power of pre-existing cultural institutions such as kinship or class to form and direct. I would still treat such institutions as constructed by individuals' cognitive use of them, individuals' continued belief in them and continued engagement in their practices. Individuals have, of course, to be taught the use of these institutions initially, but then of more interest to me is the way they become vehicles of individual expression and creativity. For in using institutions, individuals personalise them; and the institutions are themselves formed and directed by this use, reformed and redirected: individuals must continue to give them meaning and grant them causality for them to maintain social significance.

To begin, then, let me illustrate this point, (a), by referring back to two of our scenes, that in room 414 of the Sisters of the Beatitudes General Hospital (pp. 116-126) and that in the inner-kitchen of the Lightship Community Rehabilitation Centre for Ex-offenders (pp. 73-80). In the first, you will recall, Edgar Green, Gerald Hunt, Max Dawe and Bramwell Lester were chatting by their beds of a lunchtime, and in the second Norm Ward was introducing Bas Kean, a new member of staff, to the job and the premises. In these scenes, I shall say we find institutions—in this case physical ones of hospital and half-way house—used as vehicles to think about, and languages to express ideas about individuals' social worlds. For here individuals use their immediate physical space as means of interpreting a possibly tricksterish world from more personal points of view, thus transforming its potential dangers: the 'placeness' of the institution becomes an instrument through which speakers cognitively construct an orderly, safe place, distancing and delivering themselves from disorder and violence.[38]

The hospital and halfway-house are both examples of what Goffman has termed "total institutions." They are enclosed places of residence, work and recreation where a fair number of people form a collegial group, lead regularised and routine lives together, while having only meagre social intercourse with those differently located and not connected with the institution.[39] *For Goffman, such institutions are superordinate: they capture and encompass; they mortify and profane conceptions of self and proffer new worlds of institutional aims and formally administered rounds of life. However, to my mind, it is a personalisation of institution which these scenes demonstrate, with the hospital patients ending up safe in their room and ward, with nurses and doctors regulating entry, and the cook safe in his halfway-house kitchen with an army of boys to fight his battles. Speakers may be seen using what they perceive to be the physical solidity, the historical longevity, the routine regularities and the secure respectability of particular total institutions in order to distance themselves from the disorder of violence and the unfamiliar: what Bailey has called living in the middle of a series of concentric circles of trust.*[40] *That is, speakers use their institutions to help map out contour lines of relevance and intimacy in a social environment and then locate themselves in a secure and potentially dominating position at the centre, thus: self—institution—neighbourhood—city of St. John's—distant places; or again: self—institution—institution in the past—institution in the future—the future unknown; or again: self—fellow members of the institution—friends outside—strangers outside—violent strangers. It is analogous to Leach's synopses of the common cognitive mapping of nesting concentricities from that which is more familiar, more similar, more safe to that which is less so, thus: self—sibling—cousin—neighbour—stranger; or self—house—farm—field—distance; or self—pet—livestock—game—wild animal.*[41]

We find the institution figuring in a number of egocentric and graduated constructions of order in the universe, each boasting a different criterion for the gradation of space, from historical to physical, biographical and societal. In each, the institution forms part of the fortification of safe cognitive space. It stands between the speakers and the outside world in such a way that as each closer gradation is traversed, so the order of the socially familiar is progressively substantiated. Rather than media of external and coercive forces, institutions in these scenes serve for the mapping of selves in the centre of secure worlds in which it is appropriate to act.

Returning to the Sisters hospital, then, the residents of room 414 speak of it as the end-point of both their physical and biographical space. Physically they map from its windows how the hospital is bounded by the Newfoundland Hotel, the harbour, the docks, the coastguard and fishing ships, the new concrete apron and the old Southside Hills with their walks and rabbit warrens. Then further afield there lies the unfriendliness, bustle and size of the Medical Centre and the homes of outsiders. Coming closer, within the Sisters hospital, drafty and old perhaps, but still homely, friendly and familiar, and expensively furnished, room 414 is reachable only via the passing of admissions, then the nursing stations, kitchens, other wards, doctors and receptionist, and by finding one's way past the maze of other rooms such as Bramwell's daughter Clarice's and the fifty-nine other beds. Physically their room is at the centre of safe space.

Biographically, for all its residents, room 414 represents the end of long and often hard lives outside; they remember the Depression. Now, despite fearing for their health, all use room 414 to their advantage. They manage to construe it as home, and as feasible for it to be an enduring and final one. Thus, Bramwell is home here with his tobacco, cards, daughter, and Reverend Bill. And Gerald is away from the vagaries of the docks, now able to survey all with more certainty and perspective from a lofty look-out. And here Edgar, after twenty-three years of retailing and finally setting his wife up in her own home, can retire, and preserve his experience on paper for the benefit of those around him who value this expertise. And lastly, here Max finds himself on the consuming end at last after twenty-six years working these kitchens. Now it is he who can criticise while they pander for attention; he who relaxes, organises his daughter and contemplates punishment meted out to those who maltreated his son.

There is often little incentive for moving out from here anyway. Outside for Max, after all, there is mostly poverty, class difference, bills, and an immoral government. Inside is like getting away from it all, like to the suburbs, which he always wanted. And for Bramwell the way of the world outside means robberies and violence, and he has no longer the strength. While inside is more like life in a hotel. And for Gerald, outside is a dump of a world of thieves and locked doors, and of people he does not know and cannot trust. Inside, he and his peers, who were, like him, born too soon, are well-fed and cared for. Finally, Edgar sees, outside, a world of terrorism, immorality and greed. In a burgeoning city gone mad, you need to be armed to survive. It is far more worthwhile to escape the violence and stay inside where reasoned criticism is heeded.

Room 414 becomes something of a safe haven, then. From here, the outside world can be deliberated upon, graded, and set to rights. Inside, nurses can be teased and doctors scared, as these men all party together, eat, drink and sing. Families, preachers, strangers, other sick people, can all be kept at a distance. The four of them lead ordered lives at the centre of their physical and biographical worlds. They all know precisely where they are.

Similarly, in the Lightship halfway-house we found Norm Ward safe in his kitchen: the centre of his occupational, historical, physical, temporal and societal conceptions of space. For firstly, the Lightship is the culmination of a long and varied and successful occupational career for Norm: from the mines to supermarkets, hotels and bars. And it is here that he intends to end his days—a job all above board and even sanctioned by the government's manpower agency. And here, in an old Victorian house, he can align himself with the forefront of a long and distinguished historical development; for this building, passing from the upright Spencer family to the order of the Sisters of the Beatitudes and then to the Lightship organization which has made it now its own, and added new offices and so forth, accrues ever more traditional value.

Inside the building, Norm's kitchen represents the very heart. Not only must one circumnavigate the buildings and parking lots outside but then find one's way past the front offices and washrooms, the staircases and walls of photographs, the lounge and outer kitchen in order to finally achieve the inner one. And here has been Norm's home for quite a time—in the middle of ramparts of high shelves, packed fridges and freezers, sideboard, sink and oven.

The inner kitchen is also the focus of Norm's daily timetable. Having awoken, shaved and dressed, he is here for most of his day, busily working on regular meals to regular schedules: soup for dinner, vegetables on by 3:30 for fish and brewis supper, and no salads or garlic. With cribbage and shopping trips, too, this is how Norm passes the main part of his day. For here is, besides, his social centre, his family: him and the residents, and director and other staff and his personal assistant. Together they protect each other against criminals—rats, rapists, murderers, sex-maniacs—bums, and women. Strangers are kept at a distance, and the more violent of them at bay in the Big House. Here Norm finds himself most safe, surrounded by a regimen, and moreover instrumental in transforming the disorderly, the ill fed, the screwed-up into those like himself who prove themselves by getting the most out of life in orderly and law-abiding ways. As with room 414, then, Norm uses his inner kitchen as a means of dealing with violence, and transforming a potentially threatening, disorderly world into a social environment safely mapped out in terms of the intimate details of his personal experience.

Schütz has argued that people will cognitively organise their social space in terms of relevance to their own actions and potential.[42] *It is this which we witness in these scenes. The total institutions achieved significance in individual-focused worlds. Total institutions became what Wallman has called "total symbolic packages," host to a complex and rich store of diverse yet interconnected meanings which their inhabitants impart to them.*[43] *The institutions are used as shorthands, condensations of a number of egocentric orderings; a multiplication of construed criteria of order, each with its own gradation of contour lines, and each protective in different moments, each processing different threats of disorder, which together lessen the chances of breach all the more. The speakers remain socially and physically secure, at home in the control of their respective institutions, and multifariously bounded. The general point I would have taken from these scenes is that rather than regarding the institution as coercive, it is pertinent to see how it comes alive in creative individual usage: a means of cognitively constructing meaning and order in personal worlds.*

I would make a similar point with regard to language: in use the institution is personalised and becomes a vehicle of egocentric construction, affording individuals the felicity of making their own variable worlds. This is in contrast then to the overriding, custodial character of language which analysts have often been more intent upon positing, encapturing or circumscribing speakers and imposing meanings upon them. Thus, for example, B. Berger describes language as the ideal Durkheimian social fact, possessing coerciveness, historicity, externality, objectivity and moral authority in relation to its individual users. Indeed, generated, defined and sustained by society, it is she claims, the means by which all other societal institutions gain objectivation.[44] P. Berger and Luckmann concur; language, they say, is a collective repository of objective meaning, an edifice of cultural categories and social values and norms, unremittingly constraining individual experience. It is the handmaiden of cultural prescription, structuring subjective perceptions of reality into apprehension of a cohesive, typical and intersubjective order, of incontrovertible facticity, which all users then take for granted.[45]

A starting point which I prefer is Wittgenstein's definition that in most cases "the meaning of a word is its use in the language": meanings are not carried round on the words' backs but are instead imparted to them by their contexts of usage.[46] That is, the later Wittgenstein argued it was a false objectification to treat language in a vacuum, as an abstract and closed thing-in-itself. Instead, language ought to be treated as a spatial and temporal phenomenon, an instrument used with intention, a form of action. This calls for a shift in focus from the dictionary and the book of grammar to situations of linguistic performance, for it is here that the significant properties of language are to be discovered. This in turn led Wittgenstein to a rejection of the notion of language as a single, unified and integrated structure, reducible to an ideal schema and informed by an essential plan, for in performance language reveals itself as a multiplicity of different ways of speaking, with no common denomination. Units of meaning are not to be seen as words in abstract isolation, then, but rather words, phrases and sentences produced as instruments in the performance of public speech-acts. Language as a fund of names could be described as a potential means of making meaning, but it is a mere preparation for description, and only in particular situations of use does this potentiality come to life. Moreover, such situations of use must include the specific aggregation and sequence of words, the occasion and purpose of the acts of speaking, the intentions of speakers and listeners, and the actions with which the words are interwoven: only in such speech-acts, where saying is doing, may verbal meaning be located.[47] In short, relations between words and meanings are not absolute, and meaning is not to be sought in generalised denotations or reductions-to essence but rather in the idiosyncracies and situationalities of use.

From Wittgenstein, then, I learn an injunction to beware granting particular consequence to decontextualised verbal forms: to look to words in context, to the way speakers associate one word with another, for an understanding of meaning, and to make a diacritical distinction between the form of a word and its content, its sense in use; for any generalisable links between the two, of causation, of circumscription, of direction and so on, are extremely problematic. Instead, form and content may be more divorced in our appreciation, the former a matter of cultural potential, the latter a matter of bringing the word to actual social life in all sorts of individual, arbitrary and non-prescribable ways. And this applies to 'emotive' meaning as well as 'descriptive,' as Cranston differentiates — the way words make one feel as distinct from what they describe; the fact that some words are made to elicit a 'boo' and others a 'hurrah' should also be contextualised, and conceived of separately from the verbal forms *per se.*[48] So, when a group of children play 'Ring-a-ring o'roses,' for example, not only do they probably have no knowledge of the Black Death or the progress of bubonic plague to which the words superficially refer, but they also feel nothing of the horror with which the words would once have been associated.

Moreover, this is not merely a matter of historical difference, but applies equally forcefully to contemporaneous usage. Use must ever be seen as a creative process: the innovative translation of old words to new situations; and past usage need not be seen as predetermining or circumscribing future possibilities so much as providing prior sets of texts — from single words to complex exchanges — which may be drawn upon in new contexts by substituting, rearranging, inflecting and expanding the words, clauses and sentences, in line with fresh intentions. Moreover, as this occurs in unpredictable ways, so contemporaneous usage may be characterised by idiosyncrasy: by fluidity, spontaneity, pragmatism and improvisation. For here are diverse constructions of meaning, even with the same verbal forms re-occurring as individual speakers differently associate one word with another, and the verbal whole informs very different sets of activities.

The point, (b) may be forcefully illustrated by a comparison of verbal usage, and in particular perceptions of 'violence,' in two further scenes. The first is where the occupational therapy clerks Rosemary Piper and Laura Dumont were found chatting about life in Newfoundland in their craftsroom (pp. 127-135), and second where Leo Normore, ex-convict and one-time taxi-driver, trawlerman, security guard and carpenter, was seen loquaciously explaining himself to Basil Smith while being driven to the fishplant in search of work (pp. 63-72). A comparison of these speakers is made all the more pertinent by the similarities of their biographies, the relatedness of some of their behaviour. For all, you will recall, were in their early-twenties, members of the same generation, who left home in order to find work in new Canadian cities and provinces. There, all encountered violence and, as migrants, suffered from victimisation at the hands of strangers. Growing estranged from the latter, they now plan a better future with their friends, where they can act as they like without being affronted by the laws and prejudices of others. In Schwartz' terminology, Leo, Laura and Rosemary are similar

lar "migrants of identity:" part of a social movement of young people in modern society which Schwartz describes as in continual search of acceptable, authentic individual identities which are without temporal precedence.[49] *Schwartz' picture is of large-scale society as encompassing an increasing plurality of behavioural styles; there is both a diversity of experiences differentiating one generation from the next, and further differences within any one of these which he calls differences of generational style. Boundaries between generations and between styles may be indeterminate, vague and arbitrary, but they represent the making by individuals of different behavioural choices. Selecting identities, peers of a generation then divide themselves into different social movements by their preference for different miscellaneous behavioural emblems: members of different styles are those who make use of a different repertoire of cultural forms—varying preference for items of food, or clothing, or songs and musicians, or causes and heroes, or verbal slang, Schwartz suggests, or, as here, physical migrations, and the reasons for and consequences of them. That is to say, we might classify the biographies of our main protagonists Leo, Laura and Rosemary as sharing the same behavioural style; their behaviour may be aligned as part of the same social movement through their choices of certain emblems of identity. Moreover in these scenes we find their migrations similarly figuring as bases of discussion. Thus all speak of their experiences of migrating only to find distant and ignorant people; threatened with violence, they all agree it would have been better if they had never left home. However, what is more significant for me is that while all may agree that 'violence' is what one meets when their contemporaries leave home to find work—violence against oneself, violence against women—the meaning of this violence, its definition and implications, become matters of very different individual interpretation. For, indicating their migrations to themselves, speakers express and fulfil sometimes contradictory cognitive constructions of the world. In aggregating their experiences, 'violence' becomes a building block in different expectations of order, and different expositions of self.*

Reviewing the scenes more closely, we find that for Rosemary and Laura it was stimulating reaching Newfoundland and St. John's, at first. Leaving the security of their homes, they came as occupational therapists, prepared to help a backward part of the world to modernise. But, far from grateful, they found Newfoundland locals anti-intellectual and intolerant. Drunk and lazy and often on Welfare, the distant strangers were unfriendly and xenophobic, sexist, illiterate, religious and un-

aesthetic. The girls came here from sheltered families to find incest, rape, teenage suicide, blind obedience, and a passing of blame. They even found themselves victimised by violent men who would attack them on the streets, threaten them obscenely over the telephone, and endanger their lives and property on the roads. Moreover, the isolation of their work, its lack of local appreciation and comprehension was to make them fear for their own mental health. Sometimes they were made to wish they had never come here. However, at least they have each other, and their boss, Mirium Hagentasch, as a shining light to follow; and also women's activities to join, from discussion groups to marches. And they can still imagine a better future, and work towards it. It will be a world where people are free of cultural chains, where women are free to work, and free from clitoridectomies, and free to have abortions on demand, and free to walk the streets like men and talk as confidently as men; a world where Newfoundlanders, like other Third World peoples, will be free from the oppression of their traditions, their families, their churches and their politicians. They can imagine a society not dominated by a general ethos of violence, where women and children do not suffer at the hands of macho *men.*

Meanwhile, in Basil Smith's Chevy, Leo recounted how he left his Corner Brook home of girlfriends and school fights and home-cooking, and stopped being a 205-pound trawlerman and a 'cabbie,' and went to the mainland. There he found work in Ontario and on the Prairies and in the Maritimes for three years, building and doing carpentry, as well as camping and hitching over 4000 miles. But then in Toronto he was victimised by violent westerners who misunderstood his looks, and threatened to kill him; and in Nova Scotia and New Brunswick he was made the victim of his background by people who spoke differently and thought only of money. He even found the police picking on him. By the end Leo had had enough and wished he had never come. For his journey finally led him to jail—to robbing and beating his brother-in-law, arguing with his mother-in-law, and fighting and estranging his wife and child. Fortunately he found good people and friends, and his sporting buddies back home. He found people who had been in similar straits. So now Leo plans a better future for himself. His workmanlike hands will find him non-unionised work; whether it is in a store or on an oil-rig or on the roads is unimportant. And after ten weeks of that he would be free for the rest of the year through his UIC payments. Then he could find another woman, and, through her, maybe, better work; or at least drive around again in his Grand Fury picking up 'bits of fluff,' while deciding if it is to be Corner Brook and his drinking mates next stop, or Atlanta, the States, and his macho *uncle. Leo can imagine a time when he can have what he wants without having to resort to, or being threatened by, violence.*

Devereux has explained how social movements need not be composed of individuals who share beliefs or self-indications so much as people who find in the same type of activity an "ego-syntonic" outlet — an outlet suitable for the expression of diverse subjectivations and idiosyncratic expectations, which then find fulfilment in different ways and to different extents. As members indicate the experience of their social movement to themselves, the 'same' events may confirm very different constructions of the world.[50] *Thus,in talking the violence of their generation, participating in the language of a shared generational style, a common social movement, the above individuals still interpret that violence rather differently. We do not find the language of the social movement structuring their subjective perceptions of reality into a single or cohesive whole, but rather how a discordant variety of imparted meaning may be identified within the commonalities of behavioural form. Language is personalised, and the 'violence' diversified by individual interpretation and definition; different verbal associations are made with it. Using the verbal emblems of the generation becomes an act of bricolage in which the forms, aggregated in idiosyncratic ways with others are given idiosyncratic meanings.*[51] *The language of the social movement is transformed; and synthesised into different personal styles, without circumscription or limitation, it becomes the speaker's own. As Steiner puts it, however uniform the behavioural contours of a social grouping, language remains "an inexhaustibly multiple aggregate of speech-atoms, of finally irreducible personal meanings."*[52]

In reviewing our scenes, it is an idea of cultural institutions as instruments of creativity that I have been emphasising; that use is a creative process. I have argued that in use individuals personalise institutions, they construct them in terms of the meanings of their own lives, so that when, for example, the common denominations of verbal form are mediated by their speakers' individual worldviews, universality is overshadowed and replaced by diversity; use is idiosyncratic, and language becomes a vehicle for the affirmation of often diverse senses of self.

Moreover, this construction of personal meanings has often been expressly oppositionary: one opposed those outside the hospital or halfway house; one opposed those met at the end of a migration; one opposed those who differently defined Newfoundland and its violence. Boon tells us that the creation and maintenance of identity is an inherently comparative process. It always entails "playing the vis à vis": positing notions of alternatives of different others, and then juxtaposing oneself against them; admitting difference into the realm of contingency, and then inclining towards what one is not. Contrast and opposition in verbal usage may be called good to think with, then, enabling individuals to form coherent self-images, and senses of themselves as distinct.[53]

However, this does not apply only to individuals. For in the personalising of language may be found not just the construction of individual identities but also that of larger social entities in which individual speakers locate themselves. Hence, at the same time as Rosemary and Laura diverged from Leo on the above scenes over the proprieties of verbal association, the girls did align themselves with each other: *they* did share a way of speaking. In using language, I say individuals can meet each other in what I call talking-relationships; and I shall argue next that these bespeak the same acts of comparison as in the formation of individual identities but also include habitual agreements between individuals in the process thereof: the construction of contrast and opposition by a number of speakers in discussion. For our occupational therapists it was by contrasting themselves with the *macho* Newfoundland outside their window, and opposing its norms of violence that a sense of the identity of their own talking-relationship was garnered; Leo and his ilk were safely distant. However, we shall see that verbal contrasts can be constructed, and group oppositions maintained, even when individuals are engaged in conversational exchange: in the same setting, verbal associations may be far from uniform, and verbal agreements manifold.

I illustrate, (c), by returning to the party scene in Philippa Howells' apartment (pp. 25-38). Here her university friends were found discussing whether Newfoundland had suffered an increase in violence, while they drank beer in the kitchen and waited for the chilli to be served. Contained in this scene, I shall argue, is a fight to construct social reality in Newfoundland as part of a competition between certain academic disciplines to monopolise the arena of public relevance.

Eccentric as we may recall Philippa's guests were, they may be said to have been alike in resembling what Ingold calls "cultural connoisseurs."[54] *For as artists and academics, at least part of the identities which they construed for themselves involved the observing of the wider*

Newfoundland society from its interstices. They were all interested, that is, in an academic society which lived by a reification and abstraction of those standards, symbols, traditions and problems in which the wider society was found engrossed. The customs of the rest, defined and understood, preserved in amber, then served as personal assets for a negotiation of relations within a college fraternity, within a St. John's academy of arts and sciences.

The fraternity of natural *scientists has been described by Ziman as an invisible corporate matrix of social relations and obligations, owning in common that objective data which issues forth to the public.*[55] *However, according to Latour and Woolgar, the working of such a collegial corporation need not run so smoothly or so invisibly, and the fight to produce facts and construct scientific reality may be a fierce one. For it morally obliges corporate members to publicly take shares in fictional accounts of natural order, and then use the authority of the particular laboratory as a marketing tool with which to 'sell' this new property as a stable objectivation and a logical necessity. Each college thus hopes to beat contenders in the negotiations to found new givens.*[56]

Something of this may be seen in the discussions of our own cultural connoisseurs; in what Nietzsche dubs the 'unnatural sciences,' such as sociology, history, anthropology, there may be an equally fierce fight over constructions of reality. For at a time when public funding is limited and to some extent correlates with public attention and esteem, these disciplines must be seen to be relevant and to articulate with the wider society. In our scene, this competition took the form of how best to account for Newfoundland violence in technical language, how to describe this social problem in "socspeak." Socspeak is a term of Mills.[57] *Without the aura of longer-established sciences, he explains, it is by owning a vocabulary of jargon that unnatural sciences hope to emblemise their products and their distinct identities, and maintain boundaries around each. Not readily intelligible to potential competitors or laymen, these languages then provide protagonists with skills to master and replicate as a hopeful source of prestige outside the discipline as well as justification within it. However, contest is not just between sister-disciplines. Look at these two exhortations:*

> *The layman is bewildered. Two world wars, the breakdown in political, public and private morality, the ever-increasing crime rate, the development of a culture and climate of violence, together with the consciousness of an apocalyptic realisation of irrever-*

> *sible disaster, are quandaries enough to cause men to look desperately about them for some sort of answer, for some sort of explanation of the meaning, of the causes which seem to be leading man to destruction.*
>
> *Have you ever been mugged, or do you know someone who has? (...) If you answered yes to any of these questions, then you perceive crime as a real threat to you. (...) While mankind has always been afflicted with crime and evil to a greater or lesser degree, it is since the crucial date of 1914 that Bible prophecies relating to the end of the world's corrupt system of things have come to remarkable fulfilment. (Compare Matthew 24, Luke 21, Mark 13, and Revelation 6:1-8). Therefore the time is near for God's righteous kingdom government to enter into action against His enemies on earth. (...) Yes, soon the earth will be cleansed of all criminal elements—whether religious, political, or social. God's cleansing war of Armageddon...*

The first vignette, above, is the construction of Ashley Montagu, introducing a book of social science, and the second is from The Jehovah Witnesses' magazine, Awake!.[58] *It seems academicians must also differentiate themselves from what they might demean as quackery. Hence they marry socspeak with 'the social problem.' As Blumer explains it, the latter need not be conceived of as a spontaneous expression of objective social conditions such as an intrinsic state of dysfunction in an otherwise equilibrated social structure, for the social problem only becomes a problem and becomes public through a process of definition and consensual legitimisation.*[59] *Such process, indeed, not only determines the existence and nature of these problems, but also their career and their ultimate fate; and it is through the process of creating a social problem that a discipline hopes to vindicate itself, its proponents and its language. It was part of the process of constructing the social problem in the 'academy' that I suggest we witnessed at Philippa's party; and the process entailed competition: specifically, a contest over the proper definition of violence in Newfoundland. For the discipline whose theory best dealt with the problem, whose technical language could be best wed to the phrase 'an increase in Newfoundland violence,' could then hope to disseminate a new 'scientific' account of the working of local society, and extend the corporate matrix of those who agreed upon the logic and objectivity of their method and the validity of their language. Having beaten contenders to an articulation with the great-*

er unwashed society, the discipline would gain credit and respect for an explanation of a solution to its problems.

Reviewing the scene, then, first of all we found anthropologist Lance Haines describing Newfoundland as the gem of Canada: a peaceful society of tame peasants and mummers. In the traditional outport of the ethnographic monograph he knew of norms of conflict-avoidance, deference, reciprocity and a ban on interpersonal violence. The only violence which did characterise the way of life was part of those rituals of catharsis which the drinking of alcohol signalled and rationalised. Any increase of violence in urban St. John's, then, Lance would merely trace to a lowering of perceptual thresholds on the one hand, and an increase in tensions causing more emotional stress in relations of friendship and family on the other. And these, he knows, still call for cultural explanations which may be achieved without the hifalutin' and estranging structures imposed by professional sociologists!

Meanwhile, sociologists Chuck Lewis and Sam Dyke agree that the sort of violence St. John's is witnessing is a new phenomenon: part of a 600 percent increase in crime since World War Two. From the more traditional, rural and family scenario of the anthropologists, then, there has been a take-off into the domain of urban sociology. For this is meaty data—violence perpetuated by nutters and strangers. This is the archetypal Durkheimian violence against society as a whole, and not just that in the context of more familiar relationships. So, St. John's could be becoming mayhem city, and locals are right to be scared. People's commonsensical notions merely have to be replaced by sociological theory and statistical data, and then real understanding can ensue. It can be explained how this increase in St. John's violence relates to downtown cores and ghettoes, to industrialisation and unemployment, to class relations of production and false consciousness, and so on.

Then again, historians Doyle Robbins and Philippa Howells agree that explanation is worthless without a long temporal perspective. For it can be seen that the Newfoundland of the twentieth century is equivalent to the Newfoundland of the eighteenth century, merely with a different style of reporting; and thus elements of Newfoundland as the slum of the Empire, such as local violence, adhere all along. It is all very well for sociologists and anthropologists to jump on the sensationalist bandwagon, as Foucault predicted, and start popularising a more violent present and anomic future for the sake of local jobs and grants, but in fact the anthropologist is nothing but a Newfie joke in reverse, while the sociologists with their mod-con statistics forget that this rock pre-

dates Confederation! It is social history which reveals, then, that the context of present day St. John's violence, even if marginally increasing, is still the prize-fighting and rioting of the 1930s, and so on ad initio, *with their echoes in radical Ireland. It is only short memories and wishful thinking which can obscure historical truths such as these.*

The picture which this scene provides us of the St. John's college of cultural connoisseurs is a rather compartmentalised one. Squashed together in the same room, discussing 'an increase in Newfoundland violence,' a diversity of linguistic emblems was brought forward on parade; a number of different socspeaks were in use. Furthermore through these different socspeaks, a series of different social problems were constructed, each possessing its own institutional and moral orderliness, each ready for study.[60] *For as they properly unfolded their discipline's schema of rules and abstractions, speakers fashioned violence in Newfoundland into the consistencies and universals of different paradigms. The varied vested interests and intentions of the various disciplines each made the violence part of a different verbal array, in wedding it to other phrasal objectivations which they owned. Each discipline spawned a different definition.*[61]

Moreover, each individual believed that his particular discipline wielded especial vitality, currency and relevancy in solving the problem and then disseminating and publishing the solution, and such belief was oppositionary and mutually exclusive. Hence, Chuck and Sam conceived of sociology's correctness in terms of anthropology's incorrectness, and a rather lonely Lance inferred the converse, and then Doyle and Philippa discredited them all in favour of history. As socspeak was interleaved with socspeak, phrases from one abutting against phrases from another in serial fashion, there was little meeting between different disciplines over the course of the discussion beyond a slinging of brickbats. In other words, an exchange of a general language of violence in Newfoundland in this scene did not so much lessen distance between the speakers as afford them a means of maintaining boundaries around distinct ways of speaking. Thus in the reproduction of one socspeak, Sam Dyke and Chuck Lewis communicated their camaraderie with each other, while through a second Doyle Robbins could further the initiation of his neophyte Philippa Howells, and in a third, Lance Haines could continue to practice his identifying of otherness. That is, those who agreed on linguistic domains could not only reaffirm their differences to others but also extend these to include 'an increase in Newfoundland violence.' The words were personalised: diversified in accordance with the formu-

lae of different socspeaks; and through their use disciplinary members were able to share more fully with their fellows.

In short, the opposition in this scene was constructive. By using contrasting socspeaks, boundaries were built around groups in which often a number of speakers could agree to meet. Through images of difference, and exaggeration of distance, from outsiders, a number of groups came to establish identities of their own and recognise personalisations of language which members all regarded as apt and proper; and the conversation amounted to a parading of emblems of those identities along group boundaries for reaffirmations of common belonging.[62] *Furthermore, while these shared socspeaks expressed commonality between group members, they also metacommunicated disjunction from others: at the same time an agreed-upon verbal usage gave structure to internal relations of solidarity and to external relations of antipathy; so that, as Bailey put it, the "vertical cleavages" dividing discipline from discipline were formalised and legitimated.*[63]

However, this is not the whole picture which the scene provides us, for there is meeting here as well as division. Via the social problem of violence in Newfoundland, all the speakers met in their desire for social science to articulate with a wider public. Like the violence of migration before, 'an increase in Newfoundland violence' served as a knot of communication, and the social problem became a focal point of discussion on which all converged; all could agree on the arena of debate, even if they disagreed on its probable course and outcome. Hence, we are left not with a number of separate conversations so much as a single one composed of a number of parts: here are a group of individuals involved in a local drama of interdependent oppositions; their behaviours are recognised by and predictable to alien opponents as well as friends — a predictability which makes their identities compatible with each other, and a symmetry which helps ensure the continued place of each in an ideal rivalry.[64]

In sum, the scene shows us a diversity of preferred verbal association. In the same setting, personalising their language in rather different ways, individual speakers habitually meet with some in agreement and with others in disagreement.

I have been arguing that in individuals' personalised use of language can be seen the playing of the vis-à-vis for the constructing of group identities as well as individual ones; and we find speakers meeting in talking-relationships which accrue from an alignment of an individual's verbal associations with some, and an opposition to others. Moreover, these alignments have appeared finely tuned. First, Laura and Rosemary achieved precise agreement on verbal proprieties, and then our academics met in a debate in which all sides recognised each other, recognised where they agreed and where they agreed to disagree, and co-ordinated their exchange of opinion. However, I say now that such habitual meetings need not be so smooth-running, and consensus between members of a group speaking together may be far more variable. That is, some verbal exchanges may evince more explicit knowledge by the individual protagonists of where they agree with each other and disagree with outsiders, than others. In some talking-relationships, an incompatibility of members' verbal usage, and dissent over debate, may be a regular part of the interactional routine.

Let me further illustrate this, (d), by a comparison of our scene in the Salon Paris nightclub with that in Tee Cee's lounge. You may recall that in the former (pp. 89-97), we found a meeting of old friends—Shirley Blanchard, the barmaid, and Garland Jefferd, a one-time regular—chatting about the good old days while the strippers did their act behind them, and in the latter (pp. 98-107), we found Drs. Mulrooney and Steenwijk, and Terry Wells, three university pals, somewhat removed from their usual haunts, having a chinwag whilst the area's locals got drunk around them. In these discussions, I say, we can identify a common way of personalising language, a shared way of speaking which characterises the individuals as fellow group members. However, in the use of their terms of group belonging individuals cannot always agree on the niceties of application. That is, having agreed on the proper ways of talking about members and opponents, speakers do not necessarily reach consensus on precisely how a debate about the delineation of their group ought to be conducted.

In both the Salon Paris and Tee Cee's we found talk liberally peppered by tales of violent contest and combat, by fights between drunks, women, sportsmen and strangers: violence as traditional, heroic and degenerative; violence as sport, jest and destruction. Everybody seemed to be recounting lives full of dramatic incident, full of the violent, the tragic and the macabre, in which moral judgements, if present, merely played the role of so many more details, affording the happenings further piquancy. In short, violence served as dramatic prop in the conversational exchange, as colourful backdrop, as costuming; and it was a verbal technique, a way of speaking, which everyone shared. Individu-

al speakers aligned themselves with each other and met in debate through a common use of episodes of violence as spicy tidbits with which to punctuate their gossip; thence to be carried to a more interested and receptive audience. In Park's words, we found individuals guided as if by a dramatic sense, writing themselves into "reel-life melodramas" with related machinations of character and plot.[65]

Moreover, having come together via this way of speaking, I say it was information about group belonging which these individuals sought to exchange. Talking about violence, and, indeed, primarily about a certain sort of violence, the violence of play, individuals conveyed messages to each other about the terms of their relationship, about the precise nature of their common meeting within it, and about others' places outside it.

Huizinga has described fighting and warring as play's most intense, energetic and palpable forms; it is their game-like qualities which he emphasises. Play, according to Huizanga, should be conceived of as a free sphere, differentiated from ordinary life; secluded in space and limited in time, it presents a regular interlude with its own disposition. However, he urged that play not be considered in isolation from everyday life, for indeed it should be seen as a creation and a making explicit of the order and belonging of the everyday.[66] *That is, those who agree to play together in similar fashion, absorbed by the same norms and secrets, he argued, can be seen as coming together and constituting a group; in league with each other and equally removed and opposed to those outside, who play—and fight—differently. For as with other forms, Huizinga saw in playful violence the construction of relationship between people. Thus, while voluntary and fun, playful violence might also be tense, serious and solemn, and encompass strict rules of propriety. Possessing a captivating, even intoxicating rhythm, playful violence becomes regular and a matter of tradition; and a magic circle develops differentiating those who fight for us, or alongside us, from those who fight against us, and also those who fight improperly or would spoil our recreation entirely.*

Borrowing from Huizinga, then, we might expect within the intricacies of recreational fighting, for example, to be able to identify a spectrum of group belonging, of sharing and similarity: from fellow group-members who know how to fight properly, to allies, enemies, cheats and spoilsports. (Spoilsports are those who abuse one's group and its rules by denying their existence, then; cheats pretend belonging only to prove treacherous; enemies might share one's rules but still oppose one's group; and allies assist one's group but from their own, outside it.) Indeed, in reviewing the scenes, I suggest it is such circles of belonging which individuals can be seen imposing through their tales of playful violence. However, while meeting in habitual, risqué debate, speakers in the two scenes are not always in equal agreement about which violence is proper and their own, and which is not.

In the Salon Paris first of all, we found Shirley and Garland remembering the community that downtown St. John's used to represent for them. In the good old days there were folks there who knew how to play, how to drink and fight properly. There was Garland fighting the enemy bouncers, and his friend Mort fighting enemies over bets and booze and women; and Shirley's husband fighting his enemies over games of darts, even getting his hand broken over her in the Park Tavern, so that she almost became hysterical herself and joined in. And it all reminds Shirley of the good old community she knew on the Northern Peninsula, which Garland can also appreciate: fighting families of fierce fishermen living by their own rules. There were the spoilsports even there of course, the Mounties and the nagging women like Cousin Sharon, and there were the cheats such as the cowardly foulmouthers. However, generally there existed a bar life where you saw people in their true light—friends and allies like Cousin Jim and the enemies they fought and drank against such as the Saunders brothers. People knew how to behave then.

But now things are different. There are rich spoilsports overrunning Port au Fleur, all chasing status symbols and cheating with lies. Meanwhile, in St. John's, Shirley and Garland agree, bar life has been ruined. Spoilsport students destroy the furniture and stop beer bashes; cheating bands thieve and laze about; and cheating managers drink away profits and then burn their buildings for insurance. And the downtown is worst. It is full of pussies who do not know how to fight properly, and even bouncers who do not know how to behave. Everything has been cleaned up, the bars made into a kind of boring strip, with cheats and spoilsports—misfits, scuzzes, gays, thieves, transvestites from Toronto and the rest—filling the place up.

Shirley feels like leaving St. John's altogether. But going north to Labrador, she agrees with Garland, would not help: the spoilsport natives there who booze and fornicate to excess should have been shot at the start. And England, where Garland reports allies who still fight like in the good old days, is too far. So, there is Halifax; or perhaps seeking out the traditional places here, such as Brad's bar which Shirley's ally tells of good old rowdy fun, and fights against Irish and Indian enemies. And maybe even the Salon Paris will get lively again. After all, there was a friendly confusion here only recently—two big women in a recreational fight. Then again, they could pretend to be enemies for a moment, and Shirley could attack Garland with a bottle, and then make up afterwards over another drink. Help recreate the real times of yore, starting now...

Meanwhile, in Tee Cee's, Terry, Chesley and Jane's conversation contains rather more diverse ideas about St. John's and its downtown. Terry finds the latter composed of cheating, queue-barging drunks, and bikers who need booze to get the courage to go mad; and even then get beaten in fights. He feels there are no real fighting bars here at all, only spoilsports, too embarrassed and controlled to fight. The bars are bourgeois, student meatmarkets, or else full of cheating cops who go drinking together, while avoiding the rougher bars and going around pretending to be in TV mobster shows. None of them would survive in Terry's home in British Columbia. For there you find real bar fighting like his getting involved with bikers, bouncers, women and the Irish. It is real gang-warfare, even for the middle classes.

Chesley cannot agree. The hardnosed St. John's police and bar managers may be spoilsports, with all their restrictive laws about drinking ages and numbers and prices—as are the students who support them. But St. John's certainly has its traditional violent pastimes, which of course the spoilsports in the media also slander in their reporting. For example, at home in Norton's bar, Chesley finds those Newfoundland warriors, the Pride Purveyors in whose motorbike ranks one even sees Newfoundland RCMP officers. So, St. John's does possess its own way of fighting for fun, just like those allied efforts around the rest of the island: the sport of Yank-bashing in Argentia, and murder in Lourdes, and good old bar fights, especially if women, or townies or mainlanders are involved, in just about any outport. No mainland recreation need be imported.

Jane is not amused. She always thought all this macho *fighting was arranged for set times, and contained there. To find it spreading to the bars and the rest of the otherwise gentle Newfoundland social life is nothing to be proud about. It is bad enough the way men cheat and stare at women in bars, without also seeing the spoilsports take chains to each other in the streets, and then hearing of these Hell's Angels killing people and still finding the police helpless. At least men do not get up to their cheap games in the Hive bar, she is pleased to say.*

However, Terry corrects her. He and his friends do stand up for them-

selves at the Hive. They fight off drunks, for example. But Chesley would call that the staking out of territory in his home by enemies from the mainland and the nouveaux-riches. *So Terry corrects him too: the troublemaking, gate-crashing enemies are in fact Derek and Crystal from St. John's, more often than not, causing Terry's allies like Jock Fleming to beat them at their own brawling, or else defeat them in the courts. But Chesley counters: Derek and Crystal are* his *Newfoundland allies; just the sort who do quips and tricks and make violent gestures in public. And they are not the stupid spoilsports who violently destroy for the sake of it.*

Chesley and Terry are interrupted by Jane's criticism of hockey and boxing as disgusting, and ripe for stopping—played not by sportsmen but by spoilsports out for blood. The men disagree. For Terry you have your cheats like Philadelphia who fight through lack of skill and cheats who fight when the game is over, but violence is still a proper part of the game—a game allies like his brothers really enjoy. It is those in wrestling who are the spoilsports. And for Chesley, hockey is part of a Newfoundland tradition. The fine spectacle of battles at the stadium takes him back to his schooldays, and fighting the enemy Protestants. It is the rugby players of today who are the cheats, and the football supporters who are the spoilsports.

In the end, however, it is time to leave for the Hive. At least all agree that it should be more friendly and fun there than here…

Orwell once characterised the fascination and drama caused by nine killings which occurred between 1850 and 1925 as the "great Elizabethan period of English murder." For here were events so providential or coincidental that no novelist would have dared make them up; and here was to be perceived an English society full of happening and complication, and lives to be gossiped about full of memorable transcendence and surprise.[67] Our gossipers, I feel, are the same: in tales of fighting they testify to the complex drama of their own lives and those of others; and in the drama of violence at play they reflect upon community, about those who share one's definition of proper behaviour and the rules of its description, and those who do not.

Gossip may often be looked to for dramas of group belonging, according to John Berger. Continuously worked on by comment, frill and critiqué, gossip amounts to a living portrait in which speakers express and maintain their related identities, and portray the occasions on which the group meets and functions.[68] Through the intense spectacle which incidents of violence afford to the voyeur, then, and the sense of racy *drama it lends the raconteur, messages of membership in these unfolding group portraits are at once intensified, made more memorable and pregnant with significance.*

However, while all speakers were seen discussing St. John's—who they felt affinity for, and to what they were adverse—in terms of playful violence, and drinking in the city's bars when thus habitually engaged, there were still differing amounts of agreement about how precisely the city was to be described, its people and events evaluated. Thus Shirley and Garland could agree far more than could Chesley, Terry and Jane about what recreational fighting and drinking properly entailed, and who were fellow-members' allies and who were enemies, spoilsports and cheats. Chesley, Terry and Jane could be said to have switched back and forth from an agreed-upon verbal usage where their associations with 'violence' were habitual and compatible to flights of idiosyncrasy where they were not. In Paine's terms, they jumped in and out of verbal agreement, speaking in the sameness of the group in one instance, but then maybe not in the next; and pursuing more and less shared identities at the same time.[69]

Thus while sharing a way of personalising language, in this case a way of portraying 'us and them' through an idiom of playful violence, the two scenes show us groups of speakers reaching variable agreement on how this language is to be always applied, and the group boundary and proper practice of its members precisely defined. Groups of individual speakers who share ways of using language may still, it seems, be constituted of differing degrees of closeness, differing amounts of verbal commonality.

I have argued that it is through an aligning of their verbal preferences, a making compatible of their personalisation of language, that individual speakers can be seen meeting each other in conversation and coming together in habitual talking-relationships. By agreeing upon the verbal associations of 'violence,' for example, individuals may share certain meaningful conceptions of the world with some and oppose those of others. However, it has also become apparent that such verbal meetings may be of varying closeness; even in the act of alignment, agreement between talking-partners may waver, and they may maintain both a common identity and degrees of idiosyncracy at the same time—a fluid overlapping and diverging, as their intentions and priorities fluctuate. Thus, there may occur compatible personalisations of language and a convening of group ways of speaking in certain moments, and for certain purposes but then not in others. Now I want to say that such agreements between individual speakers on an alignment of their verbal practices are also situational; and as individuals engage in their daily routines, so they move from one agreement on verbal usage, one group of talking-partners to another. Each, moreover, may be characterised by a different personalisation of language, each possessing its own set of verbal practices. Hence, as individuals move from setting to setting around the city, so they may engage in different verbal association, construct different meanings and enact different identities.

As illustration, (e), I shall compare the two scenes in which we met Judge Hector Hussey. One, you will recall, found the judge delivering a criminology lecture on the notion of punishment to a class of students at the university (pp. 39-47), and a second found him meting out justice to shoplifters and armed robbers from his bench at an afternoon session of Provincial Court (pp. 48-62). In particular, I shall compare the ways Judge Hussey spoke of 'violence' and 'the system of law' in the two scenes. In each case the judge may be said to be addressing the problem of criminal activity in St. John's, but as he moves from one setting to the next, so his use of these terms differs. Associating them with different words in the two contexts, he constructs different images of violence in St. John's and different systems of law standing guard.

Reviewing the scenes, then, in the university lecture-theatre we see Judge Hussey spelling out to his class the effectiveness of the system of law, in which he finds himself to be an important part and of which he has gained mastery, in the combating of violent offenders. And when the offender is violent and the public most shocked, then the law is most protective of the latter and most strict with the former. The law punishes.

It is primarily through Provincial Court that punishment is meted out, Hussey explains. It is Provincial Court which deals with most offenders and initiates any new patterns of putting the statutes of Criminal Law into practice. The so-called superior court judges are in fact inferior in effectiveness and knowledge when compared with, say, Judge Croft, or Judge Dindale, not to mention Judge Hussey himself and his host of dedicated younger cohorts.

It is in Provincial Court then that Judge Hussey is currently meeting perpetrators of all manner of violent crime — a spate of armed robberies, more break-and-enters, more violent assaults, even more 'child-napping.' And the system of law is responding and becoming less lenient, in line with a more conservative age. Hence, Judge Hussey has use of an arsenal of means by which to curb the felon's activities in the future. For the more violent and dangerous offenders there are prisons and long to indefinite sentences; and the future may see a return to corporal and capital punishment too. For the less dangerous offenders there are still fines and probations and work camps.

This scene, then, shows a commanding portrayal by Judge Hussey of an orderly system of law before a receptive class. Class members respond as diligent pupils: course-manuals and note-pads mostly at the ready, laughter, tuts and comment on cue. And Hussey leads them through his idiosyncratic exposition, replete with jokes about precognition, District Court, women-drivers, loony Moroccans, lesbians, coin-tossing and dart-throwing and so on. In 'the system of law,' Hussey lectures his students, he implements a powerful means of guarding the public against the 'violence' of the offender.

Next, we found Judge Hussey taking part in the ritual of the court-room. The system of law here is something which involves the orderly meshing of specific players' roles; and it is Hussey who ensures the smooth-running, even when some participating individuals are newer to the game than others.

In this scene, then, the court-room is where the system of law takes place. The corridor, the foyer, the ante-rooms, all channel people towards Hussey's bench and his convening of afternoon session. The clerk gathers witnesses, the constables lead in the accused, the newspaper reporter, Salvationist and stenographer prepare to take notes. Then, when all is ready, Hussey is announced, his audience stands and bows, and his session begins. The tape-recorder runs, Hussey orchestrates counsel, witnesses and accused. He has pleas elected, oaths sworn, cross examinations and summations made, cases withdrawn, past cases cited, sentences suggested. Then, Hussey differentiates allegation from fact and pronounces from the bench. Cases are dismissed, convictions registered and sentences conferred.

The system of law entails the regular unfolding of the above ritual. Robbery-with-violence, assault-with-violence, break-and-enter, shoplifting charges are processed alike, and innocence maintained until guilt proven. The system is not to be debased. Thus, for example, a case of armed robbery once dealt with is closed, and to suggest a reversal would be to suggest an inefficacy in the law, and to insult the system.

Hussey's central role in this procedure is to ensure the system of law suffers no infringements, that no violence is done to it. It is to ensure that violent offenders are properly processed, and that decorum is maintained. Thus disrespectful laughter from the benches, and other commotion signifying the potential holding of another court in opposition to his bench, are immediately squashed. And those who refuse legal aid, chew gum in blasé ignorance, then attempt to make a mockery of pleading and sentencing are punished by banishment from the room. And those who perjure themselves in the witness box, casually lie and then attempt to reconvene court and their part in its proceedings in outside offices, in contempt of the proper course of the law, are punished by being brought to the bar at a later date themselves.

Hussey's 'system of law' in this scene, then, is the passing of offenders, 'violent' and others, before his bench. Often his enactment of this juridical procedure is punishment enough, and his performance of the law, his pronouncements from the bench, are an heuristic apparatus in themselves. Delivered with panaché, with Pepsi cups and japes about death, Mother Goose and last dollars, Hussey's exposition helps the public to learn clear-thinking ('to take' is not 'to steal'), women to learn more sensible shopping habits, and offenders to learn respect for and fear of legal procedure.

In sum, I say the two scenes provide us with a view of Judge Hussey living in two rather different contexts of verbal performance; an image of two different ways in which the judge and his talking-partners habitually align their personalisation of language. Thus we find 'violence' as illegitimate behaviour which must be punished by strict sentencing and a jail term, to 'violence' as a type of legal charge which can be corrected, negated, punished by the due process of an official court of law. Aggregated with different words and behaviours in each scene, terms like 'violence' and 'the system of law' come to inform different worlds of meaning. The difference represents two ways of exchanging words in conversation agreed upon by members of two talking-relationships to both of which Judge Hussey belongs.

However, the differences need not be overstated; there are resemblances between the meanings which the judge imparts to his words in the two scenes as well: his decisions on verbal usage are not wholly dissimilar. Borrowing from Wittgenstein, I say that we can see 'family resemblances': meanings relatable to one another in a number of overlapping and criss-crossing ways, like the features which characterise members of the same biological family.[70] *Thus there are a number of sorts of similarity between the ways in which the words 'violence' and 'the system of law' are associated in use. In both settings, then, the judge constructs an image of himself as mediating between the violent offender and the wider public, and in both his operating of the system of law effectively deals with violent crime. Moreover, in his dealings with both groups of people, Hussey conceives of the elucidation of the system of law as a pedagogic exercise. The public has an opportunity for education; and in his acts of exposition of the system, a chance for the offering of congregational responses: the public may act as Hussey's co-celebrants. Lastly, besides his familiarity with the system of law, fellow community members are also afforded the opportunity of witnessing and enjoying Hussey's personal wit and wider opinions.*

While agreement between speakers on the proprieties of verbal usage may be situational, then, it seems that individuals may be found in possession of a family of meanings, each pertinent to the enactment of a different interactional routine. As they move from setting to setting, so individuals will be seen selecting from this store and aligning themselves with partners in a number of different talking-relationships, for the maintenance of a number of different group identities.

I have been using the terms *talking-relationship* and *talking-partner* rather freely, without precisely explaining all that I mean them to imply. By talking-relationship, I mean an agreement on how words are to be associated and exchanged in interaction, their proper order and progression, and on the aptness of behaviours with which they are interleaved; and talking-partners are those who habitually come together to engage in this verbal exchange. I mean then to distance myself from the notion that it is from a lexicon that one can understand the order which words instil, and replace it by the idea that it is to their regular contexts of performance that words belong, and in which they achieve significance and legitimacy; and I have argued that the scenes recounted above encompass just such currently routine interaction between individual speakers. To return to my earlier example, children playing "Ring-a-ring o' roses" together may reveal a broad cultural background but nothing of the specific relations which the words inform: nothing of the meanings attached to the words when individual children exchange them at particular times and in particular places, of their import in particular worldviews. It is such particularity of verbal sharing that I want to acknowledge by my concept of talking-relationship. Turner writes how it is symbolic usage which creates society and calls community, calls groups, into being and doing;[71] and the most important aspect of symbolic usage is verbal: it is language which is instrumental in creating and maintaining the social world. Talking-relationships encompass the way language comes alive in individuals' personal use of it and in the alignment of the latter between particular partners in conversation. I shall call talking-relationships the building blocks of society.

Let me draw some parallels with the Wittgensteinian concept of language-game.[72] I do not mean to take the concept on board but it is useful as elucidation. An examination of social interaction reveals, Wittgenstein argued, a miscellany of what may be called "forms of life." This is, notions of truth and property, laws of inference, logic and rationality, ideas of value and sense, may be found to be of a prodigious diversity in a society. Each set of such notions, Wittgenstein continued, may be seen accompanied by its own way of speaking and behaving, its own way of using language and giving it definition and meaning. Moreover, each set of notions, each form of life may be seen to be enacted by its own group of protagonists who find it apt and appropriate to participate in exchange with each other in public. Such an exchange Wittgenstein called a language-game: the enactment of a particular, self-contained form of life; an intricate interweaving of words and actions performed by a particular group of people. Different language-games may seem superficially alike, words from one overlapping with words from another, but really this is a matter of linguistic clothing disguising the fact that the words belong to different contexts of performance, different groups of performers, different circumstances of verbal and non-verbal exchange, each representing a different world of meaning. Indeed, as with other games (football, tiddlywinks) different language-games in use at any one time, while thus superficially related, may have no common denominator. That is, between all the diverse ways that language is used in different forms of life, between all the different meanings which it expresses, there may be no common essence, or consistency, or particular closeness. Indeed, with new forms of life being created and new situations of verbal performance, there need be no fixity or common closure of the varieties of linguistic usage either. Through language-game, then, Wittgenstein firmly weds the nature of linguistic usage to particular circumstances of exchange.

The concept is a blurred one, Wittgenstein admits, but what is blurred and open to a number of interpretations may sometimes be more useful than what is not. What I take from it is an emphasis on a diversity of concrete languages in any one cultural setting, each containing its own marriage of words and behaviour, each representing a different system of information, and circle of communication. Rather than an abstract notion of a standard idiom, then, what may be said to be routinised are certain combinations of words and behaviours in particular situations of use: specific meetings of individuals in exchanges which are taken for granted as habitual and accepted as legitimate and proper. It is in these acts of speaking that people may be said to then live.[73]

What should also be emphasised is Wittgenstein's insistence on linguistic usage as public: language-games are communicative events, entailing the exchange of publicly verifiable tokens of meaning. For Wittgenstein, this means a dismissal of notions of linguistic privatisation; but I would disagree. I agree that individuals' definition of meaningful landscapes of people and events, norms and values, and their determination of courses of action, do not take place in a vacuum, but rather in a setting populated by other individuals making comparable self-indications. I agree that the cognitive process of constructing and maintaining individual selves occurs in conjunction with an interpreting of location within social space, and entails a polemical internal conversation between the individual's information on himself and that on the more and less significant others which he construes around him.[74] Moreover, all this takes place in public interaction through a formally shared language of verbal symbols, a fund of more or less commonly named objects. However, in *talking-relationships* I would like to allow for more diversity of internal perspective, and more levels of privacy than Wittgenstein entertains in language-games. I want to allow room for a variety of agreements on meaning, truth and logic within the same agreed-upon verbal exchange.

In reviewing our university friends discussing playful violence in Tee Cee's neighbourhood bar, we found agreements between individual talking-partners of variable closeness. Individuals did not always agree on how violence should be spoken about, switching back and forth from ways of speaking that were shared to those that were not. We could say that not all the individual players participate in these talking-relationships— live in these acts of discourse—on quite the same terms. In the last scenes with Judge Hussey, too, not all the partners were equally enamoured of the performances. Moreover, some occupied more central, organisational roles than others, some were newer participants, some more temporary, and so on. Putting this another way, I say that words in use should not only be seen as the habitual tokens of talking-partners' exchange, regularly associated with other words and behaviours in the context of specific talking-relationships, but at the same time should be recognised as part of families of meanings of individuals who journey between talking-relationships, from partner to partner around St. John's. For like Judge Hussey, individuals will own a family of meanings surrounding the words they use in different contexts; and, indeed, the families of no two individuals need precisely coincide. That is, each individual may possess a unique set of meanings, of personal remembrances and nets of association, and bring to one context of usage unique knowledge of others—other talking-relationships, other verbal associations, other regularly used meanings.

Moreover, this individual diversity need not be regarded as irrelevant, as negated by the routine flow of any one particular exchange. Rather, I suggest talking-relationships be conceived of in terms of partial acts of sharing; a partial coincidence of verbal association, of the expression of meanings, truths and intentions. For talking-relationships encompass verbal agreements on one level, but need not negate simultaneous misinterpretations on others. At the same time as certain talking-partners are meeting through verbal exchanges, one should imagine dimensions of meaning from other contexts of usage which are not here shared; which in terms of current agreements are private residues, private thesauri. Thus it becomes pertinent in talking-relationships to look for agreements within agreements, to expect areas of collective exchange to reveal meetings between some players only; within ways of talking that all share may be found levels of privacy of meaning through word-associations and evocations which all in fact do not share.[75] To understand a talking-relationship in all its complexity then is to know not only how words are contextualised, associated with each other, in this setting, but also to enquire about the meanings from other contexts of use which participants bring with them as cognitive luggage. For the habitual playing out of verbal exchange need not constrain talking-partners to just making one and the same cognitive journey whilst thus engaged: their shared road may be the conjunction of any number of more private ones.

In one sense, then, as talking-partners meet, they may be boasting, guarding, juggling, fulfilling and modifying very diverse expectations, constructing and ordering idiosyncratic worlds, and to this extent, interaction cannot become a matter of singular identification, of monolithic description. However, in another sense, partners are constrained by their verbal agreements, and talking-relationships do possess singularity. For they are regular and habitual, and they contain rules of right and proper exchange by which participants must play if they are to avoid risk of excommunication or of necessary renegotiation of the terms of the meeting. That is, an individual must continually achieve proportion by continuous excursion between his more private family of meanings and the publicly agreed way words are being used at a particular time, between his individual itinerary from talking-relationship to talking-relationship and the rules of the particular group is he performing in at the time; and 'only connect.'[76] He must be sure to select from his gamut of meanings-to-impart only those pertinent to the words in specific situations.

The diversity of perspective which I would introduce into talking-relationships, then, translates into a certain tension. For words exchanged are not only to be seen as shared counters but also as possible toothing stones of diversity and idiosyncrasy. Singularity of verbal form need not delimit meaning, and instead varying levels of meaning may become pertinent: there will be meanings which belong in common to all in the relationship and meanings which belong to individual partners' different 'families' as they move from relationship to relationship. Individuals' personal families of meaning then introduce an idea of the more private in the more shared. At the same time as relationships are convened and agreements expressed in terms of one set of meanings, one criterion of inclusion, there may be differentiation in terms of others; beneath the simple or superficial may be found the expansive or more involved, and the converse.

In arguing for the recognition of a prodigious diversity of language-games being used in a cultural setting at any one time, Wittgenstein also suggested a differentiation between more 'primitive' and more 'expanded' examples of such games.[77] A relatively primitive language-game, for example, may be that where a builder calls out the words 'block,' 'pillar,' 'slab,' 'beam,' and his mate responds by delivering the required items—builder and mate agreeing over the use of a primitive vocabulary, over routine names for objects, and an habitual interweaving of the expression of these with regular actions. But, we might also consider how the above could be expanded by adding more words and behaviours to the routine, such as numerals, or the pointing words 'this' and 'there'; and as it expands in this way, so we might say that the exchange becomes less primitive and more complex.

I shall use this notion of the primitive and the expanded in relation to single talking-relationships, in order to differentiate between a number of levels of agreement which, I suggest, may exist within them at the same time. That is, I want to say some talking-partners who meet in a relationship may only share in a simple agreement over a primitive association of words and interleaving of behaviours, while the terms of agreement of others may be more expanded, more complex. To return to Wittgenstein's example, then, at the same time as some meet in agreement over the relatively expanded verbal association: 'two pillars and this slab there, three blocks here,' others may agree only on the relatively primitive: 'three blocks.' Indeed one may expect the verbal practice of more speakers to be able to find alignment in the primitive, the simple form of expression, than the expanded: all may agree on the propriety of the catchphrase whereas the intricacies of more complex verbal usage may encompass commonality between the increasingly few; in the varying levels of verbal agreement within talking-relationships, we are identifying different kinds of communion between individuals in society.

Kluckhohn and Murray have written that "every man is in certain respects (a) like all other men, (b) like some other men, (c) like no other man." I want to say that this image of society as a sliding scale of similarity may be substantiated in terms of agreements over verbal usage: society as a spectrum of different kinds and amounts of common meanings.[78] I have been arguing that it is through an alignment of their personal verbal practices that individuals can be found meeting each other in talking-relationships, even though these meetings may still be situational and of variable closeness. I now suggest that it is of an aggregation of such talking-relationships that society be seen to be composed; talking-relationships nesting one within another, from the more expanded and idiosyncratic and private at the base rising to the more primitive and common and public at the top, as in Figure 1 on page 176.

Contained in this diagram is the idea that an examination of the common cultural tool of language in use reveals a spectrum of similarity about ways of speaking, so that individual speakers may be found meeting and diverging from each other regarding the properties of habitual verbal usage in a multitude of different fashions and on a number of different societal levels at the same time. Moreover, if a variety of meanings and a number of levels of agreement may be simultaneously identified in one set of words when exchanged by one group of talking-partners, then a sliding scale can be drawn by which one moves upwards from the meanings of a particular talking-relationship to meanings of broader currency, and downwards to meanings of increasing

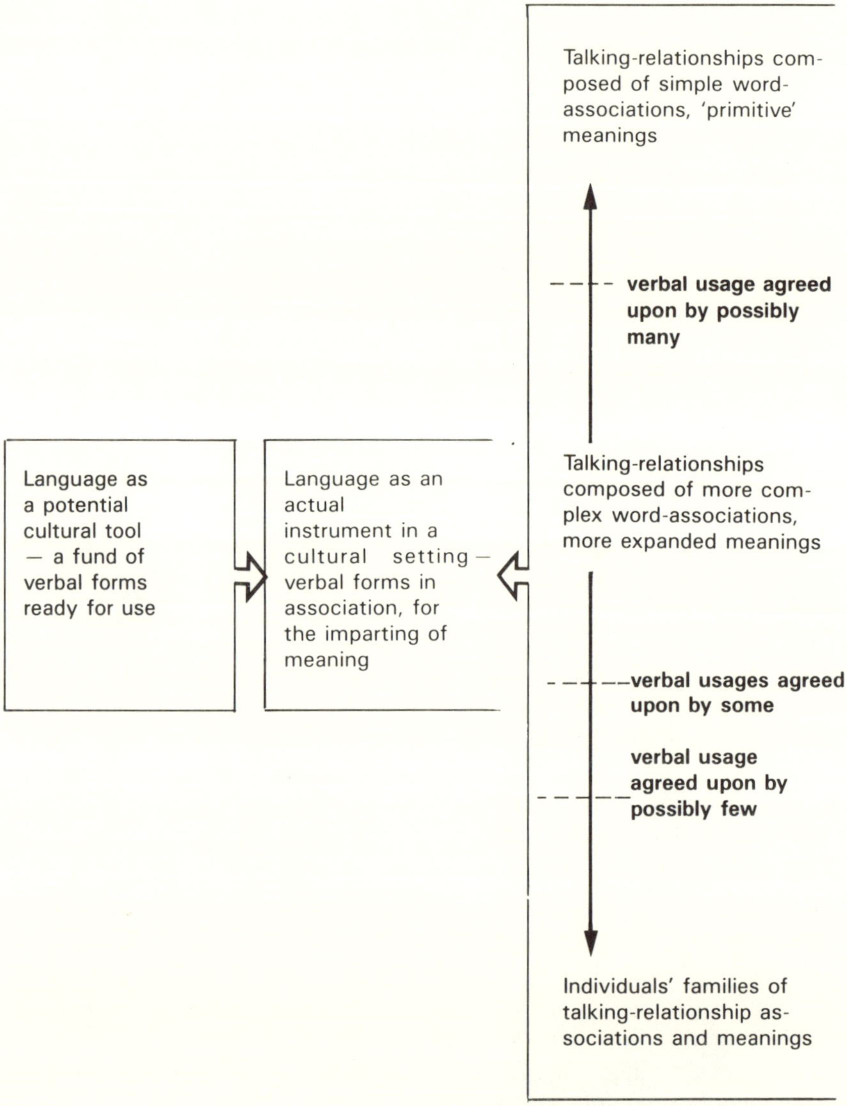

Figure 1
Language in use: society as a sliding-scale of more and less expanded verbal agreements.

privacy and individuality. That is, not only may one conceive of individuals meeting in talking-relationships, but also those talking-relationships meeting with others in more primitive verbal agreements; just as I argued our academics' different intra-disciplinary debates met each other in an agreement on how they would disagree in a public arena, and a broader ambit of comparison in which each was predictable to the other. Finally, in this way one may find very simple verbal associations in agreement over which all individuals in a cultural setting could be said to meet.

Let me further illustrate this, (b) by reviewing our two remaining scenes, that in Brady House Detoxification Centre, and that in Milligan's Irish pub. In the former (pp. 108-115), we heard an audience lectured about the abuse of drugs in St. John's, and in the latter (pp. 81-88) we found a young set enjoying an evening of drugs and drink in one of the city's downtown bars. Through an examination of the use of the word 'drugs' in these scenes, I shall argue that a number of different types and amounts of agreement over how the word ought properly to be aggregated with others in speech may be identified. These amount to a sliding scale of societal commonality; from the use of simple associations that all may be said to share, to the clustering of simple associations into longer and more complex ones that bespeak communion within narrow borders only: meanings imparted to 'drugs' which occupy a whole scale, from generality to increasing idiosyncracy and privacy.

First, of the scene in Brady House I want to say that relatively expanded talking-relationships proceed between the chatting elderly ladies Margo Halleran and Bridie O'Brien, and then between the House's director, Geoff Flynn, and his audience, and then between the RCMP narcotics officer, Corporal Duffy, and his audience. However, from these more complex acts of discourse may also be derived simpler ones from the common denomination of their separate associations of words and phrases; the above talking-relationships may also be said to meet in more primitive agreements over ways of speaking. That is, if Margo and Bridie agree on an arrangement of symbols B, C, X, N, F, and Geoff Flynn shares with his audience the aggregation A, C, X, N, J, and Corporal Duffy shares with his audience the aggregation B, C, X, N, R, then I would say the usage B, C, X, N, represents associations, meanings, that Margo and Bridie and Corporal Duffy and his audience possess in common, while in the use of C, X, N, all may be said to meet, Geoff Flynn and his audience included. In terms of overlapping verbal associations

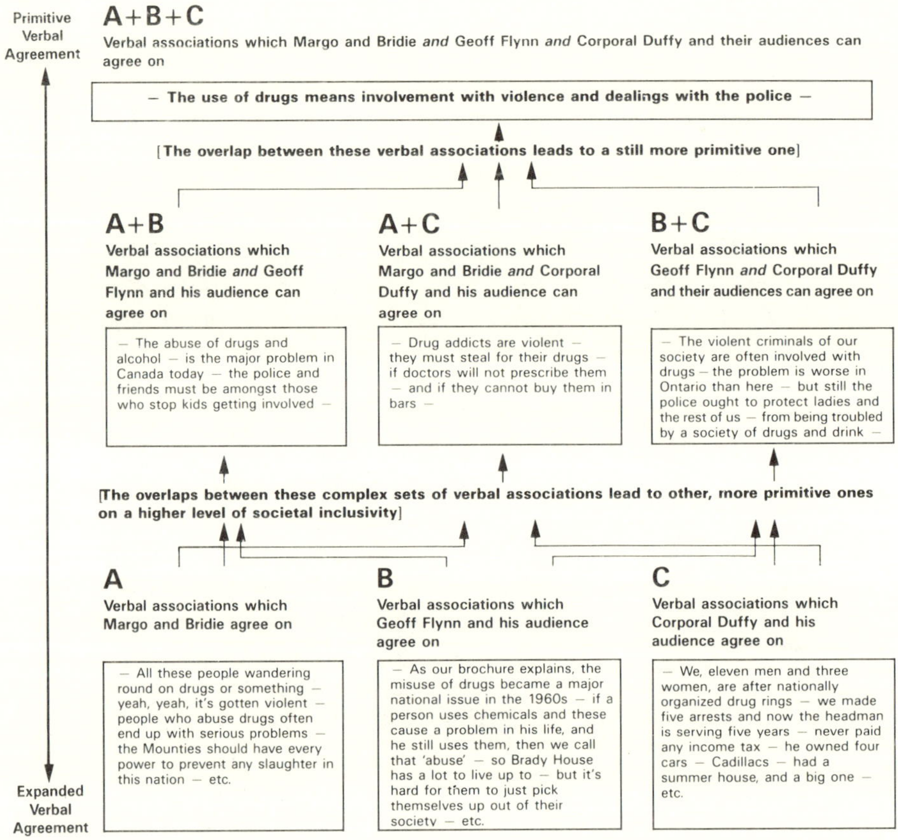

Figure 2
Meetings in Brady House: a sliding scale of verbal agreement

we may plot a scale from expanded exchanges between the few at one end, to primitive meanings on which all in the scene agree at the other. The bare bones of verbal agreement in Brady House, then, and its levels of furcating inclusivity, I would represent as in Figure 2.

I have described talking-relationships as routine alignments of meanings and identities which partners regard as legitimate; in their barest form they are agreements over the aptness of particular arrangements of words, and it is such word skeletons that I isolate in this diagram. Through the verbal structures of the different talking-relationships, I want to show how the more expanded may be said to overlap to afford the more primitive and to culminate in catchwords that include them all. Adding more detail, then, I say the scene begins with our watching the talking-relationship between Margo and Bridie. In this exchange, we hear a progression of phrases which includes the following:

—All those bars, and no shops, and all these people wandering round on drugs or something—

—Yeah, yeah. It's got violent—

—They may...get sick, have accidents, build up tolerance, get hooked, commit crimes, be arrested, become violent, go to jail, and lose friends—

—His brother was arrested for drugs— —And them with that big house and car—

—'Cause it's from them they get into drug-addicts —

—And if you don't give it them then they're likely to go steal it from you—

—The Mounties should have every power to prevent any slaughter in this nation—

—And I heard said they're the finest police force—

—I blame these doctors and psychologists for doing more harm than good—

Then the scene continues with a talking-relationship in which Geoff Flynn occupies a central role and soliloquises before his talking-partners. In this performance, he and his audience attend upon a sequence of phrases including the following:

—As our brochure explains, the misuse of drugs became a major national issue in the 1960s—

—If a person uses chemicals and these cause a problem in his life, and he still uses them, then we call that 'abuse.'

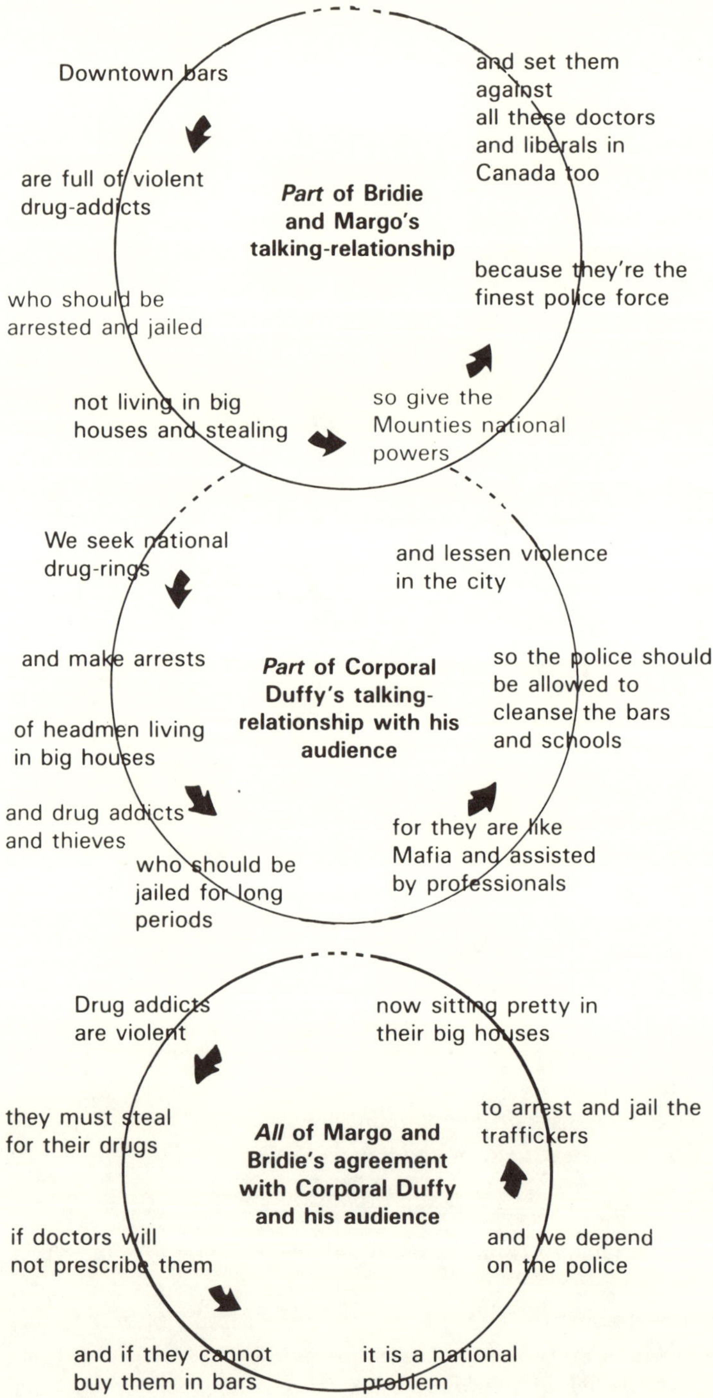

Figure 3
An overlap between the verbal agreements of Margo and Bridie and of Corporal Duffy and his audience affords another more inclusive and 'primitive' one.

—So Brady House has a lot to live up to—But it's hard for them to just pick themselves up out of their society
—And sometimes the police bring us inebriates
—Of course any violent or criminal offenders go to the lock-up—
—But remember, ladies, these horrors go on—

Finally the scene concludes with a talking-relationship between Corporal Duffy and his audience. They accompany him in the aggregation of such phrases as:
—We, eleven men and three women, are after nationally organised drug-rings
—We made five arrests and now the head-man is serving five years—
—Never paid any income tax, owned four cars—Cadillacs—had a summer house, and a big one—
—A muck-raker drug-addict, living the life of Reilly till we stopped him—
—Or his parents gave him $20 for jeans and he buys drugs, then steals the jeans—
—Scare tactics fail, so now we are hitting them with the legal angle: they can go to jail—for a long time—
—And there's bars and places you can guarantee it, day or night—
—But where would an eleven-year-old get $200, Sir?—
—We have an investigation ongoing now and they're already on the police system—
—Drugs mean more violence in the city—
—When doctors aren't smuggling it in themselves like old Dr. Wirnell down the southern shore—

Now I say that we can find overlaps in the ways words and phrases are arranged in the above, agreements by which one talking-relationship aligns itself with another and both meet in an area of commonality. These overlaps may only be partial, may represent merely primitive verbal agreements when compared to the above expanded forms but they still constitute another level of societal relationship between more people in the scene. Thus the overlap between Margo and Bridie's and Corporal Duffy and his audience's associations constitute an agreement over the propriety of the following aggregation of words and phrases:

—Drug addicts are violent—they must steal for their drugs—if doctors will not prescribe them—and if they cannot buy them in bars—it

is a national problem — and we depend on the police — to arrest and jail the traffickers now sitting pretty in their big houses —

In other words I suggest the above represents a phrasal common-denomination of the two talking-relationships; the two verbal agreements act as the building blocks of a third. Pictorally, with (opened) circles to represent the talking-relationships' self-contained and potentially repetitive circuit of verbal moves, I would portray the process as in Figure 3 on page 180.

Similarly, I suggest the talking-relationship between Margo and Bridie and that between Geoff Flynn and his audience may be said to meet in a more primitive agreement. It comprises the association of the following words:

— The abuse of drugs and alcohol — is the major problem in Canada today — the police and friends must be among those who stop kids getting involved —

Meanwhile, the talking-relationships between Geoff Flynn and his audience and Corporal Duffy and his are in agreement in terms of the following verbal usage:

— The violent criminals of our society are often involved with drugs — the problem is worse in Ontario than here — but still the police ought to protect ladies and the rest of us — from being troubled by a society of drugs and drink —

Finally, I suggest there is a catchphrase which represents a still higher level of inclusivity in the scene, an agreement constituted by the common denomination of all of the above talking-relationships. I would identify it thus:

— The use of drugs means involvement with violence and dealings with the police —

In this catchphrase all the verbal associations of all the groups of talking-partners in the scene may be said to meet.

A similar identification of relatively expanded talking- relationships and their meeting in primitive form at higher levels of societal inclusiv-

ity can be made for the scene in Milligan's Irish bar. Firstly, the scene is composed of the talking-relationship between Gord and the buddies at his table, Art and Paul, and then the one between the singer, Jerome Tirk, and his audience—his patter and their ripostés. Again I find overlaps between these two different sets of verbal associations, common denominations which represent an agreement in the preferred verbal usage of all these speakers, namely:

—Earning the bucks to buy grams of hash and then partying—by drinking beer in bars and playing videos—and smoking the drugs and getting stoned on tokes—is threatened by the police making busts—

Moreover, I suggest one can see an overlap between the above primitive aggregation and that which I said constituted an agreement between all the people speaking at Brady House. That is, one can identify the following catchphrase as the still more simple way of speaking in which all of the above talking-relationships, from both of our scenes, may be said to meet:

—The use of drugs means dealings with the St. John's police—

From individuals meeting in complex talking-relationships, then, I would build higher structures of increasing societal inclusivity, until finally a picture of verbal commonality between all the speakers in the above scenes may be drawn as in Figure 4 on page 184.

Between words used as signals and as personal speech, between the public and the private use of language, Auden would posit a dual phenomenology and imagine an absolute gulf (1986:15). Not absolute, I would argue, but spectral: between speech as primitive and as expanded; and not necessarily one thing or the other but an overlapping of the more public and the more private even within the same words.[79] *Thus, extrapolating from one level of talking-relationship to identify others of both greater and lesser commonality, I have plotted levels of agreement in verbal usage from complex associations characterising more private interaction, to primitive associations characterising what becomes increasingly public. For what I say these scenes illustrate is that a scale of societal inclusivity can be built up in terms of an interplay between a sameness and difference of verbal norms. Beginning with verbal relations between just a few individuals one can conclude with*

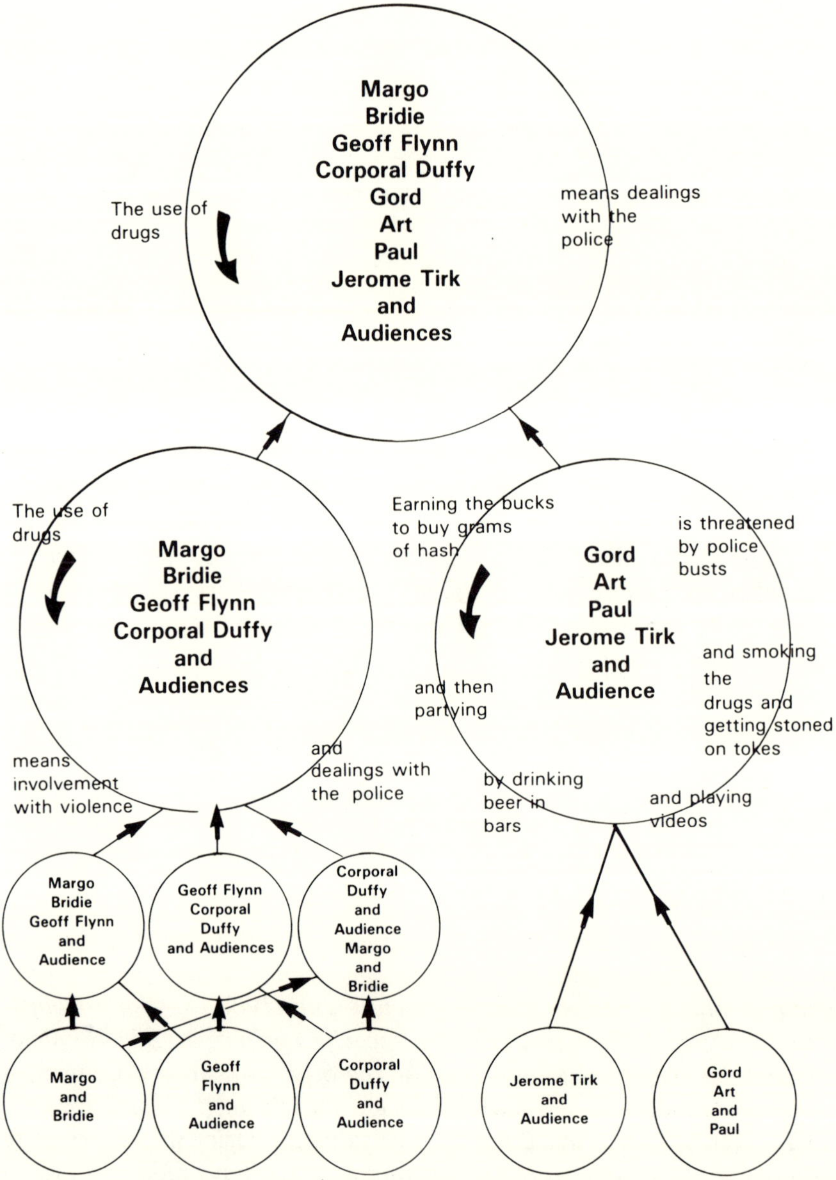

Figure 4
Levels of verbal commonality in Brady House and Milligan's Bar: a furcating structure of inclusivity.

an encompassment of more and more; until, finally, in simple catchphrases and clichés one finds nodes of communication to which otherwise very distant talking-relationships are connected—even if, as here, those catchphrases then become subject to very different if not opposite evaluation, and shibboleths of possibly contradictory intent.[80]

Much of social interaction is said to take place in terms of simple verbal exchange; "we conduct the ordinary business of life largely in terms of verbal cliché," Goodenough writes.[81] *However, I would now say that these formulaic and clichégenic occasions of primitive interaction ought to be seen as what Cranston called "incomplete pronouncements," and should not negate a recognition of more expansive verbal associations being cognitively active at the same time.*[82] *It is true that catchphrases—talking 'violence' or talking 'drugs,' for example—represent what Sapir refers to as "friendly ambiguities" in whose economy meetings of groups in society can predictably continue while their diversity is disguised, but one should also recognise larger worlds of meaning to which the ellipses of ordinary interaction allude.*[83] *Hence, while groups may meet upon the legitimate, common linguistic surface of simple phrases, they may at the same time diverge in terms of more expanded associations to which each would have their shared one relate, but which need not become apparent. To paraphrase Devereux, then, when two people say the same thing, it is not necessarily the same thing: every verbal agreement may also contain disagreement, every communication misconstrual, and thus every coming together by individuals in conversation also represent a parting of ways.*

Adapting MacIver, I assert that it is the aggregation of the countless actual doings and sayings of individuals which determine the course of social life.[84] Indeed, in my bias what individuals say is at the same time their most significant doing, and hence it is a description-analysis of their personal use of words which I have been presenting in this book. I have been examining people 'talking violence' around St. John's in habitual verbal performances which I likened to current pop 'hits' ('talking love').

However, the study has been a synchronic one: verbal constructions in St. John's from one time, and as if fixed. Yet linguistic usage is not so permanent. In Wittgenstein's metaphor, an ancient city is always subject to new building projects, while older constructions fall into desuetude and decay without the affirmation of continuous renovation.[85] (Alternatively: until possibly revived as 'golden oldies,' the cur-

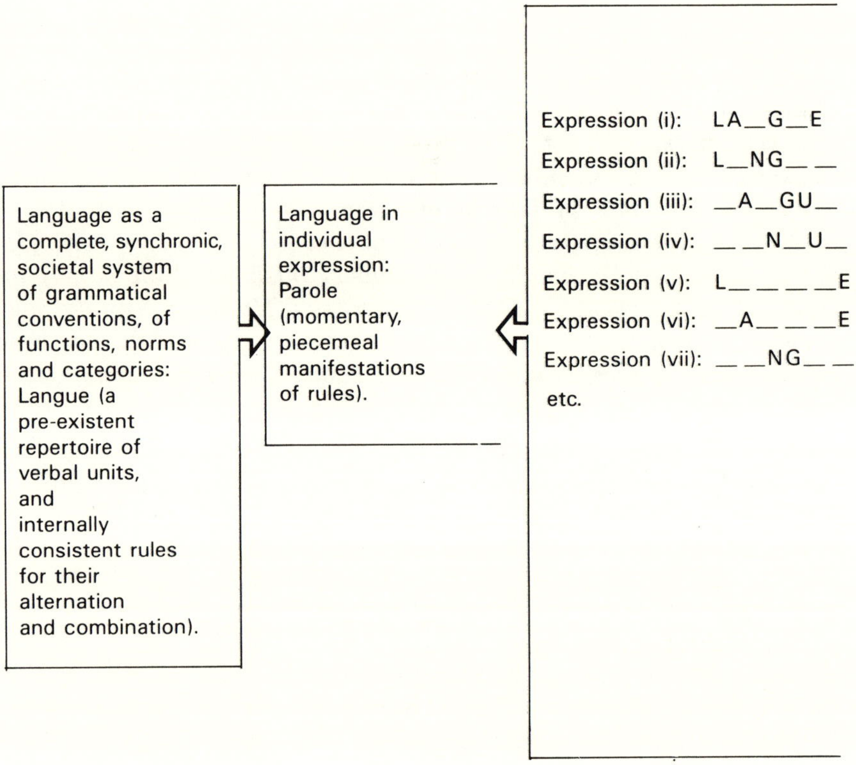

Figure 5
Language use as a manifestation of grammatical structure: individual speakers reproducing a societal system.

rency of particular pop songs is shortlived). For what does remain constant, as Harris emphasises, is the act of linguistic improvisation, the constant adapting, juggling, and amending of usage, modifying past verbal practice to suit new requirements, creating different meanings and negotiating new agreements with different talking-partners;[86] so, while words may be put to only particular uses at particular times, this may be said to represent a descriptive limit to their meanings, but not an essential one.

What may also be claimed as more constant in the diachrony of linguistic usage is vocabulary. As partners' agreed ways of talking come and go, a fund of words remains, and it is common to look to such constancy as a source of social structure and a mapping of rules and categories onto episodic expression. It is common, that is, to treat language in the abstract as a normative institution, which, in concert with other social facts such as notions of ritual and role, play and place, generation, occupation and ethnicity functions to impose a singular, morally authoritative grammar upon its users. In Saussurian terms, such a treatment might be represented as in Figure 5.

Here it is linguistic form which determines meaning and abstract denotation which is the source and guarantor of connotation, and, hence, actual verbal usage is treated as an epiphenomenon which is made possible only by compliance (however artful) with a pre-existent grammar that is assimilated and ever fragmentally reproduced. At its most vulgar, such a conception would eschew the inconstancies of episodic expression as ephemera: individual speech as a mere mouthpiece of societal objectivation and collective convention.[87]

This, of course, has not been my choice of paradigms: it does not correspond to my experiences of social interaction. Indeed, I have explained how a view of social life which emphasises the collectively *a priori,* uniform, systemic, unequivocal, orderly, dominative, denotative and circumscribed, over the relative and contextual, the heterogeneous, inventive and indeterminate, I find unhelpful and obnoxious. Hence, while it has not been within the scope of this book to explore linguistic diachrony, how language is learnt or how particular talking-relationships are initiated or sloughed off, it has not been a disinterring of archetypal, determining structures of society which I have sought either. My practice, instead, has been to emphasise what Leach calls the poetic operations of mind: imaginativeness and creativeness not trammelled by fixed or logical rules.[88] I have been less interested in individuals becoming patients or peers, academics or therapists, judges or drinkers, 'druggies' or prohibitionists, than in how these identities come alive in individuals' everyday expression and inter-individual exchange. Thus I began by arguing that rather than being imprisoned by the cultural institution of place, the latter becomes a resource, providing individuals with what Cohen describes as "the capacity to make sense."[89] Interpreting institutions within the contexts of their everyday lives, users personalise them. So that in the collective form may be found the construction of rather singular self-indications, and the fulfilment of idiosyncratic expectations. In the placeness of totalising institutions then, for example, individuals find a means of locating themselves at the centre of variously constructed safe space, and keeping violence distant.

I have treated culture as a potentiality, then; like a box of tools ready for use in the spinning of webs of significance, the making of meaning. It represents an abstract commonality, a pristine sharing. For example, in the tool of language there is the potential afforded each of its speakers to say the same things in precisely the same way, to use words as identical vehicles of meaning. For, as meaning, after Saussure, may be said to derive from the location of words in arrangement with others (an epiphenomenon of relations of contrast and similarity between associated words),[90] then from a circumscribed fund of words such as language provides, there is the potential in broad commonalities of association for broad sharing of meaning. However, I argued that in actual usage arrangements of words which individuals regard as normative are numerous, and not necessarily mutually relatable. Universality is not realised, and what must instead be emphasised is the versatility of language and its malleability. Linguistic forms are ambiguous and imprecise, and it is this which predisposes them to continued effectiveness in all manner of diverse and arbitrary usage.[91] Language may present a constant surface of collective vocabulary and conventional grammar but its content in use remains irreducibly manifold. As Steiner puts it, linguistic roots lie in the uniqueness of the "association nets" of individual speakers' minds. For behind all usage lies a concurrent flow of articulate consciousness: all comprehension entails an activating interpretation, the assimilation of words to prior stocks of meaning, and all expression is *poiesis,* the creative articulation of public signs with private sense.[92] Thus we saw how the shared language of a generation of peers is given very different meaning in different situations, and becomes part of possibly incompatible interpretations of self. In fact, even in the same situation, an academic discussion on an increase in Newfoundland violence could result in a number of mutually exclusive evaluations of verbal propriety and a number of meanings, each championing the personal expectations and identities of different speakers.

Nevertheless, in this diversity of personalisation, individuals can still be found meeting each other in talking-relationships. We saw how these were based on agreements between speakers on the proprieties of verbal usage and disagreement with that of others. Through their use of language, individuals align themselves with some and oppose others. So a discussion of the social problem of violence in Newfoundland served to maintain groups of talking-partners in predictable and routine opposition, and reaffirm their identities as comparable but distinct.

However, agreements between individuals over the proper arrangements of words in conversational exchange, over habitual meanings, may also be found to be of variable closeness, we saw next. Individuals may jump back and forth between ways of speaking they are sharing with others and ways that characterise different opinions and more idiosyncratic perspectives. Thus a discussion on Newfoundland's playful violence produced groups of differential sharing, and we found speakers switching in and out of agreement on how their partners should linguistically conduct themselves. Speakers did not necessarily uniformly agree on how the idioms of violent play-fighting should be applied, and hence how precisely the identity of their group was to be defined. Indeed, whatever the agreements which do exist on group practice, they are also situational, with individuals moving from one to another, associating words differently in each case. Thus we saw how an individual may possess a number of meanings for a word like 'violence,' a family of meanings without any generalisable norm or single common denomination to which the set may be reduced, his usage dependent upon which talking-relationship was being enacted. As Bourdieu suggested, then, we might describe individual perception as amounting to a series of profiles, of partial views, each representing a different apprehension of his social life, and between which the individual constantly moves; even if the aggregation of these profiles results more in discordant variety, a cubistic whole, than any neat coherence.[93] Moreover, as individuals make their own particular journeys between talking-relationships, so the set of profiles they carry with them may be identically shared by no one else.

Finally, we saw how individuals' conversational meetings may take place on a number of levels at the same time; in the same talking-relationship, words may be part of a number of different sets of association, and while some meanings may be common to all partners, some may derive from more private perspectives—concurrent talking-relationships that not all share. Thus, in discussions about 'drugs' we found various layers of verbal sameness and difference, and individuals met with different others in primitive and expanded agreements simultaneously. While much of social interaction may be said to take place on the level of primitive catchphrases between often distant speakers, then, we need not regard this as an impoverishment of individual creativity and its replacement by an institutionalisation of meaning, or as a dearth of meaning and its supersedure by societal function and role-bound functionaries.[94] For the appropriate formula of shared exchange on one level may be a vehicle of animation by increasingly idiosyncratic moods and identities on others. The common shorthand of everyday interaction ought at the same time to be seen as a building block in the construction of privatisation, and the differentiation and individualisation of experience. Even the cliché, used in a sliding-scale of more and more complex interpretations, can ultimately lead to the substantiation of uniquely defined objects, events and emotions. As Shelley put it, "a single word even may be a spark of inextinguishable thought;" may direct us to families of meaning in which individuals can cognitively journey as if forever.[95]

In this book, through 'talking violence,' I have wanted to explore a notion of modern, urban society as constituted by an interplay of relations of verbal sameness and difference. My arugment has been that an examination of conversation reveals the custom of individuals meeting through the habitual alignment of their preferences of verbal association. However, these meetings, to which I have given the name talking-relationships, also entail opposition: verbal agreement with some being inextricably linked to disagreement with others. It is from such diversity of verbal usage that I derive a picture of societal belonging as composed of an aggregation of shifting talking-relationships, situational, of variable closeness, and operational on a variety of levels of societal inclusivity at the same time.

Afterword

Doing Violence

In this book I have explored 'talking violence' around St. John's, and explained how, for me, talking is a most significant form of doing. However, some, even if they have read this far, may regard this as a feint, and still be courting a delineation of relations between talking violence and doing it. Of course, the aetiology of doing violence has already spawned books enough to swamp several libraries, and I cannot attempt anything of an answer here; nevertheless, a suggestion of how I think the topic should be approached might be in order.

To begin, then, violence—like all behaviour—must be seen in its social context. Violence *cannot* be regarded as a *Ding an Sich,* a thing-in-itself—an ideal type of act, a broadly defined social condition, a meaningful sociological category of behaviour which is directly investigable; nor can violence be defined outright as abnormal or pathological. For this merely leads to vulgar generalisation, and the perpetration, as Bernard Crick put it, of "bastard military sociology."[96] Violence must be seen as engendered by social interaction, and defined in terms of all the complexities of particular situations. For example, a study I find insightful is the account provided by Laurie Taylor of his descent into the underworld of the professional London criminal. Learning the 'theme-tunes' of this culture, he could explain the displays of cold-blooded butchery which he found as that which routinely overtook those who had taken liberties with a shared code of honour, and needed to be reminded of proper respect.[97]

Taylor also told us that there was a phrase regularly used in connection with the dishonourable: they were "out of order." Parodying as it does the circumscribed world of schoolboy debate, Taylor found it an odd understatement, a feeling exacerbated by the custom of treating the category as just another which people fell into, and bleached of all moral colouring; but whether used as the final phrase of condemnation prior to the butchery, or as part of the bloodthirsty tales bandied about afterwards, the words and the act were always in accompaniment.[98] A second important point of approach, then, is that the social context of violence contains gesture both physical and verbal. The item of study must include the whole gamut of behaviours, and analysis must be made of their endemic interrelations. Hence, I do not find convincing those who seek to explain societal equilibria in terms of ontological disjunctions between saying and doing: between 'symbolic' violence and 'real,' or 'figurative' violence and 'physical'; nor those who differentiate between communication by tongue and that by fist, as means of identifying neurological changes from self-control to rage—changes which those of plebian, as opposed to patrician, socialisation cannot avert. It seems to me that theories positing such neat, universal distinctions between words and actions do not stand close empirical inspection. Thus, 'symbolic' violence does not necessarily negate the 'real';[99] nor, on the other hand, does 'figurative' violence make the 'physical' necessarily more likely;[100] and resort to violence need not be correlated with modern or proletarian alienation from language.[101] For one finds the fist in the absence of the tongue in Melville's much-quoted *Billy Budd*, but also the fist and the tongue in conjunction in Burgess' *A Clockwork Orange*, and the fist and tongue in series, say with Oxford and Cambridge varsity rugby. One finds violence in partnership with stylised language—legal torture, the Inquisition, violence with minimal language—Clint Eastwood's 'Dirty' Harry Callaghan, and violence with florid, revolutionary language—*Mein Kampf* and its aftermath; and so on. No; in approaching an aetiology of doing violence, words and actions must be treated as a unity, and one should not expect particular types of distinction and correlation between the two: violence must be approached via talking-relationships. In this way, it may be discovered that any combination of behaviours is negotiable—the symbolic/figurative/lingual and the real/physical/fistical all equally routinisable, and playing regular parts in individuals' habitual interactions. The precise range of behaviours then derives from the fund of cultural forms which individuals find available for use.[102]

A more significant question of violence arises now, I suggest; one not pertaining to the differences between talking and doing but those between predictable routines within a talking-relationship and unoriented behaviour outside it. The pertinent phenomenon becomes not explosiveness in behaviour but expectability: violence as the decision to negate or to refuse to enter into a relationship of mutual predictability and orientability. In this book I have explored individuals coming together to constitute manifold types of relationship, using common cultural institutions to create and express personal meanings of greater or lesser complexity and consensuality: individuals meeting to constitute a living society. However, it seems there is also the individual who refuses the regularities of talking-relationships, and deliberately excommunicates himself by placing his behaviour outside the bounds of expectability and preventing others orienting themselves towards it.[103] That is, by random sounds, silences and actions, he flouts viable interactional convention, the habitual, the stable, and makes the maintenance or negotiation of talking-relationships impossible; he does violence to others' possible perception of routine.

This description may be seen to recall Bateson *et al.'s* conception of the schizophrenic; he is the person who does not 'correctly' label, or typologise (hence typify), his thoughts and sensations, and the level and channel of his own and others' messages, and is therefore unable to communicate.[104] The difference is that I have described the violent individual as he who achieves this by choice. This is not to say that the violent act should be defined as an instrumental one as opposed to an expressive one, or a sociological one as opposed to a psychological one; such binary selections would only impoverish our understanding. It is rather suggesting that the roots of violence may be found in particular talking-relationships and individual defiance of them: in the rejection of mutual interpretability. Moreover, doing deliberate violence to others' notions of expectability within a relationship may also be found to involve more and less extreme departures from potential norms. Hence, a sliding-scale of acts of violence may be instigated, from abusing to maiming and killing, the deviance adjudged in terms of the intended or received injury to the other individuals' abilities to mean what they choose at that time or in the future.[105]

In sum, I would describe the subject-matter of 'doing violence' as more properly the violating of existing or practicable norms of behaviour by individuals deliberately negating and eschewing the regularities of the relationship. Rather than predictive, its study is a descriptive exercise—one could not have predicted Jack the Ripper's eschewal in his dealings with the women of Victorian London any more than James Joyce's in his dealings with the English language in Ulysses; and it is the enterprise of at least another book.

Notes

1. Louch (1966:159-171, 235). Cf. Bateson (1958:96), Geertz (1975:5, 9), Honigmann (1978:325-327), Leach (1982:52; 1984:22).
2. Wittgenstein (1978:#18).
3. Poole (1982:91).
4. Smallwood (1937:1).
5. Cutler (1969:*passim)*.
6. Janes (1976:319-320).
7. St. John's Tourist Commission (1983).
8. Janes (1982:221).
9. Department of Rural Development (1983:175-176).
10. Toronto *Globe and Mail* (September 8th, 1984:8).
11. Guy (February 1985:48).
12. Szwed (1966:89). Cf. Riches (1986:15-20).
13. Firestone (1967:115-116).
14. Szwed (1966:118-120).
15. Firestone (1967:111-127); Leyton (1975:134). And cf. Fairford: "Crimes of a serious nature are seldom heard of, and murder startles the whole population, so peace-loving are the people on the whole" (1912:8). Anthropological enquiry on the island has, of course, traditionally been rural, e.g.: Chiaramonte (1970), Faris (1972), Cohen (1975), Matthews (1976).
16. Lison *(Arte verbal y estructura social en Galicia)* (cited in Fernandez, 1977:465).
17. Cf. Clark on Newfoundland "constant, low-level surveillance" (1983:5).
18. Cf. Bateson on the reversing of schismogenesis through the indiscretions of those socially apart (1936:193).
19. This is not to say that the same anthropologists did not defend Newfoundland whenever the 'backwardness' or 'introspection' of its culture were called into question; e.g. Kennedy (1983) or Park (1983) in response to Westhues (1983).
20. W.M. Williams (1963:14); Cohen (1984:26).
21. Rapport (1983a, 1983b).
22. Guy (1980).
23. Elizabeth Smart: verbal art is that pattern of order in which one word has passion for the next (public communication, MUN: April 7th, 1983). On the anthropological use of literary modes of expression, cf. Bruyn (1970:323); and then Klockars (1975:222), on such reconstruction being more meaningful than transcribed tape-recordings.
24. For a discussion of Newfoundland jannies or mummers, see Halpert and Story (1969).
25. See Paine (1986) for more on Premier Joey Smallwood and the loggers' strike of 1958-59.

26. R. Williams (1976:13, 278-279).
27. Leach (1977:*passim*).
28. Cohen (1985:104-110).
29. On the ambiguity of the boundary and its 'sacred' mission of defining identity, see Leach (1976:34-35).
30. Leach (1967:*passim*).
31. MacLuhan (1978:211-212).
32. Renek (1971:287).
33. Devereux (1978:125).
34. Durkheim: "two aspects of one and the same reality" (1964:129). Related to Bateson's discussion (1936:277-281) of 'peripheral organisation' where groups are sanctioned by other equivalent ones and 'centripetal organisation' where they are sanctioned by an hierarchical or central authority, then, could also be Sahlins' distinction between 'reciprocal' and 'redistributive' economic transactions. For the former characterises the symmetry of exchanges between two groups with centrifugal tendencies, while the latter characterises the unity, collectivity and centricity of relations within a group with centripetal tendencies; and both types of transaction can be concurrent (1972:188-189).
35. Cf. Bateson (1951:173, 250) on individuals cognitively moving objects relative to each other and hence, within wide limits, constructing the units of information and the systems of classification of the worlds they live in. Cf. Blumer (1972:*passim*) on 'self-indication'; and Kelly on individuals' 'personal constructs' classifying old events and anticipating new ones: on individuals as forms of movements who confront themselves with people and objects, and construe their replication and modification (1969:*passim;* 1970:269). Also Rapport (1985b).
36. Gluckman and Devons (1964:167-168).
37. See Rapport (1983a, 1983b, 1984, 1985a, 1986).
38. Cf. Strathern (1981:147-148; 1982:73-74) on physical village space.
39. Goffman (1961:*passim*).
40. Bailey (1971:17).
41. Also analogous, although beginning on a higher societal level, would be Sahlins' segmentary design: household — lineage — village — tribal — inter-tribal (1968:85).
42. Schütz (1944:500).
43. Wallman (1977:19-21; 1981:121-124). Cf. Turner on 'dominant symbols' (1967:22-46; 1974:55-56).
44. B. Berger (1974:77).
45. P. Berger and Luckmann (1969:66).
46. Wittgenstein (1978:#43).
47. Cf. Searle (1971:6-7; 1973:136-137) on speech-acts; Harris (1981:165-166) on the cotemporality, parity and integration of total behaviour in the act of speaking; Austin (1975:52, 145) on the propriety and rectitude of 'total situations'; Paine (1981:9-10) on saying as doing (although he would assign this only to performatory, and not propositional, speech, while for me it is more important to assert that both acts of speaking are acts of construction: both create facts); and Fish (1972:386-403,; 1979:265) on meaning accruing from participation in situational events and not from language as a transcendent and irreducible thing-in-itself (although I would dispute his positing of a necessarily generalised competence deriving from an essential Chomskian grammar).
48. Cranston (1953:16-17). Likewise, when R. Williams, tracing the etymology of 'violence', finds in the early fourteenth century that the world is in a state "Of filthe and corrupcion/Of violence and oppression" (1976:278), we should be aware that the familiarity of these decontextualised verbal forms may be superficial only.
49. Schwartz (1975:128-130; 1976:217-221).
50. Devereux (1978:126-129). Cf. Kelly (1970:3) and Cohen (1985:20). And see Blumer (1972:184) on individuals convening groupings by coordinating their different lines

of action (aligning their self-indications) at a certain point in time, and then subtracting from these collectivities by moving on.

51. Cf. Levi-Straussian *bricoleurs* (1966:16-21); and Goodenough on individuals synthesising general cultures into private ones (1963:261-262).
52. Steiner (1975:46).
53. Boon (1982:*passim*). Cf. Charney (1975:31): significance is often derived from doing violence to others' hallowed notions of morality. And on systems of homology and disjunction, see Levi-Strauss (1966:115).
54. Ingold (1976:245-247).
55. Ziman (1968:*passim*).
56. Latour and Woolgar (1979:235-258); it is in the negotiations over sales that they locate the winning and losing. It is here they see social consensus over ideas as 'objective' being generated, or else the whole founders in factionalisation. Cf. Bloor (1973:139-141).
57. Mills (1959:217).
58. Montagu (1968:viii); *Awake!* (1985:1-12).
59. Blumer (1971:*passim*).
60. Cf. Gusfield (1984:8).
61. A discussion on stylised utterances which speak to collaboration, solidarity and group identity relates this notion of socspeak to Bernstein's ideas on "public language" or "restricted code" (e.g., 1964, 1972), once Paine frees the latter from Bernstein's straightjacket of claiming their ownership by particular groups only (1976:74). On these codes as Austinian performatives, cf. Bloch (1975:12-22); and on their attractive embrace cf. Quiller-Couch (1916:142) and Bauman (1978:16).
62. On the perception of difference and the symbolic construction of boundaries for the proclamation of one's own identity and system of order, see Cohen (1978:135; 1985:117). On the exaggeration of difference, the writing large of grossly simplistic or fantastic stereotypes and the derogation of aliens as 'dirty' for the claiming of one's own more visible vitality and credible, clear-cut superiority, see Cohen (1982:13), Douglas (1966:4, 35), and Leach (1977:35).
63. Bailey (1965:9-15).
64. For other agreed-upon idioms of community rivalry and opposition, see Pitt-Rivers (1961:9) on contrastive songs, rhymes and ballads; Levi-Strauss (1978:500-501) on contrastive etiquette during menses; and Hoebel and Wallace (1958:78-79) on contrastive beadwork.
65. Park (1985); and also Louch: "complexity is a condition of any life we would think worth living" (1966:239).
66. Huizinga (1980:*passim*). This need not be interpreted conservatively. It is not only the status-quo that play reproduces, for in Turner's terminology the "ludic genre" may be poetic as well as mimetic: responsible for change as well as a cathartic release of suppressed impulses prior to a reinvestiture of the established order (1983:187). Moreover, it is not only harmony that play makes explicit but also what Briggs describes as the fantasies, tangled plots and grievous interrelationships otherwise hidden in the seriousness of daily life (1983a:10 and 1983b:13).
67. Orwell (1953:9-11). And see Foucault (1977:41-51) on the pageant of public torture in mediaeval jurisprudence achieving "an entire poetics": with stocks, racks and scaffold as props in the unfolding drama, and the intricate decoding of every agony then revealing an intense expression of the legitimacy and membership of the social order; also Camus (1972:34-37) on the transcending of neighbours' tragedies affording gossipers a narrative aperitif.
68. J. Berger (1979:9-11).
69. Paine (1976:74).
70. Wittgenstein (1978:#67); and cf. Bambrough (1968:191-195).
71. Turner (1967:22; 1974:56). Also cf. Pouillon: communication between individuals and groups is not a consequence of life in society, it is that life in itself (cited in Boon,

1973:202) (our primary communicational apparatus being word-language, I would aver).

72. Wittgenstein (1978:*passim*).
73. Cf. Steiner (1967:30); he calls the notion of a normal or standard idiom "a statistically based fiction" (1975:46).
74. Cf. Meltzer and Petras (1970:11-14) on debate between 'I' and 'me'; also Auden (1951:47).
75. See Ayer (1968:25) on the efficacy of a concept of 'private language' for describing the sharing of slangs, codes, argots and so on, by which a *de facto* restricted set of people communicate with each other, although more *could* always be included.
76. Forster's epigram from *Howard's End* (1973), wherein truth is described as deriving from proportion: the continuous movement between otherwise separate realms; and cf. Pocock (1961:101): without individuals with meanings to express there would be no interaction, while if whole words of meaning were communicated, individuals would cease to exist.
77. Wittgenstein (1978:#2, #8).
78. Kluckhohn and Murray's spectrum traced biological universals to environmental similarities to inherited uniquenesses (1953:54-56); but their image is still helpful.
79. Auden (1986:15); and cf. Becker's description of the clichés and proverbs of public language as authoritative evaluations and opinions which need no proof, as opposed to those of more private exchange (1983:135-140). (I prefer a sliding-scale wherein public and private are distinguished not by words *per se*, but by the complexity of agreement between interlocutors about their association).
80. Cf. Levi-Strauss on concrete connexions to symbolic classifications [such as agreements to disagree about symbolic evaluations — "an increase in Newfoundland violence"] sometimes being more pertinent than their exact content (1966:65-66).
81. Goodenough (1963:267); and cf. Fillmore: "an enormously large part of natural language is formulaic" — memorised and rehearsed in close associations with appropriate situations (1979:92).
82. Cranston (1953:12).
83. Sapir (1956:153); and cf. Empson on commonly using words "at a distance," to stand for vague ideas (1963:236). This is not to negate an emphasis on the simple formulae of performance as means of meeting in interaction, and communicating certain community belongings (e.g. Bauman, 1978:38-42), or the role of formulae as secure knots of communication, as shibboleths, as indispensable routines (e.g. Zijderveld, 1979:153-171), but rather to suggest that these are partial accounts which omit the levels of complexity also present; and that in Veselovskij's image (cited in Propp, 1968:116), as verbal schema are synthesised by time, so they become ever more receptive to roles in new formulations. Cf. Rapport (1986).
84. MacIver (1961:187-188): individuals are not just postulates of theory, and the stuff of history is the countless actual doings and happenings of individuals taken together; and "an ideal written history (...) would tell the whole story of everything that ever happened to every human being."
85. Wittgenstein (1978:#23).
86. Harris (1981:186-187); and cf. Gadamer (1976:174-175), and Bruner (1983:13).
87. See Culler (1976:28-31; 1977:123-124; 1981:32-33) e.g., on the necessary deconstructing, decentring and dissolving of individual speakers, whereby the macrosocial linguistic system which speaks through them, and triggers conventional responses of mood, thought and behaviour, is to be deduced. (N.B. Nietzsche: "I fear we are not getting rid of God because we still believe in grammar.")
88. Leach (1976:5); and cf. Finnegan on poetry as imaginative creation and re-creation of the world, and not the predetermined product of social, or deep, cognitive structures (1977:273-274).
89. Cohen (1985:16); and cf. Paine on culture not as a charter for consistent normative behaviour, but as a vehicle mobilisable for the attainment of certain ends, and of

use in the construction of a number of different meaningful 'wholes' (1977:50).

90. Cf. Bateson (1979:15-17) on relationship as the basis of definition, and context as fixing meaning.
91. Cf. Hawkes on symbolic arbitrariness making change unnecessary (1977:25); ambiguity as useful and constructive, then, and not some 'fuzziness' to be eradicated along with the antagonisms of social inequalities, e.g. Halliday (1978:114).
92. Steiner (1975:82, 172-173); and cf. Bruner on interactants' different "mental associations and stocks of understandings" (1983:12); also Rapport (1983a; 1983b).
93. Bourdieu (1966:233).
94. E.g. Mueller (1970:103-106) or Zijderveld (1979:*passim*), for whom an increase in the formulaic language of cliché means an increase in empty or false predefinition, and represents a removal or beclouding of the categories and concepts, the information, necessary for 'real' reflection, and leads to a reduced, or false state of consciousness; so that socio-political inequalities become mystified, the authoritative control of those in power is enhanced, and the people are destined to mundane and mindless discourse. Also cf. Partridge (1966:2-3), Orwell (1968:360-365), Howard (1977:xi-xiii), Goldschlaeger (1985:165); and then Eagleton on a necessary literary criticism to liberate from linguistic oppression (1976:76).
95. Shelley (1954:281); and cf. Bakhtin (1981:293) on the tastes, accents and intentions which belong with every word (although his contextual heteroglossia still retain more of the collective—the 'social,' the 'ideological,' the 'historical'—than I would favour).
96. Crick (1974:21); and cf. Geertz (1968).
97. Taylor (1984:148-155); and cf. Ferracutti and Wolfgang (1973).
98. Taylor (1984:156-157).
99. Frank (1976:414).
100. Wertham (1971:232).
101. May (1972:245).
102. Cf. McFeat (1974:*passim*) on the proxemics of small-group dynamics.
103. Cf. Johnson (1982:8). Also see Wallace on society as an "organization of diversity" made possible by the mutual predictability which makes behaviour 'equivalent', or compatible (1970:*passim*).
104. Bateson *et al.* (1974:32-34); and cf. Wiener and Mehrabian (1968:81).
105. Cf. Stanage (1974:229-232).

Bibliography

AUDEN, W.H.

1951 *The Enchaféd Flood or the Romantic Iconography of the Sea.* London: Faber.

1986 "A Short Defence of Poetry." *New York Review of Books,* XXXIII(1).

AUSTIN, J.L.

1975 *How To Do things with Words.* Oxford: Clarendon.

AWAKE!

1985 "Will our Streets Ever be Free of Crime?" *Watchtower Bible and Tract Society of Canada,* 66(15).

AYER, A.J.

1968 "Can there be a Private Language?" In G. Pitcher (ed.), *Wittgenstein: The Philosophical Investigations.* London: Macmillan.

BAILEY, F.G.

1965 "Decisions by Consensus in Councils and Committees; with special Reference to Village and Local Government in India." In ASA Monographs No. 2, *Political Systems and the Distribution of Power.* London: Tavistock.

1971 *Gifts and Poison.* Oxford: Blackwell.

BAKHTIN, M.M.

1981 *The Dialogic Imagination.* Austin: University of Texas Press.

BAMBROUGH, R.

1968 "Universals and Family Resemblances." In G. Pitcher (ed.), *Wittgenstein: The Philosophical Investigation.* London: Macmillan.

BATESON, G.

1936 *Naven.* Cambridge: Cambridge University Press.

1958 "Language and Psychotherapy." *Psychiatry,* 21.

1979 *Mind and Nature; A Necessary Unity.* New York: Dutton.

BATESON, G. and RUESCH, J.

1951 *Communication: The Social Matrix of Psychiatry.* New York: Norton.

BATESON, G., JACKSON, D.D., HALEY, J., WEAKLAND, J.H.

1974 "Towards a Theory of Schizophrenia." In D.D. Jackson (ed.), *Communication, Family and Marriage.* Palo Alto, California: Science and Behaviour Books.

BAUMAN, R.

1978 *Verbal Art as Performance.* Rowley: Newbury House.

BECKER, A.L.

1983 "Biography of a Sentence: A Burmese Proverb." In E.M. Bruner (ed.), *Text, Play and Story.* Washington: A.E.S.

BERGER, B.

1974 *Readings in Sociology: A Biographical Approach.* New York: Basic Books.

BERGER, J.

1979 *Pig Earth.* New York: Pantheon.

BERGER, P. and LUCKMANN, T.
1969 "Sociology of Religion and Sociology of Knowledge." In R.Robertson (ed.), *The Sociology of Religion.* Harmondsworth: Penguin.
BERNSTEIN, B.
1964 "Aspects of Language and Learning in the Genesis of the Social Process." In D. Hymes (ed.), *Language in Culture and Society.* New York: Harper and Row.
1972 "A Sociolinguistic Approach to Socialisation; with some Reference to Educability." In J. J. Gumperz and D. Hymes (eds.), *Directions in Sociolinguistics.* New York: Holt, Rinehart and Winston.
BLOCH, M.
1975 "Editorial Introduction." In *Political Language and Oratory in Traditional Society.* London: Academic.
BLOOR, D.
1976 *Knowledge and Social Imagery.* London: Routledge and Kegan Paul.
BLUMER, H.
1969 *Symbolic Interactionism.* New Jersey: Prentice-Hall.
1971 "Social Problems as Collective Behaviour." *Social Problems,* 18(3).
1972 "Society as Symbolic Interaction." In A. M. Rose (ed.), *Human Behaviour and Social Process.* London: Routledge and Kegan Paul.
BOON, J.
1973 *From Symbolism to Structuralism.* New York: Harper and Row.
1982 *Other Tribes,Other Scribes.* Cambridge: Cambridge University Press.
BOURDIEU, P.
1966 "The Sentiment of Honour in Kabyle Society." In J. G. Peristiany (ed.), *Honour and Shame.* Chicago: University of Chicago Press.
BRIGGS, J.
1983a "Conflict Management and Socialisation among Canadian Inuit." (Mimeo.)
1983b "The Management of Uncertainty in Canadian Inuit Life." (Mimeo.)
BRUNER, E.M.
1983 "Editorial Introduction: The Opening Up of Anthropology." In *Text Play and Story: The Construction and Reconstruction of Self and Society.* Washington: A.E.S.
BRUYN, S.T.
1970 "The Methodology of Participant-Observation." In W. J. Filstead (ed.), *Qualitative Methodology: Firsthand Involvement with the Social World.* Chicago: Markham.
CAMUS, A.
1972 *The Fall.* New York: Knopf.
CHARNEY, M.
1975 "Violence in other Cultures." In C. G. Weber (ed.), *Contemporary Violence: A Multi-Disciplinary Examination.* Illinois: Thomas.
CHIARAMONTE, L.
1970 *Craftsman-Client Contracts: Interpersonal Relations in a Newfoundland Fishing Community.* St. John's: Institute of Social and Economic Research, Memorial University of Newfoundland.
CLARK, R.
1983 "On Interring Westhuesian History." (Mimeo.)
COHEN, A.P.
1975 *The Management of Myths.* St. John's: Institute of Social and Economic Research, Memorial University of Newfoundland.
1978 "Oil and the Cultural Account: Reflections on a Shetland Community." *The Scottish Journal of Sociology,* 3(1).
1982 "Belonging: The Experience of Culture." In A. P. Cohen (ed.), *Belonging: Identity and Social Organisation in British Rural Cultures.* St. John's: Institute of Social and Economic Research, Memorial University of Newfoundland and Manchester: Manchester University Press.

1984 "Symbolism, Symbolic Inversion and Social Change: Matters of Life and Death in Whalsay, Shetland." (Mimeo.)

1985 *The Symbolic Construction of Community.* Chichester/London, Horwood/Tavistock.

CRANSTON, M.

1953 *Freedom: A New Analysis.* London: Longmans and Green.

CRICK, B.

1974 *Crime, Rape and Gin.* London: Elek.

CULLER, J.

1976 *Structuralist Poetics.* Ithaca: Cornell University Press.

1977 *Ferdinand de Saussure.* Harmondsworth: Penguin.

1981 *The Pursuit of Signs: Semiotics, Literature, Deconstruction.* Ithaca: Cornell University Press.

CUTLER, E.

1969 "Introduction." In G.A. England, *The Greatest Hunt in the World.* Montreal: Tundra.

DEPARTMENT OF RURAL, AGRICULTURAL AND NORTHERN DEVELOPMENT, GOVERNMENT OF NEWFOUNDLAND AND LABRADOR

1983 *Persistence and Change.*

DEVEREUX, G.

1978 *Ethnopsychoanalysis.* London: University of California Press.

DOUGLAS, M.

1966 *Purity and Danger.* London: Routledge and Kegan Paul.

DURKHEIM, E.

1964 *The Division of Labour in Society.* New York: Free Press.

EAGLETON, T.

1976 *Marxism and Literary Criticism.* London: Methuen.

EMPSON, W.

1963 *Seven Types of Ambiguity.* London: Chatto and Windus.

FAIRFORD, F.

1912 *Newfoundland.* London: Black.

FARIS, J.

1972 *Cat Harbour: A Newfoundland Fishing Settlement.* St. John's: Institute of Social and Economic Research, Memorial University of Newfoundland.

FERNANDEZ, J.

1977 "Poetry in Motion: Being Moved by Amusement, by Mockery, and by Mortality in the Asturian Countryside." *New Literary History,* VIII(3).

FERRACUTI, F. and WOLFGANG, M.E.

1973 *Psychological Testing of the Subculture of Violence.* Rome: Bulzoni.

FILLMORE, C.J.

1979 "On Fluency." In C. J. Fillmore *et al.* (eds.), *Individual Differences in Language Ability and Language Behaviour.* New York: Academic.

FINNEGAN, R.

1977 *Oral Poetry.* Cambridge: Cambridge University Press.

FIRESTONE, M.

1967 *Brothers and Rivals: Patrilocality in Savage Cove.* St. John's: Institute of Social and Economic Research, Memorial University of Newfoundland.

FISH, S.E.

1972 *Self-Consuming Artefacts.* Berkeley: University of California Press.

1979 "Normal Circumstances, Literal Language, Direct Speech-Acts, the Ordinary, the Everyday, the Obvious, What Goes Without Saying, and Other Special Cases." In P. Rabinow and W.M. Sullivan (eds.), *Interpretive Social Science.* Berkeley: University of California Press.

FORSTER, E.M.

1973 *Howard's End.* London: Arnold.

FOUCAULT, M.
1977 *Discipline and Punish.* New York: Pantheon.
FRANK, A.W.
1976 "Making Scenes in Public: Symbolic Violence and Social Order." In *Theory and Society,* 3(3).
GADAMER, H.G.
1976 *Philosophical Hermeneutics.* Berkeley: University of California Press.
GEERTZ, C.
1968 "We Can Claim No Special Gift for Violence." *New York Times Magazine,* April 25th.
1975 *The Interpretation of Cultures.* London: Hutchinson.
GLUCKMAN, M. and DEVONS, E.
1964 "Introduction" and "Conclusion." In M. Gluckman (ed.), *Closed Systems and Open Minds: The Limits of Naivety in Social Anthropology.* Chicago: Aldine.
GOFFMAN, E.
1961 *Asylums.* Harmondsworth: Penguin.
GOLDSCHLAEGER, A.
1985 "On Ideological Discourse." In *Semiotica,* 54(½) (special issue: The Rhetoric of Violence).
GOODENOUGH, W.
1963 *Cooperation in Change.* New York: Russell Sage.
GUSFIELD, J.R.
1984 *The Culture of Public Problems: Drinking Driving and the Symbolic Order.* Chicago: University of Chicago Press.
GUY, R.
1980 "Foreword." In A. Clouston, *Come 'Ere Till I Tells Ya.* St. John's: Clouston.4
1985 "Ray Guy's Column." *Atlantic Insight,* February.
HALLIDAY, M.A.K.
1978 *Language as Social Semiotic.* London: Arnold.
HALPERT, H. and STORY, G.M. (eds.)
1969 *Christmas Mumming in Newfoundland.* Toronto: University of Toronto Press.
HARRIS, R.
1981 *The Language Myth.* London: Duckworth.
HAWKES, T.
1977 *Structuralism and Semiotics.* Berkeley: University of California Press.
HOEBEL, E.A. and WALLACE, E.
1958 *The Comanches: Lords of the Southern Plains.* Norman: University of Oklahoma Press.
HONIGMANN, J.J.
1978 "The Personal Approach in Culture and Personality Research." In G. Spindler (ed.), *The Making of Psychological Anthropology.* Berkeley: University of California Press.
HOWARD, P.
1977 *New Words for Old.* New York: Oxford University Press.
HUIZINGA, J.
1980 *Homo Ludens.* London: Routledge and Kegan Paul.
INGOLD, T.
1976 *The Skolt Lapps Today.* Cambridge: Cambridge University Press.
JANES, P.
1976 *House of Hate.* Toronto: McClelland and Stewart.
1982 *Eastmall.* Hamilton: Potlatch.
JOHNSON, C.
1982 *Revolutionary Change.* Stanford: Stanford University Press.
KELLY, G.A.
1969 *Clinical Psychology and Personality: The Selected Papers of George Kelly.*

New York: Wiley.
1970 "Behaviour is an Experiment." In D. Bannister (ed.), *Perspectives in Personal Construct Theory.* London: Academic.
KENNEDY, J.
1983 "Meditations on Meditations on Meditations... " (Mimeo.)
KLOCKARS, C.B.
1975 *The Professional Fence.* London: Tavistock.
KLUCKHOHN, C. and MURRAY, H.A.
1953 *Personality in Nature, Society and Culture.* New York: Knopf.
LATOUR, B. and WOOLGAR, S.
1979 *Laboratory Life: The Social Construction of Scientific Facts.* Beverley Hills: Sage.
LEACH, E.R.
1967 *A Runaway World?* London: BBC.
1968 "Anthropological Aspects of Language: Animal Categories and Verbal Abuse." In E. H. Lenneberg (ed.), *New Directions in the Study of Language.* Cambridge, Mass.: M.I.T. Press.
1976 *Culture and Communication.* Cambridge: Cambridge University Press.
1977 *Custom, Law and Terrorist Violence.* Edinburgh: Edinburgh University Press.
1982 *Social Anthropology.* London: Fontana.
1984 "Glimpses of the Unmentionable in the History of British Social Anthropology." *Annual Review of Anthropology,* 13.
LEVI-STRAUSS, C.
1966 *The Savage Mind.* Chicago: University of Chicago Press.
1978 *The Origin of Table Manners.* New York: Harper and Row.
LEYTON, E.
1975 *Dying Hard.* Toronto: McClelland and Stewart.
LOUCH, A.R.
1966 *Explanation and Human Action.* Berkeley: University of California Press.
MacIVER, A.M.
1961 "Historical Explanation." in A. G. N. Flew (ed.), *Logic and Language* (2nd series). Oxford: Blackwell.
MATTHEWS, R.
1976 *There's No Better Place Than Here.* Toronto: Martin.
MAY, R.
1972 *Power and Innocence.* New York: Norton.
McFEAT, T.
1974 *Small-Group Cultures.* New York: Pergamon.
McLUHAN, M.
1978 "The Violence of the Media." in M.A.B. Gammon (ed.), *Violence in Canada.* Toronto: Methuen.
MELTZER, B. and PETRAS, J.
1970 "The Chicago and Iowa Schools of Symbolic Interactionism." In T. Shibutani (ed.), *Human Nature and Collective Behaviour.* New Jersey: Prentice-Hall.
MILLS, C.W.
1959 *The Sociological Imagination.* New York: Oxford University Press.
MONTAGU, M.F.A.
1968 "Editorial Introduction." *Man and Aggression.* New York: Oxford University Press.
MUELLER, C.
1970 "Notes on the Repression of Communicative Behaviour." In H.P. Dreitzel (ed.), *Patterns of Communicative Behaviour (Recent Sociology No.2).* London: Collier-Macmillan.
ORWELL, G.
1953 *Decline of English Murder and Other Essays.* Harmondsworth: Penguin.
1968 *Collected Essays.* London: Secker and Warburg.

PAINE, R.

1976 "Two Modes of Exchange and Mediation." In B. Kapferer (ed.), *Transaction and Meaning.* Philadelphia: I.S.H.I.

1977 "Tutelage and Ethnicity: A Variable Relationship." In R. Paine (ed.), *The White Arctic.* St. John's: Institute of Social and Economic Research, Memorial University of Newfoundland.

1981 "When Saying is Doing." In R. Paine (ed.), *Politically Speaking.* St. John's: Institute of Social and Economic Research, Memorial University of Newfoundland and Philadelphia: I.S.H.I.

1986 "The Mastery of Smallwood, and Interlocutory Rhetoric." *Newfoundland Studies,* 2.2.

PARK, G.

1983 "Ruminating on a Meditation." (Mimeo.)

1985 "Wee Notes on Reel-Life Melodramas." (Mimeo.)

PARTRIDGE, E.

1966 *A Dictionary of Clichés* London: Routledge and Kegan Paul.

PITT-RIVERS, J.

1961 *The People of the Sierra.* Chicago: University of Chicago Press.

POCOCK, D.F.

1961 *Social Anthropology.* London: Sheed and Ward.

POOLE, C.F.

1982 *In Search of the Newfoundland Soul.* St. John's: Cuff.

PROPP, V.

1968 *Morphology of the Folktale.* Austin: University of Texas Press.

QUILLER-COUCH, C.

1916 *On the Art of Writing.* Cambridge: Cambridge University Press.

RAPPORT, N.J.

1983a "Are Meanings Shared and Communicated? A Study of the Diversity of Worldviews in a Cumbrian Village." Ph.D. Thesis, University of Manchester.

1983b *Fred, Doris and Florence: Of Worldviews in an English Dale.* St. John's: Institute of Social and Economic Research (xerox).

1984 "Under Tarn Fell: A Chronicle of Voices in a Cumbrian Dale." MS., St. John's: Institute of Social and Economic Research, Memorial University of Newfoundland.

1985a "Waiter, Farmer, Drinker, Spy: Personae and the Meaning of Fieldwork in an English Village." St. John's: Institute of Social and Economic Research, Memorial University of Newfoundland (Mimeo.)

1985b "Sergeant Hibbs and the Details of Truth: the Rite of Oracular Lie-Detection in St. John's." St. John's: Institute of Social and Economic Research, Memorial University of Newfoundland (Mimeo.)

1986 "Cedar High Farm: Ambiguous Symbolic Boundary: An Essay in Anthropological Intuition." In A. P. Cohen (ed.), *Symbolising Boundaries: Identity and Diversity in British Cultures.* Manchester: Manchester University Press.

RENEK, M.

1971 "Reflections on Violence as a Literary Tool." In G. F. Estey and D. A. Hunter (eds.), *Violence: A Reader in the Ethics of Action.* Waltham, Mass.: Xerox College.

RICHES, D.

1986 "The Phenomenon of Violence." In D. Riches (ed.), *The Anthropology of Violence.* Oxford: Blackwell.

SAHLINS, M.

1968 *Tribesmen.* New Jersey: Prentice-Hall.

1972 *Stone Age Economics.* Chicago: Aldine. Atherton.

SAPIR, E.

1956 *Culture, Language and Personality.* Berkeley: University of California Press.

SCHÜTZ, A.

1944 "The Stranger: An Essay in Social Psychology." *American Journal of Sociology,* 49(6).

SCHWARTZ, T.

1975 "Cultural Totemism: Ethnic Identity Primitive and Modern." In G. de Vos and L. Romanucci-Ross (eds.), *Ethnic Identity-Cultural Continuities and Change.* Palo Alto: Mayfield.

1976 "Relations among Generations in Time-Limited Cultures." In T. Schwartz (ed.), *Socialisation as Cultural Communication.* Berkeley: University of California Press.

SEARLE, J.R.

1971 "Editorial Introduction." In *The Philosophy of Language.* Oxford: Oxford University Press.

1973 "What is a Speech Act?" In P.P. Giglioli (ed.), *Language and Social Context.* Harmondsworth: Penguin.

SHELLEY, P.B.

1954 "A Defence of Poetry." In D. L. Clark (ed.), *Shelley's Prose.* Alburquerque: University of New Mexico Press.

SMALLWOOD, J.R.

1937 *The Book of Newfoundland, Volume 1.* St. John's: Newfoundland.

ST. JOHN'S TOURIST COMMISSION AND CONVENTION BUREAU

1983 *City of St.John's* [street-map].

n.d. *Our New Flag.*

STANAGE, S.M.

1974 "Violatives: Modes and Themes of Violence." In S.M. Stanage (ed.), *Reason and Violence: Philosophical Investigations.* Totowa, New Jersey: Littlefield, Adams.

STEINER, G.

1967 *Language and Silence: Essays 1958-1966.* London: Faber.

1975 *After Babel.* London: Oxford University Press.

STRATHERN, M.

1981 *Kinship at the Core.* Cambridge: Cambridge University Press.

1982 "The Place of Kinship: Kin, Class and Village Status in Elmdon, Essex." In A. P. Cohen (ed.), *Belonging: Identity and Social Organisation in British Rural Cultures.* St. John's: Institute of Social and Economic Research, Memorial University of Newfoundland and Manchester: Manchester University Press.

SZWED, J.

1966 *Private Cultures and Public Imagery.* St. John's: Institute of Social and Economic Research, Memorial University of Newfoundland.

TAYLOR, L.

1984 *In the Underworld.* Oxford: Blackwell.

TORONTO GLOBE AND MAIL

1984 "Unarmed Police Push for Guns." September 8th.

TURNER, V.

1967 *The Forest of Symbols.* Ithaca: Cornell University Press.

1974 *Dramas, Fields and Metaphors.* Ithaca: Cornell University Press.

1983 "The Spirit of Celebration." In F. Manning (ed.), *The Celebration of Society.* Bowling Green: Popular.

WALLACE, A.F.C.

1970 *Culture and Personality.* New York: Random House.

WALLMAN, S.

1977 "The Shifting Sense of 'Us': Boundaries Against Development in the Western Alps." In S. Wallman (ed.), *Perceptions of Development.* Cambridge: Cambridge University Press.

1981 "Refractions of Rhetoric: Evidence for the Meaning of 'Race' in England." In R. Paine (ed.), *Politically Speaking.* St. John's: Institute of Social and Economic Research, Memorial University of Newfoundland and Philadelphia: I.S.H.I.

WERTHAM, F.

1971 "The Goddess of Violence." In G.F. Estey and D.A. Hunter (eds.), *Violence.* Waltham, Mass.: Xerox College.

WESTHUES, K.
1983 "Meditation on Newfoundland." (Mimeo.)
WIENER, M. and MEHRABIAN, A.
1968 *Language Within Language.* New York: Appleton-Century-Crofts.
WILLIAMS, R.
1976 *Keywords.* New York: Oxford University Press.
WILLIAMS, W.M.
1963 *A West Country Village: Ashworthy.* London: Routledge and Kegan Paul.
WITTGENSTEIN, L.
1978 *Philosophical Investigations.* Oxford: Blackwell.
ZIJDERVELD, A.C.
1979 *On Clichés.* London: Routledge and Kegan Paul.
ZIMAN, J.M.
1968 *Public Knowledge.* Cambridge: Cambridge University Press.

ISER BOOKS

Studies

35 **Listen While I Tell You: A Story of the Jews of St. John's, Newfoundland** — Alison Kahn

34 **Talking Violence: An Anthropological Interpretation of Conversation in the City** — Nigel Rapport

33 **"To Each His Own": William Coaker and the Fishermen's Protective Union in Newfoundland Politics, 1908-1925** — Ian D.H. McDonald

32 **Sea Change: A Shetland Society, 1970-79** — Reginald Byron

31 **From Traps to Draggers: Domestic Commodity Production in Northwest Newfoundland, 1850-1982** — Peter Sinclair

30 **The Challenge of Oil: Newfoundland's Quest for Controlled Development** — J.D. House

29 **Sons and Seals: A Voyage to the Ice** — Guy Wright

28 **Blood and Nerves: An Ethnographic Focus on Menopause** — Dona Davis

27 **Holding the Line: Ethnic Boundaries in a Northern Labrador Community** — John Kennedy

26 **'Power Begins at the Cod End': The Newfoundland Trawlermen's Strike, 1974-75** — David Macdonald

25 **Terranova: The Ethos and Luck of Deep-Sea Fishermen** — Joseba Zulaika (in Canada only)

24 **"Bloody Decks and a Bumper Crop": The Rhetoric of Sealing Counter-Protest** — Cynthia Lamson

23 **Bringing Home Animals: Religious Ideology and Mode of Production among Mistassini Cree Hunters** — Adrian Tanner (in Canada only)

22 **Bureaucracy and World View: Studies in the Logic of Official Interpretation** — Don Handelman and Elliott Leyton

21 **If You Don't Be Good: Verbal Social Control in Newfoundland** — John A. Widdowson

20 **You Never Know What They Might Do: Mental Illness in Outport Newfoundland** — Paul S. Dinham

19 **The Decay of Trade: An Economic History of the Newfoundland Saltfish Trade, 1935-1965** — David Alexander

18 **Manpower and Educational Development in Newfoundland** — S.S. Mensinkai and M.Q. Dalvi

17 **Ancient People of Port au Choix: The Excavations of an Archaic Indian Cemetery in Newfoundland** — James A. Tuck

16 **Cain's Land Revisited: Culture Change in Central Labrador, 1775-1972** — David Zimmerly

15 **The One Blood: Kinship and Class in an Irish Village** — Elliott Leyton

14 **The Management of Myths: The Politics of Legitimation in a Newfoundland Community** — A.P. Cohen (in North America only)

13 **Beluga Hunters: An Archaeological Reconstruction of the History and Culture of the Mackenzie Delta Kittegaryumiut** — Robert McGhee

12 **Hunters in the Barrens: The Naskapi on the Edge of the White Man's World** — Georg Henriksen

11 **Now, Whose Fault is That? The Struggle for Self-Esteem in the Face of Chronic Unemployment** — Cato Wadel (ed.)

10 **Craftsman-Client Contracts: Interpersonal Relations in a Newfoundland Fishing Community** — Louis J. Chiaramonte

9 **Newfoundland Fishermen in the Age of Industry: A Sociology of Economic Dualism** — Ottar Brox

8 **Public Policy and Community Protest: The Fogo Case** — Robert L. DeWitt

7 **Marginal Adaptations and Modernization in Newfoundland: A Study of Strategies and Implications of Resettlement and Redevelopment of Outport Fishing Communities** — Cato Wadel

6 **Communities in Decline: An Examination of Household Resettlement in Newfoundland** — N. Iverson and D. Ralph Matthews

5 **Brothers and Rivals: Patrilocality in Savage Cove** — Melvin Firestone

4 **Makkovik: Eskimos and Settlers in a Labrador Community** — Shmuel Ben-Dor

3 **Cat Harbour: A Newfoundland Fishing Settlement** — James C. Faris

2 **Private Cultures and Public Imagery: Interpersonal Relations in a Newfoundland Peasant Society** — John F. Szwed

1 **Fishermen, Logger, Merchant, Miner: Social Change and Industrialism in Three Newfoundland Communities** — Tom Philbrook

Papers

16 **Fish Versus Oil: Resources and Rural Development in North Atlantic Societies** — J.D. House (ed.)

15 **Advocacy and Anthropology: First Encounters** — Robert Paine (ed.)

14 **Indigenous Peoples and the Nation-State: Fourth World Politics in Canada, Australia and Norway** — Noel Dyck (ed.)

13 **Minorities and Mother Country Imagery** — Gerald Gold (ed.)

12 **The Politics of Indianness: Case Studies of Native Ethnopolitics in Canada** — A. Tanner (ed.)

11 **Belonging: Identity and Social Organisation in British Rural Cultures** — Anthony P. Cohen (ed.) (in North America only)

10 **Politically Speaking: Cross-Cultural Studies of Rhetoric** — Robert Paine (ed.) (in Canada only)

9 **A House Divided? Anthropological Studies of Factionalism** — M. Silverman and R.F. Salisbury (eds.)

8 **The Peopling of Newfoundland: Essays in Historical Geography** — John J. Mannion (ed.)

7 **The White Arctic: Anthropological Essays on Tutelage and Ethnicity** — Robert Paine (ed.)

6 **Consequences of Offshore Oil and Gas — Norway, Scotland and Newfoundland** — M.J. Scarlett (ed.)

5 **North Atlantic Fishermen: Anthropological Essays on Modern Fishing** — Raoul Andersen and Cato Wadel (eds.)

4 **Intermediate Adaptation in Newfoundland and the Arctic: A Strategy of Social and Economic Development** — M.R. Freeman (ed.)

3 **The Compact: Selected Dimensions of Friendship** — Elliott Leyton (ed.)

2 **Patrons and Brokers in the East Arctic** — Robert Paine (ed.)

1 **Viewpoints on Communities in Crisis** — Michael L. Skolnik (ed.)

Mailing Address:

ISER Books (Institute of Social and Economic Research)
Memorial University of Newfoundland
St. John's, Newfoundland, Canada, A1C 5S7